THE EYE OF THE
TIGER

THE EYE OF THE

TIGER

The Story of
JOCK SHAW

Ian Stewart

First published by Pitch Publishing, 2021

Pitch Publishing
A2 Yeoman Gate
Yeoman Way
Worthing
Sussex
BN13 3QZ
www.pitchpublishing.co.uk
info@pitchpublishing.co.uk

A CIP catalogue record is available for this book
from the British Library.

ISBN 978 1 78531 990 7

Typesetting and origination by Pitch Publishing
Printed and bound in India by Replika Press Pvt. Ltd.

Contents

Dedication

To the memory of Adrianna Haxton, the brightest star in the sky. There is not a day goes by I don't think about you. Grandpa x

Acknowledgements

I WOULD like to thank the Campbell and Shaw families for their co-operation writing this book. With special thanks to Elaine and Margaret.

I would also like to thank all those who helped me with research and information, in no particular order: Robert McElroy, Craig Innes, David Leggat, Frank Bennett, Neil Stobie, Ian Manson, Tom Purdie, Maggie McGinty, Archie Wiseman, Ian Manson and the late great Bobby Brown.

I would also like to thank Donald Caskie, Ewan Gibbs, Robert McElroy, Archie MacPherson and David Leggat for material used in the book, along with DC Thompson and the Airdrie and Coatbridge Advertiser.

Thank you to Paul and all at Pitch Publishing for your support.

Finally, Yvonne – thank you for your patience and support, as always.

An Absent Friend

Sadly while finalising the book Tiger's daughter Margaret passed away peacefully on 22 June 2021.

Margaret was a huge help to me during the drafting process keeping informed with anecdotes and personal family photos used within the book. She was keen to see Tiger's story told, and it's a matter of deep regret she did not live to see the final version in print. I can only hope she would have approved. Rest in peace.

Introduction

IN 2013 Yvonne and I were looking to downsize, as only our youngest daughter Iona remained at home. Our house on the Southside of Glasgow sold far quicker than we ever imagined, so the race was on to find our new home.

So it was, more than anything, that we stumbled across Glenboig. I actually at first got it confused with Glenbuck in Ayrshire where the great Bill Shankly was from.

First impressions were that it was a lovely village with a pub only five minutes' walk from the house, commuting to Glasgow was no problem for work and there was a good school.

So, in August 2013 we moved to 'The Boag'.

I had an amusing encounter shortly afterwards with one of the parents of Iona's classmates. He asked would I be going to the pub to watch the football. I asked if, as a Rangers supporter, would I be in a minority, to be told 'there would need to be more than one of you to be described as a minority'. Not quite true as it so happens, as I was about to find out, but it made me laugh.

After *Mr Struth: The Boss* was published in 2013, I contemplated what or who the subject for my next book would be.

The answer was staring me in the face, as not long afterwards I found out a bona fide member of Rangers Royalty had lived in my new home village.

Jock 'Tiger' Shaw was one of my father's favourite players, and whenever Rangers were struggling or not quite putting in the effort you would expect he would invariably say, 'Ah he's no Tiger Shaw.'

So, this takes us to where we are, and the publication of this book. I enjoyed writing it immensely and hope you equally enjoy reading it. I especially hope that is true for the Campbell and Shaw family: I really hope I have done the great man proud and this meets with your approval.

So, as Mr Struth used to say to Tiger, 'Lead them out captain.'

Foreword

I WAS both proud and privileged to not only play for Rangers, but captain the club from 1990–1998.

I had grown up in South Africa, hearing tales about Scottish football from my father and his Scottish friends in Johannesburg. I heard all about the passion for the game and Rangers were the team I wanted to play for.

Luckily, I was able to fulfil that dream and also be incredibly successful in doing so.

When I joined the club in 1987, I very quickly became aware of the standards expected at Rangers, and the crucial role the captain of the club fulfilled. I also knew that the jersey of the captain, in particular, was a heavy one to fill, as among those who had gone before me and who had worn the jersey with pride were Terry Butcher, John Greig, Bobby Shearer, Eric Caldow, George Young and Jock 'Tiger' Shaw.

All of these men epitomised what it meant to be a Ranger – those qualities you needed in the marrow so to speak – leadership, dignity, a never-say-die attitude, will to win and fair play.

I know from speaking to folk around Ibrox, and indeed to Jock himself over the years, that he had these qualities in abundance, and I also know how much he loved the club. Next to his family, Rangers were his life.

For me in particular he was generous with his time and was always available for advice.

He spent 42 years of his life working for Rangers in various roles and gave his all to each one, whether it was as a left-back or groundsman.

He was one of the first three players to be inducted into the Rangers Hall of Fame, in 1999, which gives you some sense of the esteem in which he was held.

Jock 'Tiger' Shaw was a true Rangers legend and I was extremely humbled and honoured to follow in his footsteps.

Richard Gough
March 2021

Eye of the Tiger – The Life and Times of Rangers' First Treble-Winning Captain, Jock Shaw

THIS IS the story of one of the most legendary figures in Rangers' long history, someone who epitomised what it meant to be a true Ranger. It could be argued he was a man carved in the image of his manager Bill Struth.

This is not just the story of a football player but an insight into life in the industrial central belt of Scotland, straddling two world wars and without the riches today's footballers enjoy.

John (Jock) Shaw was born in Annathill on 29 November 1912.

Jock was a no-nonsense full-back whose fierce uncompromising tackling earned him the nickname 'Tiger' from the club supporters. He joined from Airdrie in 1938 for £2,000, having started his senior career there five years previously, after signing from junior club Benburb.

He was a key figure in the Ibrox defence in the immediate post-war years. That defence was dubbed the 'Iron Curtain' because it was seen as being as unyielding as the barrier which divided Europe at this time. When he signed for Rangers, it started a remarkable association with the club which lasted over 40 years and saw him serve as team captain, third-team coach and groundsman. Tiger also captained Scotland and he and his brother David filled the full-back roles in the Victory International win over England in 1946.

This is the story of a man absolutely dedicated to his trade in general and Rangers in particular: a very humble man, despite his achievements, and one who was held in the highest esteem by the football fraternity and the local community where he stayed in Glenboig, North Lanarkshire.

The book will describe his career from the humble beginnings, turning out for Annathill Guild, to treble-winning Rangers' captain and captain of his country three times against England.

It will also look at his role in the community and his Glenboig village shop. I have spoken at length with surviving family to give me an insight into the man, not just as a professional sportsman but as a husband, father and papa.

It says much for the esteem in which he is held that he was one of the first inductees into the Rangers Hall of Fame after over 600 games for the club.

When he passed away in June 2000, Ally McCoist, despite being busy abroad on European Championship TV duty, returned for the day to Scotland to attend the funeral and pay his respects to someone he held in the highest regard.

The following words were printed on the back of his funeral service: 'If the captain is the man he should be, the example he sets can be of priceless value. Rangers are fortunate in having had John (Jock) Shaw, the type of leader who fulfils the essentials – never-say-die, fair to all (opponents and team-mates alike), quietly proud in victory and no bitterness in defeat.'

A fitting epitaph to a true member of Rangers Royalty.

Birth

ON FRIDAY, 29 November 1912 at 11.50 am, John Shaw arrived into the world – the first child of David and Alice Shaw. Four years later the family was increased by the addition of brother David, on 5 May 1916, then later by another brother, Charlie.

There was nothing of particular significance which happened on the day of John's birth, but this year was the year the *Titanic* sank and the Pulitzer Prize was introduced.

Rangers sat atop the Scottish League, which they would eventually win by four points from Celtic, though the following day they would succumb 0-2 to Falkirk at Brockville.

John, henceforth to be referred to as Jock, was born into the mining community of Annathill and the adjacent Bedlay Colliery, a harsh and tough life, and his father David was a miner.

Annathill early years

Annathill is a small village on the banks of the Mollins Burn, a tributary of the Luggie Water. Annathill was primarily famous for coal, as it was home to Bedlay Colliery. The majority of miners from Bedlay Colliery came from Annathill and there were three 'Miners' Rows' of houses along with various shops, a butcher's and a pub, which were all built around the same time Bedlay Colliery's shafts were sunk by William Baird and Company in 1905. With its neighbouring coke ovens, Bedlay was established to produce high-quality coking coal for nearby Gartsherrie Iron Works. The colliery employed over 1,000 workers as recently as 1969, and produced around 250,000 tons of coal annually.

The Shaws lived in one of the houses located on what was referred to as Miners' Row Annathill. There were three rows of houses built by Bairds to house the mine employees and they were collectively known as Annathill Terrace, with the addendum, front, middle or back to distinguish the location.

The houses were generally comprised of two rooms (a living room and back room), a scullery and a cupboard with a sink and running water sited in the living room, so conditions were very cramped. There were eight larger houses located on the back row which had three apartments, indoor toilets and front and back doors.

Annathill is now scarcely recognisable from the village it was when Bedlay was at its peak. Then there was a bowling green, recreation ground, grocer's, post office, chip shop, two Co-ops, a confectioner and a cobbler. In addition, for recreation there was a social club and football pitch. It was clear this was a thriving community, albeit one totally dependent on the pit.

As I have said, Jock's father David was a miner, married to Alice (nee Wellwood). David was one of eight siblings – three sisters, Alice, Maggie and Jeannie, and four brothers, Jock, Rab, Will and Charlie.

All the men were accomplished footballers and all five of the boys turned out for a junior team founded in the village.

The sports periodical of the time, *The Scottish Referee*, reported in its 14 July 1911 edition, 'Bedlay Juniors, a new club in the Glenboig district, are looking forward to a successful season. They have secured D. Shaw (Croy Celtic), M. Sloan (Rutherglen Glencairn), and other class players, and with a good pavilion and the ground nicely set off with barricade etc., the juniors should do well in their first season. I have to thank Mr John Crawley, the secretary of Bedlay Juniors, whose address is 36 Annathill Terrace, Glenboig, for a copy of the club's membership card.'

There did seem to be a degree of nepotism at play right enough as a team photo of the time included only three surnames: Shaw, McGowan and Marshall. Ten of those were Shaw and McGowan, who were cousins.

The First World War brought devastation and heartbreak to countless families across the country. The Shaw family sadly were no different. On 2 November 1917 the *Airdrie and Coatbridge Advertiser* reported the death of Jock's Uncle Jim as follows:

Deep sympathy is felt for Mr Shaw and his family in the loss of two sons in a little over two years.

> Bedlay soldier Mr J. Shaw, 129 Annathill Terrace, has received the news of the death of his son, Pte James Shaw, Argyll & Sutherland Highlanders, who was killed by rifle fire at an advance on the morning of October 31. In conveying the sad news Lieut. Hunter expressed the deep sympathy of B Company, with whom Pte Shaw was popular, being so cheerful and a willing soldier. Pte Shaw was well known in junior football circles, being one of five brothers who have played with Juniors. Previous to enlisting in February, 1915, Pte Shaw was a miner in Messrs Wm. Baird & Co.'s Bedlay Colliery. The sympathy of the inhabitants of Annathill is with Mr Shaw and family in the loss of two sons in two years – Q.M. Sergeant J. Brodie, in a letter to Mr Shaw, states: 'As all the officers of the company were casualties, thought it my duty to write. Your son was very popular with both officers and men of his company, who held him in high esteem, was such a cheerful and willing lad, who could be depended on doing his duty, no matter how dangerous. He will be missed very much; know he will be missed more at home. I have to offer you my own deepest sympathy, hoping the knowledge that he died doing his duty may help to lighten the blow. Your son met his death while advancing towards the German

trenches, and was shot by rifle fire. He suffered no pain, being instantly killed.'

While the news would have been heartbreaking, at least there would have been some comfort in the kind words articulated by the army.

After the Great War, life returned to something approaching normality and on 31 July 1920 there was the spectacle of the Bedlay, Annathill and District Highland Games which took place at Carrick Park, Glenboig. There were also plans underway to form a brass band in Annathill, and there was a plea for this not just to be a pipe dream but turned into a reality.

Life down the pit for Davie (senior) and his surviving brothers was difficult and soon his sons would follow him underground. Ewan Gibbs penned a comprehensive review of mining in his paper *Coal Country – The Meaning and Memory of De-industrialisation in Post War Scotland* from which he kindly approved publication of the following extracts, to give a bit of a sense of the dangers and also some personal testimonies about Bedlay specifically and some of the employment practices, which I found fascinating.

> Coal mining has always been a dangerous enterprise and from the mid-1800s, as technology allowed miners to dig deeper, the dangers increased. Terrible tragedies such as a collapsed pumping engine at New Hartley Colliery, Northumberland in 1862, in which 204 men and boys died, trapped underground, and the explosion at Blantyre in 1877, which claimed 207 lives, highlighted not only the dreadful loss of life but the inadequate provisions for rescuing survivors.
>
> The Coal Mines Act 1911 was a major step forward in mines safety, consolidating previous legislation to create a clearer framework of regulation. The Act made mines rescue stations compulsory, and dictated that no colliery could be more than 15 miles away from one.

The importance of having a rescue team nearby had been brought home by an explosion in Somerset in 1908 which killed ten men and boys. Because there was no mines rescue team, workers at the pit spent ten days searching for survivors.

At the time of the Coal Mines Act the Lanarkshire Coal Field was the most important in Scotland, accounting for more than half of the country's production. The industry reached its peak level of production in 1913. At that time 146,000 people (2,000 of them women) in Scotland worked in coal mining. This was how extensive and vital to the economy mining was. The Lanarkshire Coalmasters Association opened Coatbridge Mines Rescue Station in 1915.

The Mines Rescue Station was called to deal with many terrible incidents during its lifetime and those mentioned below are just a few of them.

The first call-out after Coatbridge Mines Rescue Station opened in 1915 was at Bedlay Colliery. A roof fall had blocked a vital ventilation tunnel with the result that four men were overcome by carbon monoxide, and became unconscious. The rescuers drove from Coatbridge with breathing apparatus and were able to rescue three of the men alive.

In the National Coal Board (NCB) era, Coatbridge was the main rescue station for the Scottish Area which also included stations at Cowdenbeath, Kilmarnock and Heriot-Watt, Edinburgh. These were manned by part-time staff.

The Coatbridge brigade consisted of three teams of seven men and an instructor, plus a full-time superintendent. Aside from their own equipment the brigade also serviced extinguishers and safety equipment from area mines.

The full-time rescue men lived in the station and their families received free passes to the Regal cinema just along the street. Training was hard, with the men wearing full breathing apparatus in a replica mine working, which was housed inside the building. The brigade also trained Scotland's fire brigades in the use of breathing apparatus. At the back of the building there were garages for the brigade's rescue vehicles and an aviary which housed canaries for testing the air in the mine.

The alarm bells were ringing toward the end of the 1960s when the future of Bedlay became shrouded in doubt.

Then in September 1969, H. J. Henson of the Board of Trade Office for Scotland wrote to the department of industry expressing concern at the 'seriously aggravated' male unemployment that he expected to develop in Kilsyth, North Lanarkshire, over the following months. Henson detailed the expected closure of Cardowan Colliery, with the immediate redundancy of 1,200 men, due to the pit being put onto 'jeopardy' status regarding its financial losses. The adjacent Bedlay Colliery, which employed Kilsyth men too, was also expected to close due to a gas problem. There were only limited employment opportunities in the area. Henson noted that just less than half, 80 of 180, available local jobs were classified as 'male' and most of the local advance factories were oriented towards 'women's work'.

Deep coal mining ceased in the northern core during the early 1980s. The striking differences in the responses to the closure of Bedlay in 1982, and Cardowan in 1983 were due to the broad adherence to the moral economy at Bedlay and a clear transgression of its customs by the NCB at Cardowan.

Bedlay was the last moral economy closure in Scotland, with all those that followed being marked by managerial hostility to union consultation and workforce opposition.

The colliery had traditions of collaboration between managers and anti-communist trade unionists. Cardowan contrasted with Bedlay.

It was a large cosmopolitan colliery and was a stronghold of politicised left-wing trade unionism. Descriptions of these distinct ideological alignments were present in the oral history interviews. For instance, Pat Egan, an NUM youth delegate at Bedlay, recalled, 'Cardowan was always quite a militant pit. Bedlay wisnae, and Bedlay was run by *pause*, Cardowan's mainly a communist pit and Bedlay a lot a Catholic group, the Knights of St Columba, all these kindae organisations. It wis probably Knights of St Columba. They used tae say if you wanted overtime at Bedlay go for a pint at the Knights on Saturday night or a Friday night and you'd ask "how much is that?" Most ae the management were all in the Knights of St Columba or the Masonic Lodge … Union and management wis pretty much what would be termed right wing noo. Cardowan was always left wing.'

These distinctions were not the fundamental cause of the differing responses to closure. It was the difference in the treatment of closure by the NCB, through their relative adherence to the moral economy at Bedlay, and clear breach of it at Cardowan, which was fundamental in determining the stance taken by the NUM and within the communities affected.

For those unfamiliar with the term 'moral economy', this relates to economic decisions made which have cognisance of both the moral and material impacts of any decisions.

In the case of Bedlay, the closure was less controversial as it took place on geological rather than economic grounds. Extensive consultation and discussions with all unions were spread over several months, while a joint examination of all possible areas of reserves took place with the involvement of the union's mining engineers. Closure was agreed due to 'insurmountable geological issues'.

Attention was then directed to employment practices and the continued significance of sectarianism during the latter half of the 20th century.

> [Dr Elinor] Kelly defined sectarianism as 'a social setting in which systematic discrimination affects the life chances of a religious group, and within which religious affiliation stands for much more than theological belief.' [Kelly is Honorary Research Fellow in race and ethnicity at the University of Glasgow and this refers to her work published in 2005: 'Sectarianism, Bigotry and Ethnicity – The Gulf in Understanding'.]
>
> This is an appropriate basis on which to construct an analysis in the context of the Scottish coalfields. Sectarian trends were especially concentrated in Lanarkshire where different Irish ethnic backgrounds, Catholic and Ulster–Protestant, intersected with residence, work patterns, and political affiliations.
>
> Sectarian practices figure significantly within the oral testimonies collected for this study, especially as they relate to the private industry. Jessie Clark recalled that in the South Lanarkshire mining village of Douglas Water, her father, a blacklisted trade unionist, felt 'the members of the Masonic Lodge were the ones that always got the work, you know. And that was a fact of life in the village that I lived in.'
>
> Jessie's father had rejected such a path, breaking with his father's affiliation in favour of socialist politics through the Independent Labour party, but sectarian connections

retained some bearing on colliery employment into the nationalised period.

Pat Egan's memories of the influential role played by a Catholic fraternity, the Knights of St Columba, at Bedlay Colliery, are demonstrative of the pit's social embedding through strong links between workers and management. These practices were informed by a defensive and divisive mentality, which protected access to premium employment and promotion for those of a particular ethnic background and religious–political affiliation. Pat's contentions about Bedlay are corroborated by the memories of John Hamilton who was originally from Lesmahagow in South Lanarkshire.

John had worked alongside his father at Ponfeigh Colliery, adjacent to Lesmahagow, but took up employment at Bedlay during the early 1980s. His recollections also confirm that sectarian affiliations were embedded in other collieries. Before Bedlay closed, John transferred to Polkemmet in West Lothian. In contrast to Bedlay, it had a Protestant loyalist character.

'I'm of the Protestant religion. I worked at the Bedlay and it was, the majority was Catholic religion. Big time. So you couldnae even talk aboot Glasgow Rangers when you were doon the pit. You'd just to watch what you were saying when you were saying it! So, when that closed, I got transferred to Polkemmet. And in Polkemmet they've got pictures o' the Queen in every corner you can think ae … But you were accepted nae matter where you came fae, didnae matter to who you were working wi'. No. That was okay, as long as you were daein your job and aw that. There was never any trouble.'

John's eagerness to stress that sectarianism did not contribute towards serious divisions in the workforce is indicative of elements of composure, especially in which Bedlay was a colliery invested with community and familial significance.

(Here is a link to the full report, which does make fascinating reading covering both the social and economic impact of the pit closures. *Coal Country: The Meaning and Memory of De-industrialization in Post-war Scotland* by Ewan Gibbs (https://humanities-digital-library.org/index.php/hdl/catalog/book/)

On 11 December 1981, Bedlay Colliery was closed by the then Conservative government and was left abandoned until 1982 when it was filled in (or 'capped') and the complex demolished. Material from the bings, or slagheaps, was used as bottoming for the M80 construction. Post-closure, in the 1990s, the land on which Bedlay Colliery sat (owned by the National Coal Board) underwent an operation to restore the ground to what it looked like before the colliery was sunk.

When Jock was 14 he left school and life down the pit commenced for him with all the perils and dangers that involved. By this time, with some coaching from his Uncle Willie, he had started to show some real ability as a footballer, and was consistently playing a starring role for the local Boys' Brigade team – Annathill Guild – and others were starting to sit up and take notice.

From Bedlay to Broomfield

Benburb

After a short spell shining locally for Annathill Guild, Jock's reputation was gaining more and more momentum. Clubs were starting to sit up and take notice and top junior side, Benburb, came calling for his signature in August 1931, when he was 18, and introduced him to the rough and tumble world of junior football. Even as a young man this did not present an intimidating prospect to Jock, who absolutely relished the opportunity to star in a Bens side who played at Tinto Park, Govan, in the shadow of Ibrox Stadium.

So keen were Benburb to capture his signature they travelled to Bedlay Colliery to sign Jock immediately after he had finished another tough shift. The interest and signing came as a complete surprise to him as he had no idea his play for the local Boys' Brigade team had attracted this attention. So it was that Jock set off on the first steps of what would become a glittering career.

Life was truly much simpler back in the early 1930s, and it was reported in the local press that a Whist Drive and Dance had been arranged in the local school at Annathill to raise money for Glasgow Royal Infirmary. It was recorded as a very popular event with 25 tables and 60 couples taking part. Among the associated activities on the night were such quaint events as a 'Guessing' Competition – quite what the guess was around was not revealed. The music was to be provided by the superbly named 'Mr Taggart's Imperial Savoy Quartet'. There was also news of a further fundraising event where the Junior Choir of the Mission under the able leadership of Mr William Wilson would stage the Japanese operetta *Princess Chrysanthemum*. The performances were given on Thursday and Friday of that week in the local hall. It was reported by *Airdrie and Coattbridge Advertiser*, 'The platform was literally converted into stage with sides and front-raising curtain, back and side scenery affording easy access for principals and troupes. This was the work of Mr McLuskie, the local handyman. Electrical footlights were fitted and maintained by battery. The stage effect greatly enhanced the performance. The chorus and solo work reflect great credit on both conductor and choir. The singing was tuneful and effective and well sustained throughout. The principals were well suited to their part, and acquitted themselves in true artiste fashion.'

One interesting participant in this local extravaganza was Jock's younger brother David, who was name-checked in the press reports as 'carrying his spirits with him' – in other words taking part with great enthusiasm – as a Sorcerer. No hint of the distinguished football career which was to follow.

Jock quickly made his mark in the juniors and, while not tall at 5ft 7in, his muscular physique coming in at 11st 9lb stood him in good stead to stand up to the rough and tumble of a season in the Central League.

At the end of the 1932/33 season, representative honours came his way for the first time when he represented the Scottish Central League against the Irish Intermediate League on Saturday, 6 May. It should be noted that while researching the book, as with *Mr Struth: The Boss*, I trawled through a lot of publications for information, and it is a great pity that many are sadly now defunct, as the report of this match, which ended in a 5-5 draw, has to be one of the most bizarre yet entertaining I have ever read. For that reason, I have reproduced it almost in its entirety, grammatical errors and all, and it is from the *Northern Whig*, an Irish newspaper which ceased publication in 1963.

Goals Galore at Grosvenor Park, by Justice.

Representatives of the Scottish Central and the Irish Intermediate League met at Grosvenor Park on Saturday, the conditions being which side give away most goals for a period. The contest was exceedingly keen, and the Scots had to fight hard to earn the spoils, and only succeeded having a penalty kick and very doubtful goal awarded against them. There was precious little good football but amount of good-natured chaff amongst spectators, as one defence and then the other faltered, until double figures were and one was reminded that the ticket season had arrived. That goals were equally divided gave the spectators full value and their goal scoring form standing out. It made Belfast Celtic and Linfield look very small in their matches in the County Antrim Shield final they can score only four goals between them. Glentoran and Distillery could only muster but eight goals in three games to decide the destination of the Irish Cup. How the forwards of these four leading senior clubs must have turned green with envy, and how the defenders of the same clubs must have wondered what fate would have befallen them if they had given such a feeble display as the defences on view at the Distillery ground. Of the clubs from which the visitors were drawn, I had to rub my eyes to discover if I was not asleep and dreaming that I had wandered up Shankill way. Such names as Petershill and Glencairn seemed strangely familiar. 1 was quickly disillusioned, however, when I came to beautiful names like Kirkintilloch Rob Roy and Duntocher Hibernians. What's in a name?

A cricketer's comments: now for the story of how both teams went on the goal standard. It's mercy no one was killed in the rush. The scoring was so prolific that I feel justified in using cricket parlance. Six minutes, McCaffer, the Scots left-half, opened the innings with low drive that went clean to the boundary. Seventeen minutes, Kimlin made the scores level. Nineteen minutes, Gavin was no-balled when he bowled Gough. (This was not a maiden over.) Whiteside drove the ball in the air, and Farquharson failed to bring off catch. Twenty-two minutes, there was an exciting race between Lyttle and Gillick, and the 'keeper had great chance to run his man out, but dropped the ball and the run counted in favour of Gillick. Scores again level. Twenty-eight minutes, the Scots appealed in vain that Kimlin had got his leg front, but Umpire Sam Thompson allowed the run. Fifty minutes, Lyttle failed to field the ball from Ross. Fifty-two minutes, the 'keeper was again at fault from Gillick's drive and the Scots regained their slight advantage. Fifty-six minutes, Kimlin nicked the ball past Farquharson. Fifty-eight minutes, great shot from Rowbotham travelled the whole way to the boundary. This was the biggest and best drive of the match.

Seventy-four minutes, Caskie brought the innings to end by driving the ball past Lyttle. It was a masterly stroke and deserved to give the Scots a draw. And the Ashes remain on the pitch Grosvenor Park.

I not take much interest in horse-racing but just as the match started a colleague in the press-box told me there was a tip for a race called Relief. This horse had been running after the game I should have had a flutter, as I should have taken for the match as a tip in itself. Ten goals, and four of them in 13 minutes, afforded great relief, not without its comic side, after the recent Marathon games between Glentoran and Distillery, and Celtic and Linfield. The one man for whom I felt sorry was McMillan, the secretary of the Intermediate League, whose splendid organising abilities merited a much bigger crowd. I heard, though not officially, that the guarantee for the Scots was £100. As the receipts amounted to only just that amount, it does not require Solomon to arrive at the conclusion that the match was not a success financially. Better luck next time.

During his time with the Bens, Jock played in the same team as John Jackson, father of Mike Jackson, and Tiger made a point of looking after young John on the pitch.

Also featuring in this remarkable match, scoring the final goal of the afternoon, was Jimmy Caskie of Ashfield. Caskie would later become a team-mate at Ibrox many years later.

They were, though, to be team-mates again the following week, when Central League this time took on the Leinster Senior League at Firhill in a match watched by 4,000 spectators. This was a much more sedate affair with the Scots running out 2-0 winners with goals from Caskie and Cassidy.

Their paths had of course crossed on league duty back in Scotland and the first record of facing each other was early in 1933 when Ashfield drew 1-1 with the Bens at Saracen Park.

Benburb had a reasonable degree of success during Jock's time there and in 1931/32 won the Glasgow Junior Charity Cup against Vale of Leven 8-6 on corners, after a 0-0 draw. Then the following season they lost in the final of the Elder Hospital Cup to Clydebank 0-4 in a replay following the original two-legged final finishing all square. They would also lose the Glasgow Junior Charity Cup to Rutherglen Glencairn 0-1. What is unique is that both the Hospital Cup replay and Charity Cup were played on 10 June 1933, one match in the afternoon and the other in the evening. It would be a very weary and downcast Jock who turned up for his shift at Bedlay the following morning.

The season after he left, Benburb won the Blue Riband event of the Scottish Junior calendar, the Scottish Junior Cup, defeating Bridgeton Waverley 3-1 in front of 13,000 spectators at Ibrox. Jock was, of course, in the crowd cheering on his old team-mates.

Among Jock's team-mates who would then go on to the senior ranks were John Glass (Kilmarnock), James McGregor (St Mirren), David McKenny (St Mirren), James Smith (Hearts), George Torrance (Bradford), Thomas Brownlie (Rangers), Tommy Devers (Aberdeen), William Moore (Airdrie), William McRitchie (Clyde) and Jack Montgomery (Manchester Utd). The junior game at this time was a rich source of talent for the Scottish League and in many respects was the well-established path of transition for so many into the professional ranks.

Airdrie

Jock's development continued apace and it was not long before interest from senior clubs was pricked, and he was invited to play in a trial match for local side Airdrieonians.

It has also been speculated that it was while with Benburb that Jock first came to the attention of Bill Struth, who spotted the raw potential and glimpsed into the future the type of character who would be welcomed and indeed thrive at Ibrox. It was further a matter of some contention that the wily Mr Struth may have facilitated the move to Airdrie as part of Jock's development, similar in a sense to how clubs use the loan system for developing talent in the modern game. Knowing Mr Struth, that would have been a distinct possibility as he was constantly looking to evolve and develop his teams.

The *Coatbridge Express* of 8 August 1933 reported, 'A jury of something like two thousand attended at Broomfield Park on Monday to pass verdicts on twenty-two players on trial as to fitness or otherwise to claim Airdrie's colours in the coming League campaign which opens on the 12th inst. There were many new faces in the game, which ended in a struggle. Possible Defenders were Morrison, Calder and Shaw (Benburb), Newman, Sharp and Todd (Newton Grange Star). The Possible Attack line comprised Johnston, Barnum, Newman, Law, and Mooney. To criticise a bunch of new men on their first game would be unfair, but it may be that Mooney was the only forward of the five that shone in any way. It was his shooting and Morrison's defending that gave some spice to the game. Both of the new signed players – Shaw and Todd – displayed worth and suggested themselves as coming men.'

So Jock had taken his chance and local press on 26 May 1933 reported that when Jock finished his junior season he would be donning the red of Airdrie after his signature was obtained following a starring role in the trial match. It was also reported that the Benburb treasurer would be happy with the move to Airdrie and went on to say he was the son of David Shaw, the ex-Croy Celtic full-back, and noted that 'young Shaw should go far in senior football'.

That same day, the Glenboig Fire Clay Company reported it had started making common bricks for house building and had secured large orders and output was expected to reach 16,000 a day.

Once his signature was obtained Jock then eagerly awaited his introduction to senior football in Scotland. In a pre-season preview in the now-defunct *Evening Telegraph* it was noted that Airdrie veteran George McQueen was missing from the list of players for the new season.

For the previous dozen years McQueen had been the Broomfield left-back and an outstanding mainstay of the side. He held a unique place in Diamonds history as the only man to lead them to national trophy success via the Scottish Cup in 1924. Then, aged 37, in season 1932/33 his appearances dwindled, and it was clear a replacement was required. 'John Shaw, a Benburb junior, will open the season in McQueen's place,' it was reported. So the die was cast and it would not be the first time Jock would replace a legend.

Jock would go on to spend four very happy years at Airdrie, making his league debut against Aberdeen at Broomfield on 19 August 1933, with the Dons winning 1-0 in front of 4,000 spectators. He made his competitive debut in the Lanarkshire Cup Final first leg against Motherwell at Fir Park on 16 August 1933. He had missed the opening game against Rangers at Ibrox where the Diamonds were thrashed 5-1, which no doubt hastened his promotion to the first team. He did get his chance against the light blues on 23 December 1933 but this was to prove even more traumatic than their trip to Ibrox, as Airdrie were thrashed 7-2 at Broomfield.

The experience was certainly a chastening one for Tiger and over 50 years later he was able to recall with a grimace 'being run dizzy by right-winger Bobby Main'.

The season would prove to be exceptionally challenging for the Diamonds and they escaped relegation by the proverbial skin of their teeth, finishing third bottom, only one point ahead of Third Lanark.

Rangers finished the season as champions, while local rivals Albion Rovers were promoted as Second Division winners.

Despite the team struggling, and they would end up conceding 103 goals in their 38 league games, Jock's performances were continuing to improve and it was reported envious eyes were being cast in his direction. Typical of reports in the local press was: 'Airdrie's young recruits, Shaw and Todd, continue to please. Both give great promise. Shaw was a bit special on Saturday with powerful directional punting.'

I think in modern terms this was saying Jock was pretty adept with his long-range, accurate passing. That same week it was reported that a writer of football in the south of England said, 'Association football can be brightened! Look, for example, at the influence Arsenal have been in adding spice to the game, as a feast for the fan. Arsenal, by their publicity stunts, have done more to keep football a popular spectacle than any other club. That was probably written before the Rangers went down South last week and gave the "Gunners" a second pungent lesson on how to play and win.'

Rangers winning 3-1 at Highbury.

In January 1934 there were reports of Sandy MacFarlane, the Blackpool manager, being in Scotland on a scouting mission for a full-back. MacFarlane hailed from Airdrie, and his playing career had seen him turn out for Airdrie, Arsenal, Newcastle, Dundee and

Chelsea and he was capped five times for Scotland. After retiring he stepped into the managerial ranks and had two spells each at Dundee and Charlton Athletic before becoming Blackpool manager in 1933. He had a serious rebuilding job to do at the Seasiders to lead them out of the Second Division back to the top flight and his sources had alerted him to the outstanding left-back now plying his trade at Broomfield.

It was reported that two players were on his radar in particular, 'questing for a full-back, and the names on his list of likely defenders were Matt Smith, Clyde, and Shaw, of Airdrie. I should not wonder if he reports very favourably of both players. Smith is a stalwart, and is playing well this season. Shaw is a sound young defender. Would Clyde part? I think so, and would Airdrieonians? I'm certain they would.'

Nothing was progressed, however, and in Jock's case I suspect the fact he was a home bird would have meant the chances of him moving south were remote. The interest in him from elsewhere would, though, be a feature of his four years at Broomfield.

Season 1934/35 was to prove much more successful for the Diamonds as they finished in a very comfortable position in the table, 14th of 20 teams and the Lanarkshire Cup was also won.

The promotion of Albion Rovers meant a local derby and the New Year's Day version of that resulted in a 3-0 win at Cliftonhill, in a rousing match, it was reported, with Jock being Airdrie's biggest influence with his drive and determination.

Later that month in a Scottish Cup tie against St Bernard's in Edinburgh, the Diamonds ran out 3-1 winners, scoring twice in the opening eight minutes. This was a tough tie but Airdrie were reported as having a brilliantly performing defence within which Tiger excelled. All the goals came in the first half and Airdrie appeared to settle for what they had, and played out time relatively comfortably, as was reported in the *Airdrie and Coatbridge Advertiser*: 'There were times when Saints came near to scoring, but Wilson, Calder, and Shaw put up the bar. Wilson was cool and confident. Surely there isn't a better pair of backs, than Calder and Shaw. Calder's positioning and control of an emergency were supreme. Shaw didn't put a foot wrong. Crosbie was a grand Airdrie right-half.'

Airdrie would fall at the quarter-final stage, losing 2-3 to Hearts at Broomfield, but Jock had another outstanding game, and there was said to be interest from the Jambos in himself and his team-mate, outside-left Tom Mooney.

There was some joy in February, however, as Airdrie completed a league double over Aberdeen, romping home 4-1 at Broomfield, having won 3-1 at Pittodrie the previous September. Conditions were atrocious in the first half, with torrential showers of snow and sleet, but it did not dampen the Diamonds' spirits and by the interval they were three ahead. With 16 minutes remaining Jock sent a raking 60-yard pass into the Dons' penalty area which was snapped up by striker Connor to settle the contest. Aberdeen netted a consolation in the final minute. The summing-up of the match noted that again the full-backs Calder and Shaw were outstanding while the Dons' display was reckoned to be too bad to be true.

The season would end on a high against Albion Rovers in the two-legged Lanarkshire Cup Final. Played over successive days, Airdrie won 2-0 at Cliftonhill on 29 April 1935, and played out a 3-3 draw at Broomfield to clinch the cup comfortably, and provide Jock with his first senior honour.

While season 1934/35 had been one of progress for Airdrie, 1935/36 was to prove an unmitigated disaster for the club, as they were relegated, finishing second bottom, one point behind Clyde. On a personal level this was really the first setback Jock had experienced in football terms but nonetheless his own star remained on the rise, and despite a poor season for the club, the interest in their tough as teak talented left-back did not diminish.

In the pre-season preview of 10 July 1935, in the *Airdrie and Coatbridge Advertiser*, it was noted, 'It is a bit premature to talk about players who may be capped for Scotland, but knowing how players live in the minds and eyes of talent spotters, it is being suggested that Shaw, the Airdrie left-back, is on the way to 'National honours. Popular Jock has most of the attributes of a great player, and I would not be surprised if he falls for a decoration in the course of the coming season. Scottish footballers of quality are still replying to calls from England.'

It was the Saturday preceding this which brought that rare commodity, a Tiger goal, this time in a comfortable 3-1 victory in a friendly against Alloa Athletic on 6 July – the visitors racing into the lead after only 30 seconds through Black. This merely served to jolt Airdrie into action, and less than a minute later they were level, Angus shooting past Muir from close in. Both sides then settled down to less spectacular play with a few fruitless attacks before Moffat of Airdrie sent in a pile-driver of a shot which defender Kerr stopped with his hands. From the resultant penalty, Jock took responsibility and put Airdrie ahead in the eighth minute. The scoring was completed before half-time through McEwan. As for Jock it was reported that the visitors' attack had a pretty poor time of it against the confident play of Devine and Shaw, any aggressive attempt they made being quickly frustrated by the clean-kicking Broomfield backs.

Throughout his career, goalscoring was never an attribute that was particularly noteworthy for Jock, as a full-back's role during his era was principally to defend; the days of overlapping defenders were at least 30 years into the future. Goals, though, did occasionally arrive and, of the five he scored for Airdrie, one was netted in a rip-snorting game at Broomfield, where Aberdeen gained some measure of revenge for the previous season's double defeats by winning a seven-goal thriller 4-3. It is worth noting that this game, played on 14 September 1935, was the seventh league match of the campaign and only one other full-back had scored by that stage of the season.

As a recognition of his growing influence at Broomfield, Jock took over as club captain from Tommy Calder in early October 1935. This served not just as an acknowledgement of his football abilities but his qualities as a leader and organiser on the park in an era when players very much dealt with the tactics.

As an indication of his growing profile within the game, Jock was then featured in *The Sunday Post* of 27 October 1935 as follows: 'Once upon a time there was a wee, short-trousered fellow called Johnny Shaw. Johnny was the favourite nephew of an uncle who had brought much renown to Annathill, a little hamlet in the Lanarkshire backwoods, by some great defensive play for Armadale. And little Johnny Shaw told his uncle that he, too, wanted to be a back. So it happened, on a stretch of turf at the rear of his Annathill home, this lad was taught football by his uncle – how to kick right, to head cleanly, to dodge with a fancy feint. That's how Johnny Shaw, of Airdrie, Scotland's left-back for this week's league 'National with England, started football. I was first to tell him of his honour. First thing he said was, "I'll have to run along and wire uncle." Of course, football is a part of the Shaw make-up. His dad played with Bedlay Juniors; there was the uncle who coached him, and David, his kid brother, plays right-half with Banknock juveniles. Johnny was sixteen when he started with Annathill Guild team. They saw his worth in a season. Transferred him to Benburb. In another season he was an Airdrie player. That was three seasons ago. Since then, he's missed only one game – through injury.'

Jock was to succumb to a lengthier injury lay-off for the first time and sadly he missed the league international with England but international honours would not be too far away. He was out of the first team for several weeks while recovering but it was noted in the *Airdrie and Coatbridge Advertiser* of 20 November 1935, previewing the upcoming weekend's matches, that 'with Calder and Shaw on the field there may be a chance'. It went on to state that 'Shaw, Airdrie folks will be glad to learn, is again punting the ball, and it is not unlikely that he may appear on the field this week-end. That will be against Partick Thistle at Firhill Park, where the Thistle have only lost one and drawn one this season.'

Jock had returned to the first team by the time they faced Hibernian at Broomfield on 14 December. Airdrie quickly raced into a two-goal lead after 15 minutes. First, Tom Mooney hit a shot from a free kick wide on the touchline which rebounded off the underside of the bar; referee Riley was well up with play and gave a goal. However, Hibs strongly disputed that the ball had crossed the line but to no avail. Still harbouring feelings of injustice, five minutes later Hibs fell further behind through Connor.

In 34 minutes, the complexion of the match changed. Walls sent over a simple shot, and goalkeeper Hawthorn clutched the ball on his line. He then delayed clearing the ball despite appearing to have ample time. Hibs forward Black raced forward and barged into him, and he dropped the ball, McCaffer kicked it away, but there was general bemusement as the referee pointed to the centre of the field awarding a goal. Reports of the time expressed bewilderment that the referee was able to make such a decisive decision, that the ball had crossed the line, as he was fully 35 yards away from the action. Nonetheless Hibs were back in the match. After 62 minutes they drew level. Jones was fouled, and the free kick reached Walls, who in turn slipped the ball to Gowdy, and he whipped the ball into the net from close range. Both teams then went all out for the winner and Hibs almost broke through on several occasions but the Airdrie defence held firm with Jock being reported as outstanding. In the final minute Airdrie grabbed the precious victory through Jones.

This should have been a pivotal moment in the season as it completed the double over Hibernian who Airdrie had also defeated 3-2 at Easter Road earlier in the season. Hibs were at the foot of the table fighting for survival. They were to pull themselves clear of danger though and finish two points ahead of Airdrie in the final analysis

Despite Airdrie struggling badly, Jock's form remained of a consistently high standard and, after a narrow 2-3 defeat to Celtic at Broomfield on 7 March 1936, it was reported that, 'The form of Shaw, the Airdrie left-back, against Celtic on Saturday warrants him being watched for national honours. He was selected for a cap last year but was foiled of its accomplishment by an injury that prevented him playing.'

Such personal plaudits meant very little to Jock as the season ended in heartache, joining Ayr United in relegation after finishing in 19th place.

So it was that 1936/37 saw Airdrie in the Second Division and along with Tiger they were determined to get back into the top league at the first attempt. However, reports during the close season again linked Jock with a move away from Broomfield with Hearts once more to the fore showing significant interest. The Tynecastle club were showing real ambition, being linked too with ex-Third Lanark and Manchester United striker Neil Dewar who was at the time plying his trade with Sheffield Wednesday. The reports, though, concluded that it was unlikely Airdrie would sell as they strove to get promotion, while the Dewar transfer fee was considered too rich for Hearts to afford.

So, life in the Second Division commenced and an early-season meeting on 22 August 1936 with Dundee United at Broomfield saw the Diamonds emphatically winning 4-0. The first half was an evenly matched contest until the 36th minute when Mooney's strike changed the complexion of the match as the winger cut inside the full-back, and scored from an acute angle. In the second period Airdrie took control, scoring four times without reply, and it was noted that Devine and Shaw were superb at full-back, along with a faultless display from keeper Fleming. Another report described the triumvirate as a grand trio who never yielded while United were still in the game in the first half.

Airdrie then had a tough encounter at Broomfield with league leaders Ayr United on 22 October. While Ayr were firm favourites, Airdrie made a strong start to the match and could have scored in the opening minutes but forward Stewart only succeeding in spooning the ball into the keeper's arms from close range. Both sides had their spells of superiority and it looked more and more as if the game could go either way; however, the match ended with honours even at 1-1, but again mentioned in despatches were Fleming, Devine and Shaw for their sterling performances.

It was becoming apparent that Airdrie and Jock were going to have a tough time securing the promotion they all hoped for.

In the midst of this campaign, though, national recognition for Tiger finally arrived. It came in the form of a call-up to the Scottish League side to play the English League at Ibrox on Wednesday, 21 October 1936.

The match was to be the 41st between the League representatives of Scotland and England, and, of the 40 played, England had won 22, the Scottish League 10, with eight games being drawn. In the course of these matches the English had scored 102 goals, with the Scots getting 70 in response.

These games have now disappeared entirely from the football calendar and it's hard to believe that at one time the annual Scottish League International against the Football League was second in importance only to the full international fixtures between the same countries.

The key difference with the League contests was that nationality was irrelevant; selection was based upon the league you were playing in. For example, John Charles and Denis Law turned out for the Italian League against Scotland in November 1961 at Hampden in front of 67,000 fans, the match ending in a 1-1 draw.

The introduction of European football in the mid 1950s signalled the beginning of the end in terms of interest in the fixtures and they disappeared from the calendar almost entirely during the 1980s.

In 1936, though, this was a key fixture and there was significant prestige at stake. The previous year England had won 2-1 at Stamford Bridge and the season before at Ibrox the match had been a 2-2 draw.

Scotland's last victory had been at old Trafford in 1933, so a win was long overdue.

The withdrawal of Andy Anderson of Hearts through injury left the selectors with a headache and they had no choice but to draft in a replacement, though there were concerns this would disrupt a promising international defence, where Anderson and Cummings were looked upon as the best bet as a pair of defenders Scotland had had for a number of years. For this match, though, there would be a new pairing in front of Jerry Dawson: Cooper, of Aberdeen, who was reserve to Anderson, would be the right-back, and Shaw of Airdrieonians was the choice for left-back. Cooper had played in the corresponding game the previous season, but this was the Airdrie man's first honour. Quite an achievement to be selected, for someone playing outwith the top league. It's worth listing the line-up in which Jock was to feature: Dawson (Rangers), Cooper (Aberdeen), Shaw (Airdrie), Massie (Hearts), Simpson (Rangers), Brown (Rangers), Main (Rangers), Walker (Hearts), McGrory (Celtic), Venters (Rangers) and Reid (Hamilton).

There was an expectation that there would be the usual invasion of English club managers and directors at this game, to cast their eye over the talent on show. Also present was Rangers manager Bill Struth.

The match itself ended in a 2-2 draw and Jock was said to have acquitted himself really well against a high standard of opposition and contained his direct opponent Birkett of Middlesbrough with great aplomb.

Back to the bread and butter of league duty, and the week before Christmas, on 19 December 1936, Airdrie were at Boghead, and despite the sides being at opposite ends of the table this was a really tough fixture and featured a penalty from Jock saved by keeper Lang. The keeper pushed the ball out but Tiger could not capitalise on this second chance and hit the ball off the upright where it rebounded to safety. In an engrossing encounter Airdrie eventually triumphed

3-2 with once again the defence of Devine and Shaw receiving commendations for proving a pair of steady backs.

New Year's Day 1937 did not bring the usual swashbuckling local derby for the spectators but instead Cowdenbeath were the visitors. What subsequently ensued was a tough match in which, if truth be told, the final score of 2-2 flattered the hosts. On this occasion Jock was noted as finding the opponents from Central Park a little more troublesome than normal – even the very best occasionally have an off day.

The chat on the football grapevine at the end of January was that clubs south of the border were taking a keen interest in the Broomfield left-back. This was no doubt as a result of his Scottish League performance, and Reading in particular were credited with a strong interest in Jock. That interest would not be reciprocal though, as Reading were a team operating at the time in Division Three South of the Football League and Jock would be set for much greater things.

A meeting at the end of January against bottom club Edinburgh City would provide a hammer blow to Airdrie's promotion ambitions. The amateur side would only win two games from the entire 38-match league card and this proved to be one of them, by 3-2. Airdrie's performance was described in pretty scathing terms in the *Coatbridge Leader*: 'There can be little doubt, as said, that, on the day's showing, 'Onians only got their desserts, whereas this match, we imagine must have been the Amateurs' best display this season. Airdrie, on the other hand, were in anything but championship form, and this defeat, it is to be feared, may prove fatal to their promotion prospects. Fleming revealed all his accustomed ability, and was in no way to be blamed for any of the shots which got past him. Shaw, while the better back, was often troubled by Douglas. McCaffer played well, but Carruthers led him a gruelling chase. The forwards, as a bunch, were disappointing, and did not adapt themselves to the conditions.'

So, the much hoped for promotion never materialised and Airdrie were consigned to another season in the Second Division. They completed the campaign in a disappointing fourth place behind champions Ayr United, Morton and St Bernard's – seven points adrift of promotion. This was hugely disappointing to Tiger who, while happy at Broomfield, had ambitions beyond Second Division football. A constant feature of matches during the campaign had been the consistently impressive newspaper reports of his performances, and scouts continued to hover around Broomfield as his reputation grew. His ultimate ambition though was in one place and one place only, to the west in Govan with his boyhood heroes, but he did wonder if the call would ever come.

The next year proved to be almost a mirror image of the previous campaign with the promotion race being a little closer, but frustratingly Airdrie missed out by a point to local rivals Albion Rovers with Raith Rovers going up as champions. The team were again their own worst enemies shipping points to teams far less talented from the lower half of the table.

For the first time Jock now appeared to be feeling some level of strain with the team's inability to mount a real challenge for promotion, particularly as he was club captain. Reports from the first half of the season suggested the new responsibility was weighing heavily on his broad shoulders. By the turn of the year, however, his form seemed to flourish and return to the standards of excellence that all had previously become accustomed to expect from him.

There was a little consolation in that Tiger picked up a runners-up medal in the 1936/37 Lanarkshire Cup. The final was delayed until 30 August 1937 and the second leg on 20 September 1937, the Diamonds going down 2-0 and 4-1 to Motherwell respectively. A measure of revenge was enacted in the 1937/38 tournament when the Steelmen were vanquished 4-2 in the semi-final on 20 April 1938.

The first leg of the final was played at Broomfield on 27 April, where Hamilton Accies were comfortably beaten 3-0. The second leg and conclusion of the tournament would be held over until the beginning of the following season, by which time Tiger would be plying his trade in more illustrious company.

At the end of the season Jock declined to re-sign for Airdrieonians as the club were financially unable to give him the benefit payment which he was due after five years of service, and he was subsequently transferred to Rangers, for a fee of £2,000, in mid-July,1938.

In the *Airdrie and Coatbridge Advertiser* of 13 July (a few days before he signed for Rangers) the question was posed, 'Will Johnny Shaw leave Airdrie? The followers of Airdrie are anxiously awaiting news as to what is to happen. Is he leaving Broomfield or will he remain until he sees the old club back in the First Division?' The paper, of course, at that time was unaware of the contract issues and that he had kicked his last ball for the Diamonds.

In total, during his five full seasons with the club (1933/34 to 1937/38 inclusive), he played in 174 league fixtures (109 in Division One, and 65 in Division Two), 11 Scottish Cup ties and 14 Lanarkshire Cup ties.

He scored five league goals (one in Division One, and four in Division Two – three of those from penalty kicks).

His final appearance for the club came in the last match of 1937/38, the Division Two game against Dundee United at Tannadice on 30 April 1938, after appearing in all 38 League fixtures.

While Airdrie were sad to see Jock go, they at least put his transfer fee to good use, and built a new stand from the proceeds.

Struth and Ibrox Come Calling

JOCK ENTERED the summer with a degree of uncertainty following the contractual issues with Airdrie. The timing could not have been worse as a young woman from the nearby village of Glenboig had come into his life and there were wedding plans afoot. Margaret Elizabeth Hutchison was employed as a live-in children's nurse for a wealthy Jewish family, the Silversteins from Glasgow, and Jock and she had plans to marry in July.

It was not only in Annathill, though, where there was uncertainty afoot, but also in the oak-panelled office of Rangers manager Bill Struth in the Ibrox Stadium.

The season of 1937/38 had been a poor one by Rangers' high standards. They finished third in the league, 12 points adrift of champions Celtic, were beaten by Kilmarnock in the semi-final of the Scottish Cup, lost the Charity Cup Final to Celtic and were despatched easily by Everton 2-0 in the end-of-season Empire Exhibition Tournament. The only crumb of comfort was a Glasgow Cup triumph when they narrowly beat Third Lanark in October 1937.

Rangers were without a doubt a club in transition, and this would be a season where the winds of change would sweep through the club, as household names such as Dougie Gray, Bob McPhail, Jimmy Simpson, Jimmy Smith, George Brown and Bob McDonald were reaching the end of their careers.

Struth knew he had to act and decisively, carrying a firm belief that he could not speculate on potential but needed high-quality experienced men equipped to fill the positions in the starting XI immediately. As *The Sunday Post* of the time reported, 'It is admitted by Manager Struth in his annual survey that the first team is in a state of transition, but he is confident the present lean period will be as successfully bridged like others in the past. Now that he has made a start in his search for "ready-mades" his further efforts will be awaited with interest. It is recognised generally that Rangers must make substantial additions if they are to maintain championship pace.'

News of the contract issues alerted several clubs as to Jock's availability and he had been coveted for some time by a number of teams as the left-back role was a notoriously difficult one to fill. Hearts in particular had been tracking him for several seasons and Arsenal would also now table their interest with a formal offer to Airdrie, but when Rangers entered the race there really was only going to be one winner, and Struth moved for a player who was to become one of his and Rangers' best-ever signings.

There was another life-changing contract, though, which Jock had to attend to before Rangers, and on Glasgow Fair Friday, 15 July 1938 he made his own best-ever signing. At New Monklands Manse, Glenmavis, Airdrie, he married the love of his life Margaret Hutchison, with brother David attending as best man. Margaret was now recorded on the marriage lines as a brick worker and coming from Glenboig that would have been the primary source of employment at that time in the world-famous brickworks, having given up her role as a children's nurse. Ever the wily old fox, in order to avoid a lot of press intrusion on his big day, he told the press he was getting married on 22 July.

On the Monday of the following week, he then got the telegram which would change both his professional and personal life forever.

This was the summons from Mr Struth inviting him to Ibrox on Wednesday, 20 July to discuss signing. As far as Jock was concerned there would be no need to have much discussion; newlywed or not, this was a dream come true.

He had grown up a proud Rangers supporter and now at the age of 26 he was an experienced professional footballer, one who had done the 'hard yards' at a provisional club and all the trials and tribulations that involved. Now he had a chance and, as Jim Baxter memorably once said, 'if you get a chance to get a bite, make sure you take a good bite'. It would also mean he could go professional on a full-time basis and give up work in the Gartsherrie Iron Works to dedicate himself to his craft.

The Iron Works was just north of Coatbridge, still close to home in Annathill and owned by the same firm who owned Bedlay Colliery – William Baird and Sons.

Hearts were also now in contact to offer him terms but there was no contest as Ibrox was where Jock's heart lay. There was even a formal bid from Arsenal, higher than Rangers were prepared to pay, but Jock made it abundantly clear there was only one club for him.

The signing was quite a coup for Rangers at the time and was extensively reported in the press; from the *Press and Journal*, 'Rangers yesterday signed John Shaw, left-back of Airdrieonians. Shaw is a player of ripe experience, and the transfer fee would be considerable. Three seasons ago he was chosen to play for the Scottish League against the English League but had to forego the honour through injury. A studious type of defender Shaw is usefully built, standing 5ft 7in, and weighing 11st. He returns to his proper sphere in First League football, and should do well at Ibrox. This signing may be taken as part of Rangers' new scheme of reconstruction. The left-back position has given them much anxiety recently, and Rangers have decided to go for the ready-made article.'

The Sunday Post reported, 'Rangers strike out in their bid for greater power by securing the transfer of John Shaw, Airdrie left-back, and one of the foremost defenders in Scottish football. Good news for expectant followers, and a sound transaction that may have involved a sum of £1,500. Shaw has been a top-line performer in recent seasons. He played his first game for Airdrie in 1933. His desire for advancement has not been disguised. He assisted the Scottish League against the English League in 1937, and since that time Airdrie officials have had many inquiries regarding his future. He graduated from the popular Benburb. Already the light blues have three players for the position – Winning, McDonald, and Cheyne. Who'll come first in the coming campaign?'

Bill Struth was the master of recruitment and had noted for some time that there was a left-back needed as Rangers had struggled to fill that position ever since Archie Macaulay had departed for Chelsea in 1933.

Mr Struth, though, had even greater plans for Jock: he also recognised that the time was ripe for a new inspirational leader, his man on the park so to speak. Ever since Davie Meiklejohn had retired in 1936, Rangers had been unable to find a suitable long-term replacement. Jimmy Simpson had been carrying out the role but he was in the twilight of his career and a new captain was required. Jock had been identified to fit the bill on both fronts.

In the end the transfer fee to secure his registration was £2,000, which in 1938 was not an insignificant investment for a football player. The fee, though, did not impress Airdrie as Arsenal had offered much more money but Jock made it clear there was only one destination for him. 'I told them no way; I was signing for the team I wanted to join.'

Rangers supporters welcomed the news and speculated if this latest signing from Airdrie proved to be as successful as Bob McPhail, who had made the same journey 12 years previously, then Rangers would have themselves a bargain. One of the true greats of that era and the great all-conquering Rangers side of the 1930s, McPhail had also started his career at Airdrie, and while he was coming to the end of his playing days, he still had plenty of friends at Broomfield and in conversations they spoke very highly of their left-back. McPhail mentioned this to Struth. Struth had been keeping a close eye on Jock but also arranged for further scouting and made his customary enquiries to establish the character of the man. Was he the sort Struth wanted as a Ranger? In Jock's case it soon became apparent that he fulfilled every one of Struth's demanding criteria.

As Jock himself said, 'I was signed and told right away that I was to be the new Rangers captain. I hardly had time to think about it as I was making my debut in the big match against Arsenal at Ibrox.'

Jock then went on to further describe the signing: 'I had been with Airdrie as a regular first team player for five years. It was part-time and I worked down the pits in Lanarkshire, but when I was told Rangers wanted to sign me it meant an escape from the pits, so I didn't take much convincing that it was the right career move for me. If I had needed anything to convince me, it came when I was first introduced to Mr Struth in his office at the top of the marble staircase. I had played at Ibrox for Airdrie a few times but this was the first time I had ever climbed those stairs, and looked around to see how grand everything was, at least compared with Broomfield.

'When I met the manager what he told me made a big impression on me, and made me feel a very special person [classic Struth]. He told me he was going to sign me not only to be his left-back but also to be the new captain of Rangers. He told me that such a position was a great honour and that he had every faith in me conducting myself in the right manner off the field, and also of being the leader on the park.

'I remember he made it clear to me what would be expected in terms of setting an example, and he also said that he had been looking to replace Davie Meiklejohn who had retired two year earlier. The very fact of being mentioned in the same breath as Meek made me grow a few inches. He had been the giant of Scottish football when I was growing up in the 1920s, and when I started playing in the early 30s. The very notion of me, a laddie from Lanarkshire, being chosen by Bill Struth to replace Davie Meiklejohn was quite something for me to think about.'

David Leggat observed in his book *Mr Struth*, 'Struth, despite those claiming he was a man of his time, displayed traits and insights which actually placed him ahead of his time. His introduction to Ibrox of Tiger Shaw was one such trait and Struth's reading of the measure of the man's character he was signing, and handing the captaincy to him. Far from inhibiting Shaw, being told he was being signed to replace such a legend as Meiklejohn would only serve to make the new skipper all the more confident in his ability to succeed.'

One can only imagine how this must have made Jock feel; he must have grown in stature. A full-back from a Second Division team being signed by the mighty Rangers and furthermore he was to become club captain.

Jock went on to reflect upon that very aspect: 'If Bill Struth said it was so, then that is exactly what it was going to be.'

It would be the following season (1939/40), though, when he would officially become captain. He was given a season to settle, as the big-money move along with assuming the captaincy was viewed by Struth as too much of a burden all at one time. The honour remained with veteran centre-half Jimmy Simpson for one final year. Having had a season to acclimatise at Ibrox, the captaincy passed to Tiger for season 1939/40 as Simpson's appearances reduced to two league games (one league and one regional league), before leaving Rangers in 1941.

The summer of 1938 would prove to be a momentous one as Jock joined up at Ibrox along with some figures who would go on to achieve legendary status – Willie Waddell, Scot Symon and Jimmy Duncanson, two of whom would, of course, also go on to manage the club with great distinction.

Jock and Meg started married life by moving into a new flat at 12c Ronald Street, Coatbridge, where a year later their son David would be born, followed by a daughter, Margaret, in 1944. Their home sat just behind where the current Lamberton's factory is sited, near Sunnyside train station.

A First Title

IT WAS generally accepted and recorded that Jock's debut was in the friendly at Ibrox against Arsenal on 29 August, however, that is not quite correct. Officially Jock's debut was at Muirton on 13 August in a 3-3 draw, and then he made his bow at Ibrox in another draw, this time 2-2, on 20 August against Motherwell. His third appearance saw Rangers winning 4-2 against St Johnstone in front of 18,000 spectators at Ibrox.

So, by the time the Arsenal game came around, Jock had already got three games under his belt and was settling in nicely. These annual jousts with Arsenal were originally set up by old friends Bill Struth and Herbert Chapman – who had died in 1934 – and were considered highly prestigious; a great relationship between the clubs had built up as a result of the friendship.

It was a warm, late-summer evening as 41,000 spectators gathered on the terraces. Jock was not confident or assured of his place in the team yet, particularly as the defence had conceded seven goals in those opening league games. Jock recalled sitting nervously in the dressing room before the match. 'It was the usual process for the manager Mr Bill Struth to come into the dressing room about half an hour to three quarters of an hour before kick-off. That was the case that night and my name was the third he read out after Jerry Dawson and Dougie Gray. It was quite an experience for me because this was a big game, and because it was Rangers I was playing for now, we were expected to win. It was when we were lining up at the start of the game that I realised Bryn Jones was to be my direct opponent, because I hadn't really given it much thought beforehand.'

Bryn Jones was a Welsh international whose exploits for Wolves had earned the attention of George Allison's Arsenal, who were looking for a replacement for Alex James, and paid a then British record fee of £14,000 to take him to Highbury in August 1938.

Jock said: 'Arsenal had just signed a winger called Bryn Jones. He had cost them £14,000 which was quite a lot of money. Fortunately, I played quite well against him and never looked back. I wasn't in any way overawed, just quietly determined that I would come out on top.'

Come out on top he duly did, as Jones had very little impact on the game, being closely marshalled by Jock, and Rangers triumphed 1-0 through a goal from Willie Waddell, who was making a real dream debut that night aged only 17.

The Rangers line-up on that memorable night was: Dawson, Gray, Shaw, McKillop, Simpson, Brown, Waddell, Fiddes, Smith, McPhail and Kinnear.

At 5ft 7in, Jock was perhaps physically not as intimidating as, say, Willie Woodburn, but that simply belied someone with the heart of a lion and a never-say-die attitude. When you match those attributes with no little skill, then you have a potent cocktail.

Which brings me to the new moniker he attracted shortly after his arrival at Ibrox, which to all intents and purposes forever more was what the supporters referred to him as – Tiger.

The legend was not too long in being established, as it was during this match against Arsenal that the 'Tiger' nickname was born, due to his ferocious but fair tackling, and never-say-die attitude. Jock recalled, 'At Airdrie I had never been anything other than Jock. I was christened John but in Lanarkshire in those days John soon becomes Jock, but that soon changed to Tiger when that is what the Rangers supporters started calling me.'

Struth, some years later, commented about how he remembered Jock hardly ever being injured and he put this down to his fierce tackling. He recalled, 'Shaw went into every tackle with perfect timing, braced and ready for it. The chaps who got hurt are those who went in half-heartedly with the leg loose and flabby.'

The league campaign got off to a mixed start with draws against St Johnstone (3-3) and Motherwell (2-2) at Ibrox and defeat was only avoided by a last-minute Davie Kinnear goal. It seemed that the team were taking time to settle but there were signs of future promise. For example, it was noted in the press that Shaw was the best back in the encounter with Motherwell and that Willie Woodburn was showing promise as a potential successor to veteran Jimmy Simpson. Bob McPhail was noted as providing valuable experience even if he was no longer as mobile as he once had been.

There then followed three wins against St Johnstone (4-2), St Mirren (5-1) and Ayr United (4-1) before a chastening trip to Parkhead where the light blues were soundly thrashed (2-6).

Far from being a setback, as it most assuredly could have been, that defeat seemed to galvanise the team and only a further three defeats were suffered over the remainder of the season.

The return Old Firm match, on 2 January 1939, was a special affair as it marked the official opening of the new Archibald Leitch-designed Main Stand in front of a record league crowd of 118,730 spectators. The majority left elated as the light blues triumphed by 2-1 with goals from Davie Kinnear and Alex Venters, while Carruthers replied for the visitors. This win propelled Rangers to the title on the back of a 13-match unbeaten run, ended only on the final day of the season by the Dons.

Rangers notched up some mammoth victories during their march to the title, including scoring 12 against Albion Rovers. The championship was won by 11 points from Celtic and by scoring 112 goals over the 38 matches.

The cups were not as kind, as Rangers only managed to annex the Charity Cup on the basis of corners won. Queen's Park were beaten 2-1 in the semi-final before a 0-0 draw against Third Lanark in the final in front of a crowd of 29,448 at Hampden. No extra time was played then and the corner count was 7-4 in Gers' favour so the trophy was Ibrox-bound.

In the Scottish Cup Gers beat Raith Rovers 1-0 at Stark's Park, then Hamilton 2-0 at Ibrox before a calamitous 4-1 defeat to Clyde at Ibrox. Clyde were worthy winners and would go on to lift the cup, with the goal Rangers scored the only one they lost on their march to glory.

The Glasgow Cup was lost in the first round when Rangers were defeated 3-2 by Queen's Park at Ibrox following a scoreless draw at Hampden.

All in all, though, it was a hugely successful first season for Tiger with winner's medals in both the League and Charity Cup safely tucked away. He played in every single match Rangers played – League (38), Scottish Cup (3), Charity Cup (2), Glasgow Cup (2) and friendly (1).

As the season concluded, Tiger would have purred in contentment, if you can excuse the terrible pun, but only a few short months later the world would be plunged into turmoil.

War

THE FOLLOWING is reproduced from the sadly now-defunct *Rangers Historian* of 1989, with the kind permission of Robert McElroy.

When Great Britain declared war on the Third Reich on 3/9/1939 the football season was already in full swing. After five games of the season Rangers led the table by a point from Falkirk with Aberdeen, Celtic, Hearts and Partick Thistle close behind. Dundee, after four games, led the Second Division followed by Dunfermline and King's Park. An international had already been played, the Scottish League having beaten their Irish rivals at Windsor Park but on that fateful afternoon the management pulled down the fire curtain on the show and called 'finis' to normal life for the next six years.

The next day the SFA advised its member clubs that the government had put a ban on all places of entertainment, including outdoor sports and in consequence all players' contracts were cancelled although their registrations would remain effective. Any further moves would need to await the government's decision.

Four days later the Home Secretary gave permission for friendly matches to be played in what were described as neutral areas, which were those not deemed likely candidates for air raids. Banned areas were Glasgow, Edinburgh, Dundee, Dunfermline and Clydebank.

On 13 September an emergency meeting of the SFA confirmed the ban on any competitive match in the neutral areas and the Scottish League management committee abandoned the 1939/40 league competition, but formed a sub-committee to investigate the possibility of regional competition, and the following day sent out feelers to its clubs on the matter.

Sensibly the authorities realised that if football was allowed in neutral zones, it should be permitted in the danger zones too, and as long as crowds were kept small no vast civilian concentrations would present themselves to enemy pilots who escaped the early warning system.

Logic prevailed, when on 15/9/1939, the Home Office gave its approval for competitive football even in the danger zones. Several clubs had pointed out that if football was to be permitted there was no reason why it should not have a competitive edge; if such games were banned, they would have to fold up.

The Scottish Secretary duly gave his approval for full competitive football on 21 September setting down limits for the bigger grounds such as 15,000 at Hampden, Celtic Park and Ibrox, and 8,000 for all others. Two days later friendlies were played at Ibrox (Rangers 1-4 Falkirk, Celtic 4-2 Partick Thistle, Queen's Park 3--4 Third Lanark and Hearts 2-4 Hibernian).

The final step on the road back to something passing as normal came on 26 September when agreement was reached for two regional leagues to be formed, commencing on 21 October.

Regional League South and West consisted of Rangers, Queen of the South, Hamilton, Motherwell, Clyde, Albion

Rovers, Morton, Kilmarnock, Third Lanark, Celtic, Partick Thistle, St Mirren, Queen's Park, Ayr United, Airdrie and Dumbarton. The North and East League was Falkirk, Hearts, Aberdeen, Dunfermline, St Johnstone, Alloa Athletic, East Fife, Dundee United, Hibernian, King's Park, St Bernard's, Raith Rovers, Arbroath, Stenhousemuir and Cowdenbeath.

Even as a contingency plan it wasn't much of a solution and by the 1940/41 season the format had been altered, although not as the Scottish League had hoped, as in the summer of 1940 it was proposed that a return to the promotion and relegation between the First and Second Division should be agreed. Things had a nasty habit of changing rapidly that summer.

In their very first wartime match, which saw Rangers succumb to Falkirk, Rangers lined up as follows: Dawson, Gray, Shaw, Bolt, Woodburn, Symon, Waddell, Gilmour, Thornton, Venters and Kinnear. Alex Venters got Rangers' only goal from the penalty spot in a 4-1 defeat.

The Glasgow Cup, incidentally, which had commenced in peacetime, continued unaltered on 7 October when Rangers, in their first competitive wartime game, faced Third Lanark at Ibrox in the semi-final. A 2-2 draw was played out with Gilmour and Waddell netting for the light blues, and Waddell also missing a penalty. The replay seven days later, again at Ibrox, saw the home side win 2-1 with Waddell and Gilmour again the scorers.

The final was played on Christmas Day 1939, with Queen's Park providing the opposition, again at Ibrox. Rangers brought some much-needed festive cheer to their supporters, winning 3-1 with goals from Gilmour, Thornton and McNee to record their first trophy success during what was to become known as World War Two. It is surely a remarkable coincidence that it was the now late-lamented Third Lanark whom Rangers faced in both their final peacetime match (a 2-1 win at Cathkin on 2 September 1939) and then their first competitive wartime match.

Other clubs who at the time were full-time members of the Scottish League but are sadly no longer in existence are King's Park (from Stirling), and the Edinburgh duo of St Bernard's and Leith Athletic.

Edinburgh City could also have been added to the list, as the incarnation present at the outbreak of the war was an amateur side who dropped out of the league in 1940 and played in the Lothian Amateur League during the hostilities. They were re-admitted to the Scottish 'C' League in 1946, but only lasted three years before setting up as a junior side, and ceased playing in 1955. A new club called Postal United was formed in 1966, while the Edinburgh City Football Club Ltd had continued to trade as a social club since the football team stopped playing. A vote was passed in 1986 following an application to allow Postal United to utilise and take over the name of Edinburgh City. The new Edinburgh City gained promotion to the Scottish Professional Football League in 2016.

The world changed for everyone with the outbreak of the war and life would never be the same again. Jock recalled, 'When war broke out, I went with my brother Davie to join the army, but if you were a miner, they preferred you to work in the pits. So, we went back to our original jobs. It meant I could only play football part-time. We were down the pits from 7am, trained twice a week at Ibrox and played on a Saturday.

'It was tough going but I always enjoyed it. For training we would run up and down the terraces starting at stairway one at the Celtic end and finishing at stairway 20 at the Rangers end. We hardly ever kicked a ball. Occasionally we would go on to the red ash school park across from Ibrox, or else play a game together at the car park on the Copland Road.

'I think standards did decline during the war years because teams were forced to field guest players or their own lads, home from leave, or even laddies too young to join up. We were quite fortunate. Willie Thornton was stationed in England and played a number of games for teams down there but players such as Willie Waddell, Andy Cheyne and George Jenkins all had engineering backgrounds and were put to work in the local shipyards so they could still play for Rangers. As far as I am aware we never struggled for players. The only one who ever guested for us was Stanley Matthews, as Bill Struth always had a supply of players.'

So the disrupted 1939/40 season reached a conclusion with Rangers champions of the new Regional League West, while Queen of the South were runners-up, eight points behind. Celtic finished a dismal 13th, only five points ahead of second-bottom Ayr United.

Rangers reached the Emergency War Cup Final by defeating Alloa, Falkirk, St Mirren and Motherwell and the light blues were confidently expected to dispose of the Tannadice team at Hampden, but the Tayside men were to emerge from the final with their reputation enhanced due to a spirited performance.

Showing scant regard for the reputations of the illustrious Ibrox line-up, United took control of the game in the early stages and wingers Glen and Fraser looked very busy on the flanks. Their nimble footwork had Rangers in trouble and from their crosses centre-forward Milne threatened to cause havoc in the light blues' goalmouth.

Twice in the course of the first five minutes he had headers on target, but he could not match that accuracy with power and Jerry Dawson saved both efforts easily.

The United half-back line of Baxter, Littlejohn and Robertson was also showing up well, winning possession and spreading passes, which had the Ibrox defence all at sea and Milne once more came close when he fired a powerful shot into the Rangers side net.

After that early flurry, United had to go on the defensive when Jimmy Smith took a pass from Willie Waddell and bustled through the defence only to be thwarted by a timely Littlejohn tackle.

Back came the underdogs from Dundee with Milne and Adamson linking up well only for the latter to shoot wildly past when he had two team-mates in better positions. Nobody could complain about a lack of entertainment in the opening spell but you got the impression that Rangers were holding something in reserve, allowing their opponents to commit themselves to attack before punishing them on the break.

So, everyone knowing the resources of the Ibrox players waited for the Rangers onslaught and waited, and waited. United continued to look the more impressive of the two outfits, stringing passes together and pinning the light blues in their own half of the field.

Wing-half Robertson broke through, taking a pass from Adamson but, with the way to goal clear, he opted for returning the ball to Adamson and Willie Woodburn cleared the danger. Then the Ibrox centre-half was caught in possession and Milne shoved the ball through to Gardner but again United showed a reluctance to shoot and Woodburn recovered in time to slide in and tackle the forward.

As half-time approached, the faces of the Rangers fans grew longer as their heroes remained under pressure, then two minutes before the break the long-awaited 'crack' appeared to show.

United were awarded a free kick on the edge of the penalty area after Milne had been fouled. Every Rangers player dropped back into their own goalmouth as Milne prepared to take the kick.

He shot for goal but his effort cannoned off the Rangers wall. It broke to Adamson and from eight yards out he confidently placed the ball out of Dawson's reach.

The United players turned cartwheels of joy as they celebrated the goal, only to be brought back to earth with a thump as referee Webb stood on the spot where Adamson had been and indicated that the Tannadice player had been offside. A lucky break for Rangers but a tragic blow for United. There was little time to get play back in motion before the half-time whistle sounded, and as the players trooped off there was certainly plenty for the manager Bill Struth to discuss with his players in the pavilion during the break.

Seldom had there been a more one-sided cup final, Rangers being mere spectators as United dominated the game, but to their credit they were still on level terms and now the fans looked to see them show their true form in the second half.

While there was an improvement in Rangers' play, United were still getting too much time on the ball for the Ibrox faithful's liking.

Full-backs Dougie Gray and Jock were the men breaking up the Tannadice attacks and United were now paying for their insistence of making one pass too many instead of getting a shot at goal.

At the opposite end of the field Jimmy Smith was causing problems for the Tayside rearguard as he took advantage of the service from wingers Willie Waddell and Adam Little.

Willie Thornton came close with a header almost inevitably from a Willie Waddell cross, but keeper Thomson was equal to the effort, tipping it over the crossbar.

It was now apparent that only something out of the ordinary was going to lead to a goal but, with both sets of players appearing to lack that extra special touch, a goalless draw was on the cards.

Then 14 minutes from time Jimmy Smith supplied that much-needed quality.

Alex Venters sent an accurate through ball to the Ibrox centre-forward who raced on to it as Littlejohn moved in to tackle but the Ranger beautifully sidestepped the defender leaving himself with only the keeper to beat.

As the crowd roared 'hit it', Jimmy kept going and drew Thomson from his line before neatly jinking round him and slotting into the empty net.

The roar which greeted the goal mirrored the opinion that the first goal would indeed be the only one and that's exactly how it turned out, with Rangers holding on to comfortably register a 1-0 win, taking the Emergency War Cup to Ibrox.

Dundee United could quite justifiably feel aggrieved at having lost a game in which they had so much of the play but Rangers proved once more that it's goals that count and when all is said and done clever lead-up play means nothing if you can't put the ball in the net.

A clean sweep of honours was completed with the Glasgow Cup and Merchants Charity Cup also being annexed. Jock only missed one match that entire campaign, a league encounter with Dumbarton at Boghead on 24 April 1940.

A New Look League

THE NEW Southern League kicked off on 10 August 1940 with Rangers meeting Falkirk in their augural match of the revised league format at Brockville. The light blues turned out in the rather unfamiliar garb of Queen's Park-style hoops. Rangers were right up against it from the start and only some superb goalkeeping from Jerry Dawson kept the Bairns at bay until the 17th minute when a superb Keyes pass sent Napier through, and he sidestepped Willie Woodburn before firing a fine shot into the net. With their tails up Falkirk poured forward.

Only a last-ditch goal-line clearance by Dougie Gray prevented Falkirk going two ahead. When you also consider Falkirk hit the woodwork three times in the first half it shows how dominant the Bairns were, but somehow Rangers reached the interval only one behind.

The second half started, following a familiar pattern with the home side swarming around the Rangers goal and Dawson coming to Rangers' rescue yet again, with a fine diving save from winger Carruthers, after his shot looked destined for the bottom corner. That save, though, appeared to dishearten Falkirk and in the 55th minute Rangers capitalised on some lax marking, and Jimmy Smith with his back to goal managed to hook the ball high past keeper McKie for the equaliser and the momentum of the match shifted significantly.

In an attempt to change the pattern of the match the home side switched centre-forward and right-winger. This was counterproductive as Marshall on the right had been causing Rangers all sorts of problems but the move backfired and the switch nullified that threat. Rangers then went on to capitalise. Left-winger Charlie Johnstone raced for a 50/50 ball with the home keeper and the Ranger duly won the race before lashing the ball into the empty net. Rangers then tightened their grip on the game and hit the crossbar twice, the post twice and had what looked like a perfectly good goal disallowed.

With six minutes remaining the points were secured after neat work by Waddell and Torry Gillick on the right and ended with the latter lashing a vicious shot into the Falkirk net.

That ended the match as a contest but not the talking points. On 87 minutes, Falkirk's Napier and Rangers' Johnstone clashed and the Ibrox man ended lying on the ground in agony. The referee was left with no option but to order the Falkirk man off in a sad end to an enthralling contest.

This opening match served as a marker for the season and Rangers would again prevail. Their closest rivals for this new league title were Clyde and it was a close contest; however, Rangers all but clinched the title when they beat Clyde 3-0 at Shawfield on 15 February in the 27th match of the 30-game season. Rangers won the title by three points from the Bully Wee.

In April 1941 Rangers faced St Mirren in a Southern League Cup semi-final tie having beaten Third Lanark 2-1 in the quarter-finals. Gers had the added bonus of Willie Thornton being available for selection as he was on seven days' leave from the army and Struth had no hesitation in including him. There was a crowd of 36,823 at Hamden that day to see the action.

Lining up in opposition was another legendary Ibrox figure in Bob McPhail, and he came close to giving Saints the lead, but his normally deadly touch deserted him and an almost certain chance was lost. Rangers wasted no time taking the lead in the 17th minute through Charlie Johnstone, then increased the lead through Thornton, justifying his short-notice selection. While supporters back then were much more restrained than these days, the sight of Thornton's goal had them throwing their hats in the air in jubilation and scaring the Hampden pigeons.

Soon after half-time Rangers went further ahead through Willie Waddell. Saints refused to buckle though and it was Jimmy Caskie who hit a wonderful volley from the edge of the penalty area to reduce the deficit.

Rangers refused to simply see out the tie, though, and restored their three-goal lead through Jimmy Smith, who finished off a neat interchange of passing to slot home from close range and ensure Rangers ran out emphatic winners by 4-1.

The light blues would go on to clinch the trophy in the final, defeating Hearts 4-2 in a replayed final following a 1-1 draw. The goals to ensure another winner's medal for Tiger came from Venters, Smith, Thornton and Johnstone in front of a healthy crowd of 70,000. *The Sunday Post* newspaper report of the time described the first match.

> The final we had all dreamed about stopped as most dreams do, at the most interesting part, but that was good stage-management. If it had lasted a few minutes longer the cup might have been won, and that would have diddled us out of an hour and a half of, I hope, the same next Saturday.
>
> As time wore on I felt that Rangers were bound to get the all-important goal before the 90 minutes were up, but it didn't happen. The way I figured it was that men like Jimmy Dykes, Archie Miller and Tommy Brown didn't deserve to finish on the losing side after such a display.
>
> The first half was a genuine test between two good teams. In the second it was only the unflagging effort of the Hearts defence that prevented the cup going to Ibrox. Of the two halves the first had everything. Rangers forward moves that fascinated. Forked lightning stuff from Johnstone, many

Walkerisms. Delectable Dougan dashes. Goalmouth stuff that made the shivers run down your back.

During one Thornton-Gillick-Smith move Waugh was standing open mouthed waiting for the inevitable to happen, and then up popped Tommy Brown to kick past for a corner. That was Hearts' first big escape.

The greatest thrill of all was when Johnstone went tearing past McLure like a tornado and swept the ball across goal. Dykes tried to intercept but his long legs weren't just long enough and Gillick came careering on to miss it by a fraction and landed headlong in the back of the net.

It would be about 15 minutes from the interval before the Tynecastle fellows settled into a really confident game. Wee Dougan started to show Johnny Shaw a trick or two that the latter didn't know very much about. Walker was endeavouring to make good his puerile display in last week's International while George Hamilton was beating Woodburn surprisingly often in the air.

The one blot on the landscape was the left wing. Massie was allowing himself to be beaten for the ball time and time again by Bobby Bolt with the result that Christie was left outside rather than outside-left. Yet Massie was right in at the death when the goal came along, after Walker made great play on the right, the ball fell between Massie and Dawson. Massie lofted the ball over his shoulder to leave the goal uncovered and as Walker rushed in to finish the job Woodburn stuck out his foot, and thus was credited with the score – an own goal.

Hearts should actually have turned around two-up as a minute or two later Hamilton flashed the ball across the goal with the Ibrox defence hopelessly lost. Massie and Christie made for it simultaneously, but it was a one-man job. The Hearts pair got flanked, and the chance of the game went a begging.

I won't go into detail about the second half because you would only get bored of the repetition of Rangers did this, Rangers did that, but the equaliser, you must get the slant on that.

Eight minutes after the interval and Gillick going flashing through Dykes took him in somewhat agricultural fashion just on the 18-yard line. Rangers claimed a penalty and I thought their restraint quite remarkable when Peter Craigmyle refused to listen to them.

The infringement was so palpable. In clearing, Dykes had conceded a throw-in however I for one did not have any regrets when after Massie had dillied and dallied instead of clearing first time Bolt's throw-in, young Marshall got possession took it first time, and banged it into the roof of the net.

From then on it was one-way traffic. I completely lost count of the number of times Johnstone's immaculate crosses were either headed or kicked away by the blond giant who rose above everyone else in the Tynecastle defence.

And then there was Archie Miller constantly popping in to prevent Gillick from becoming dangerous, though it is highly questionable whether Gillick can be dangerous these days.

To Philp and Brown, full marks, though they never showed the subtlety of their opposite numbers, Symon and Bolt. I cannot remember having seen Bolt play a better game. There was really no comparison in the forward play, which was hardly to be wondered at since Hearts had to rely on Dougan, Walker and Hamilton.

I didn't see much of young Marshall in the first half but he pushed himself into the limelight after scoring the equaliser. Rangers' best forward was Charlie Johnstone. He ran McLure quite dizzy, but if Mac usually came second best he took his medicine like a man.

There were 75,000 of us there and I fancy most will be in our places on Saturday. We may not see a Rangers victory but I reckon we ought to.

So, it was back to Hampden for the replay.

Five minutes from the finish we were all set for an extra half-hour, and we certainly needed it. Yeah, to recover from the shock of seeing the trophy won 'inside the distance' by Rangers. The light blues ought to have gone down on their bended knees last night and given thanks to all the good fairies who look after their welfare on occasions such as this. Occasions when they are beaten and somehow manage to survive. The picture I have of the last four minutes is more than a trifle hazy, and even yet I can scarcely believe it's true. Last week it was Rangers who were the second-half team. Hearts with a gallantry I have seldom seen equalled by any Tynecastle side, had fought and conquered a deficit of two goals.

Hamilton's dream equaliser 25 minutes after half-time put them in such a mood that subsequent defeat looked out of the question, and then to lose as they did.

A chancy Rangers right-wing raid, a quite uncalled for infringement on the part of a defender, a quite perfectly placed free kick by Bobby Bolt and a header from Willie Thornton. That was all, but it was enough to break the hearts of thousands of fond Hearts from Edinburgh.

Even though there were only four minutes left after that, the Tynecastle fellows still had a chance, but what happened? Walker instead of having a 'go' on his own, tried to tee up the ball from Massie. An Ibrox foot intercepted, and in a flash, play was away at the other end, and a corner won.

A lot of indecisive poking at the ball by defending and attacking men alike, until it came to Charlie Johnstone. The winger gathered it perfectly and hit it low and true as steel through a ruck of players into the net. Seconds more and Rangers had officially won the cup by four goals to two.

Hearts will dwell on their misfortunes for a long time to come. I have no doubt, ah me. As somebody or other said to me at the finish 'It would take tommy guns not Tommy Walkers, to beat a side with that amount of luck'. An excusable expression under the circumstances. Hearts were a better all-round team than they were last Saturday. They lost two goals in the first 20 minutes, and yet never displayed any signs of inferiority. I had the feeling that Waugh might have prevented the first – he lost the ball after having it in his grip, leaving Venters to walk the ball into the net.

The second may have looked a bit on the soft side but I am convinced it wasn't. Between them Gillick and Thornton made space for Smith and the big fellow veering to the left to outwit Dykes hit the ball from a terribly difficult angle with his left foot.

Hamilton whose wily leadership was putting furrows in the forehead of young Woodburn rose to a free kick by McClure six minutes from half-time to keep Hearts in the game. It was a well-deserved and long overdue reward.

Yes, Rangers were distinctly rattled round about this time. The fact Scot Symon could do very little with Walker made things a trifle too hot for some of the others, and for a time the tactics of the Ibrox defence weren't exactly kindergarten.

In the early stages of the second half it looked as if we were in for a repetition of last week. Willie Waugh made one of the most daring dives of his career to rob Venters of a goal and then there was Jimmy Smith getting all tied up when he had a little more to do than hit the ball straight in front of him, but it was little more than a passing phase. Before long Hearts were given more than they were getting.

The equaliser was well on the cards and it came delectably in 69 minutes.

Massie started it; Walker added his touch with a beautiful pass to Dougan. The winger then lobbed one across, Dawson moving out, the watchful Hamilton closing in. They rose almost simultaneously but Hamilton's judgement was better and the ball spun unerringly off his head into the net. The remainder I have already described. I might devote screeds more to the ifs and buts of it all. Instead of doing that I may want to say that apart from the result it was a grand finale.

While at times Hearts backs and halfs brought added work on themselves with faulty releasing of the ball, they all performed heroically. Walker was something like the glamour boy of old, and he had the perfect foil in Dougan.

I very much question if there is a better outside-right in the country today than Dougan. Christie's form was well in advance of last week's but I'm afraid Alec Massie was very little better.

Rangers didn't move with nearly the same assurance. One of the more noticeable changes was that Johnstone didn't get half the rope he got a week ago. Venters wasn't quite 100 per cent, but Thornton was Dandy and Smith as big a problem as before.

It is interesting to note that the trophy presented to Rangers at the end of the match was utilised in the guise of the Victory Cup in 1946.

On the day of the semi-final four Gers were named in the international squad to face England on 3 May – Dawson, Gillick, Smith and Venters, while Jock was named as a reserve. This was the first time full international recognition had come Jock's way, and was another sign of his progress.

These were obviously terrible times for everyone to live through, and Clydebank in particular was recovering from the Blitz while

London continued to suffer heavy bombing. Rangers played a match against the RAF on 23 April to raise funds for the Clydebank Air Raid Distress Fund in front of 25,500.

It was against this background that football at least provided a degree of escapism.

Jock was again an ever-present, and in addition picked up a winner's medal in the Merchants Charity Cup.

The First Clean Sweep

HEADING INTO the 1941/42 season Rangers were supremely confident, and rightly so, as, with the exception of the odd cup result, they were completely dominant across the Scottish Football landscape. This was in no small part due to Mr Struth's shrewd recruitment and sustaining a strong pool of players, and not relying on 'guests'.

Over the years there were several challengers to their throne. One such challenger was Hearts, and the Edinburgh side's visit to Ibrox on 15 November 1941 was particularly crucial, both Rangers and Hearts being locked together at the top of the table with 22 points apiece, so the objective of both teams was clear, a victory to be top of the league.

It was to be a match in which two players stole the show, the respective inside-rights Torry Gillick and Tommy Walker of Hearts. Their skills did much to give the big crowd a memorable afternoon's football.

With no more than four minutes played, the fans' cards were well and truly marked with each side getting on to the scoresheet. The scorers of the goals: Messrs Gillick and Walker.

The Hearts man put his side in front when he capitalised on good work by inside-left McCrae and beat keeper Jenkins with a fierce shot from just around the penalty spot, bringing grimaces to the Ibrox faithful. But if the visitors thought they were on their way to a comfortable victory, they were soon to realise the folly of such thinking.

Torry Gillick picked up the ball some 25 yards from goal, took two paces forward and unleashed a rocket of a shot which almost demolished the goalpost before flying into the net.

That set the scene for the day's entertainment, both sides playing wonderful attacking football and, if anything, Hearts looked the likely winners in the early stages as they swept Rangers aside with Walker playing a pivotal role in the Jambos' forward thrusts.

There were several near things in the Rangers goalmouth with the light blues having good cause to be thankful to keeper Jenkins on more than one occasion.

The Ibrox keeper covered himself in glory in the 20th minute when McCrae barged through the Rangers defence and fired in a powerful shot which appeared destined for the roof of the net until Jenkins leapt to touch the ball onto the crossbar.

The danger was still there as the ball rebounded from the bar into the path of the onrushing Adams but Jenkins threw himself at the Hearts man's feet and smothered the effort, to the cheers of the fans.

Hearts were to pay dearly for their failure to capitalise on the chances they created.

In a five-minute period near the end of the first half, Rangers struck with a vengeance scoring three goals in quick succession to sink Hearts' table-topping aspirations.

The first of the trio was scored by Jimmy Smith who outjumped centre-half Dykes to nod a Charlie Johnstone cross into the postage-stamp corner of the net and three minutes later Gillick again showed the power of his shooting, cracking the ball home from outside the penalty area. With Hearts now reeling, Gillick sent McIntosh clear on the right and the winger sent a superb cross to the far post where Johnstone raced in to make it four. To Hearts' credit they continued to fight but with their tails up the Ibrox men had no intention of conceding their advantage and the visitors were right up against it.

Tommy Walker did get his name onto the scoresheet again when he crashed a Gillies cross past Jenkins from ten yards out, and there were flickering signs of a Hearts fightback as the Edinburgh men tried to repeat Walker's effort.

However, with full-backs Jock and Dougie Gray, along with centre-half Thomson on top form, Hearts were banging their heads against a brick wall particularly with keeper Jenkins emulating his defenders.

It must have been very frustrating for the Hearts players because, make no mistake about it, they were playing well and were matching Rangers in every department of the game except where it mattered most – in front of goal.

Rangers proved that point four minutes from time when the McIntosh/Johnstone combination which had produced the fourth goal reversed roles to net the fifth, McIntosh heading a Johnstone cross past the diving Anderson.

So Rangers ran out convincing winners but there was no lack of sympathy for Hearts having met the Ibrox men on a day when a player of the calibre of Torry Gillick was at his best.

Torry was the man who had made Rangers tick that day, spraying passes to both wingers and serving up shooting of an accuracy and power second to none.

Only he could have overshadowed Tommy Walker in the way he did and remembering the high class of football for which Walker is renowned it's a great tribute to Gillick's ability that he was able to do so.

Having opened up a two-point gap by virtue of the 5-2 win over Hearts, Rangers held on to their place at the top to register yet another title win with the procession of success maintained. Highlights during this campaign were Jock's first goals for the club, as he notched three times. These strikes were in a 7-0 home win against Dumbarton, then penalties in the 6-0 home win against Hamilton Accies, and an 8-2 victory at Shawfield against Clyde.

In addition to the league title, the club completed a clean sweep of all the honours available which include the Southern League

Cup, Glasgow Cup, Glasgow Merchants Charity Cup and the Summer Cup.

The Summer Cup victory was achieved via the toss of a coin after a 0-0 draw with Hibernian at Hampden and corner-kick count in extra time being equal at 2-2. This was a modicum of revenge for defeat by the same opponents in this competition the previous season. So, the curtain came down on a hugely successful campaign on 4 July 1942.

Season 1942/43 to the End of the War

THE COUNTRY was now three years into the war and football continued as near to normality as possible with the league set-up regionalised. Clubs saw their player pools depleted and with some experienced players away in the services, youngsters with limited experience were often introduced to first-team duties. Rangers were no different although most of the time they managed to field a relatively stable side with many players, such as Jock in the mines, having reserved occupations. Contemporary match reports of the time often listed the Rangers side as 'Defence as usual, forwards were...' That defence was, of course, Dawson, Gray, Shaw, Adam Little, Young and Symon.

New Year's Day in 1943 brought a game of huge significance, war or no war, as it saw Rangers achieve a record score in an Old Firm match. The crowd was restricted at the time and therefore only 30,000 were present on the day. However, if you had arrived a little late you would have missed the first two Rangers goals as the light blues streaked into a quick-fire two-goal lead after only four minutes through Duncanson and Waddell. Celtic fought to get back into the match and pulled a goal back in the 11th minute through Duncan, to reduce the deficit. Rangers then took a stranglehold on the game and came close to increasing their lead on several occasions but stout defensive work by Celtic kept them at bay till the interval. The crowd eagerly awaited the second half as, although Rangers were dominant, there was only one goal in it and the next goal would be crucial.

No one, though, could have foreseen what would unfold over the next 45 minutes, and the complexion of the match was about to change dramatically. Torry Gillick scored a third soon after the restart injuring himself in the process by striking his head on an upright. He refused to leave the field and as things turned out he remained to make quite a mark on proceedings. A further 11 minutes had elapsed when George Young swept a free kick across the Celtic goalmouth, and Waddell deflected the ball into the net to make it 4-1, much to the annoyance of Celtic's McDonald. For reasons known only to himself, the Parkhead full-back disputed the validity of the goal and the protests were so vociferous he was eventually dismissed.

Three minutes later the visitors' wing-half Lynch met the same fate, again for remarks to the referee. Interestingly, post-match, there were reports that Rangers forward Duncanson felt the second dismissal was rather harsh and sent a letter to the SFA pleading for leniency on Lynch's behalf.

While the gulf in class was obvious prior to the dismissals, with Celtic now down to nine men it became a yawning chasm.

Rangers were in no mood to take it easy and a great Waddell run ended when the winger crashed the ball past keeper Miller to complete his hat-trick and soon afterwards George Young converted a penalty to make it 6-1. The Rangers fans in the crowd were in full voice, really enjoying themselves now, and to a man they rose to acclaim the injured Torry Gillick who despite being dazed added a further two goals to also complete his own hat-trick.

The only crumb of comfort for Celtic was that Willie Thornton was serving abroad at the time of the match; one can only speculate what the final scoreline may have been had he been available.

Rangers' domination of the football landscape was total during this period and over the next three years the cavalcade of trophies and success continued. Titles were won in 1942/43, 1943/44 and 1944/45. Success in cup competitions also continued with only the odd set-back along the way. Over these three years the Southern League was won twice, the Glasgow Cup three times, and the Glasgow Merchants Charity Cup twice.

An impressive haul of honours and no mistake but unfortunately, due to wartime restrictions and shortages, there was not always a medal to go along with the trophy. Speaking in 1972, Rangers outside-left Charlie Johnstone recalled that players often got savings certificates instead of medals. On that basis, the Rangers playing staff must have been very wealthy men. During this period a quite remarkable run came to an end for Jock. On 18 December 1943 Jock missed Rangers' home match with Airdrie, which brought to an end an ever-present record for Rangers stretching back to 27 April 1939. Over a period of four years, which spanned five seasons, Jock appeared in 173 consecutive matches for the club in all competitions including friendlies and benefit games. A testimony to his dedication and supreme fitness levels.

Of the war years, Jock said, 'During this spell we simply dominated the game, and we won everything going. There were some great names around then. There was Jerry Dawson in goal, and Dougie Gray at right-back, while at centre-half there was either Willie Woodburn or George Young and then there were the half-backs like Ian McColl and Sammy Cox.

'On the right wing there was Willie Waddell, and when he intermittently came back from the war Willie Thornton. Alex Venters was in the team when I arrived and Torry Gillick. They were all terrific players and there were others who came through into the side, like Bobby Brown and Billy Williamson. It was a magnificent team.

'For as well as everyone being a top-class player, we were a team as well. We all worked for each other and helped each other too. And the players could take a telling. It didn't matter who they were or what their reputation was, if they did something wrong on the park they were told in no uncertain manner, and they listened.'

There were also changes afoot in Tiger's life, as in 1944 the Shaws were blessed with the birth of a daughter, Margaret, to be joined by a son David not long afterwards.

War Ends and the Dynamos Visit, Season 1945/46

AT LAST the hostilities and heartache of the previous six years came to an end with Germany's surrender on 8 May 1945, which prompted Winston Churchill's announcement of VE (Victory in Europe) Day and street parties were held all over Britain to celebrate the end of the war. In truth, the World War did not formally come to an end till September 1945, when US General Douglas MacArthur accepted Japan's formal surrender aboard the US battle ship *Missouri* anchored in Tokyo Bay. The general public rubbed their hands in anticipation of a return to a normal life, and that, of course, included the football-supporting public.

It would take some time to demob all the national servicemen, but with the war over the man on the street could look forward to going along to a match without the thought of an air raid or wondering how relatives were faring on the battlefield.

So, when 25 September was declared Victory Day a series of exhibition games was arranged across the country to celebrate the event and on that date Newcastle United came to Ibrox to take on Rangers.

The Geordies were one of England's top teams and just the day before arriving in Glasgow they had annihilated Stoke City 9-1, so there were absolutely no doubts this would prove to be a tough match.

A crowd of 48,000–50,000 (depending upon reports of the time) turned up and all the admission money was donated to the King George VI Navy Fund, a worthy charity which benefitted immensely from the large crowd.

Newcastle, though, were less than courteous visitors in the opening stages when they showed they were interested in only one thing: to beat Rangers. After five minutes, winger Jackie Milburn took a pass from Stubbings and from 20 yards he sent in a fierce left-foot shot which left Dawson helpless as the ball nestled in the net behind him.

The gauntlet had well and truly been laid down and Rangers did not take long to respond. Four minutes later Scot Symon sent a superb pass through the middle and Billy Williamson raced on to it, to send a powerful shot goalwards. Keeper Swinburne got a hand to the shot but could not stop it crossing the line; 1-1 and the game was well and truly on.

Now we had the exciting spectacle of both sides attacking each other for all they were worth and Dawson was forced to make a fine save from Milburn, just before Ibrox winger McNee had a net-bound shot deflected wide of the posts.

In the 23rd minute Rangers took the lead. Great work by Jimmy Duncanson left three Newcastle defenders in his wake, and his cutback across the face of goal left Billy Williamson the easiest of chances. Rangers now had the upper hand and the visitors had no answer to the right-wing duo of Waddell and Gillick, who were taking the Magpies' defence apart. After the half-time break the light blues continued to press forward and in the 50th minute the woodwork again denied Williamson. Three minutes later Waddell raced into the penalty area but was impeded by full-back Smith. There was to be no celebration though as Young's spot kick was saved by Swinburne.

This seemed to galvanise Newcastle and they clawed their way back into the game. A lapse in the Rangers defence allowed inside-forward Welman space to shoot and his effort flew into Dawson's net to tie the scores.

Disappointed though the crowd were, they couldn't help but appreciate the quality of football on show, and Rangers were not prepared to settle for a share of the spoils.

Towards the end the light blues forced a corner and Willie Waddell's cross into the box was met by the high-flying Jimmy Duncanson, whose thumping header restored the Ibrox side's lead. The roar which greeted the goal was said to almost split the skies and Newcastle just could not come back from the killer blow, and Rangers ran out worthy winners. The big crowd got a glimpse of what normality was to look like and were hugely appreciative of what both sides had served up and the Scottish press acclaimed Rangers having beaten one of the top sides in England.

Next up in the spirit of introducing some glamour matches for the masses were the famous Russian side Moscow Dynamo.

The press of the time originally suggested that Dynamo would perhaps play against a Glasgow Select XI, before it was settled that the match would be against Rangers.

This match is engraved in the annals of Rangers' colourful history, and Jock recalled: 'Aye, it was quite a game. They were a bit different to what we had been used to playing against. But we had to settle down to the match and take everything in our stride. There was no question of spy trips back then to find out how the opposition played. We had to find out ourselves.'

Nothing at all was known about the Russians when they arrived in Britain except that they were also supposed to be good ice-hockey players. As it turned out they played in a very modern style with a deep-lying centre-forward, Beskov, who would go on to be the national team manager. They had a tremendous centre-half in Semichastny and a remarkably athletic keeper in Khomich.

By the time they arrived at Ibrox on Wednesday, 8 November 1945 they had drawn 3-3 with Chelsea before 85,000 at Stamford

Bridge, thrashed Cardiff City 10-1, and then beaten a star-studded Arsenal side, which included Stanley Matthews as a guest player, 4-3.

So, it was very clear this would be a serious test for the Ibrox men.

The Russians were making themselves awkward guests upon arrival to the UK. In addition to complaints about accommodation (which were to an extent justified) they also had a list of demands; they wished to only play on the day which was normally a football day in England (Saturday), wished the referee who accompanied them to officiate in at least one match, wished substitutes to be permitted, and to have an assurance that the teams would not be changed from the names submitted to them before each match. They had also insisted on training on the pitches they were to play on, and were to astonish the home crowds at each game by coming out some time before kick-off and having an intensive warm-up with several balls, something no British team ever did in those days.

Around this time Rangers were in negotiations to bring Jimmy Caskie to Ibrox from Everton. Prior to their arrival in Glasgow the Russians had been sent a list of 18 players and as Caskie's transfer had not yet been completed his name was not on the list. After realising both Chelsea and Arsenal had strengthened their teams with guest players, the Russians insisted they would not be agreeable to such a thing happening for the Ibrox clash as they considered those previous encounters had been strictly against the representations they had made in advance. Accordingly, they advised Rangers 'Niet' and that if Caskie played they would not.

The match at Ibrox had caught the public imagination as no other had in the history of the Scottish game. People had queued for hours to obtain tickets so it was unthinkable the game could not go ahead.

Journalist Hugh Taylor recalled in his book *We Will Follow Rangers*:

> The visit of Moscow Dynamo was like no other before and I was constantly being harassed for match tickets so answered yet another call wearily. 'It's about the Dynamo game,' and I

automatically interrupted and wearily said, 'I am sorry I can't get you a ticket.' The voice on the other end said 'Is that Mr Taylor?' In a tired voice I repeated, 'No can do, I couldn't get you a ticket for £50,' and the voice on the other end said, 'I don't want a ticket for the match, I've got one. I want to tell you about a picture you can get, of the first picture of the Russians.' I jerked up; this was different, this promised to be a real story, especially when the voice said the picture was located in of all places, a public house in Paisley. The voice on the phone unfortunately didn't know in which public house was to be found the valuable picture. So I set off, starting at one end of the town and making sure I didn't miss any places of refreshment on my way to the other end. Rather unfortunately for my thirst I found my objective inside ten minutes, but then soon I realised I was on the track of a really good story.

The Palace bar was owned by the George Walker whose brother was none other than Bobby Walker one of the greatest forwards ever to play for Hearts and Scotland. It was a tavern with a real football atmosphere. Displayed in the bar were many valuable trophies, including most of Bobby's numerous international caps. Then Mr Walker told me how football started in Russia. Yes, it was the Scots again, the race who had taken their national game to countless countries. Coats the famous Paisley thread firm had a factory in Russia and Scots who went out at the beginning of 20th century to establish the factory made it their missionary work to teach the Russians our national game. [Coats had a factory there between 1889 and 1917, set up to avoid import duty.]

They were good coaches but as with many other nations who had been taught in the first place by Scots the pupils were now the masters and as proficient in all the arts and crafts of the game as the old Scottish masters themselves. Now the Russians were meeting a Scottish team on level terms.

What about that picture? 'Oh yes,' said Mr Walker, they had a picture. Would he mind if I took it back to the *Evening News* office to use with my story? He gave me an odd look but replied 'not at all'. He then proceeded to produce the picture which then explained the odd look he drew me. At least Mr Walker and two barmen produced it. No wonder Mr Walker looked at me oddly, what a picture this was. It seemed to me to be about six feet long, and two feet high, but it didn't lack detail. It showed two full teams lined up in a field near the Coats works in Russia (though it was not possible to tell if it was the site at St Petersburg, Riga or Lodz). This was the first informal Russia v Scotland international. It was a real panoramic effort, even the spectators were clearly seen. They were composed mainly of spectacularly dressed Russian officers. It made a fine exclusive story and then I had a brainwave. Why not ask Rangers to hang the picture in the Dynamo dressing room at Ibrox before the match by way of a small gesture to make the Russians feel at home. I got in touch with Ibrox and Mr Struth the Rangers manager liked the idea. So, we got the huge picture down to the stadium and the caretaker hung it in the dressing room the Russians were to occupy.

Upon arrival the Dynamo received a heroes' reception from the excited citizens of Glasgow. They looked superbly fit, these footballers with strange-sounding names who were surprised as we stood and gazed, in our utility suits and patched shirts compared with how smart the Russians were, debonair in leather coats and wide brimmed hats.

The Russians smiled and exchanged compliments with their hosts in Glasgow, but they had an iron-curtain complex: their officials were aloof and it was difficult for reporters to glean much information from them, though they were not lacking in courtesy.

When they reached their hotel their chief officials immediately disappeared into a private room. We learned later that a special phone had been installed, and the line to Moscow was busy both day and night. The Russians were leaving nothing to chance. It may only have been a football match, but it had been planned with typical Soviet thoroughness. National prestige was at stake. Dynamo were expected to win, or Moscow would want to know why. Anyhow there was no lack of instructions from their experts in Moscow.

No detail was too small for the Russians to overlook. They even brought their own food. My mouth watered; my own lunch consisted of whale steak as I watched the Dynamo players sit down to their first meal. There were mountains of eggs, fountains of chocolate drinks, mounds of butter.

The Russians also impressed the onlookers as they trained at Ibrox prior to the match which would prove to be one of the most exciting ever played in Scotland.

These practise sessions were anything but light hearted. The Dynamo team boss was a tall fair-haired man, Merited Master of Sports Mikhail Yakushin, and he had a guard sergeant's outlook on life. I saw him smile once. He didn't train his players – he drilled them; everything was done with regimental precision. For more than an hour at a time, he put the players through it. They lapped, exercised and practised with the ball with grim-faced concentration. There was no time for humour. Even when the pretty girl who was one of the interpreters posed for photographers after one training session, happily kicking the ball, Mr Yakushin only frowned. The coach knew his job, and he certainly hadn't earned his highly impressive title for nothing.

I actually gasped the first time I saw him in action. In the Ibrox dressing room he signalled his players to go out on to the pitch. There were two footballs lying on the floor. Neatly he put his foot over one, and flicked it into his hands. Then he put his left foot over the other, and the next second that too was magically in his hands. A football master indeed this Merited Master of Sports.

Well, the Russians looked good at practise. Every expert who saw them, and few know more about the game than the people of Glasgow, admitted that, and realised that Rangers were in for a test as stiff as any they had ever faced in their long and illustrious history.

No one could doubt the fitness of the Russians. Every one of them was a superb athlete, product of a diet balanced to vitamins, and a training schedule planned to the most trifling detail supported by a panel of experts whose ideas were revolutionary. And it was in fitness in particular that some feared they would score over Rangers.

There was nothing military about the training of the Rangers players. Indeed, their workouts would have shocked the serious-minded Russians but there was little the Ibrox staff could do about it. All the Rangers players were working at that time. They could snatch an hour or two off for training when they could, and they arrived in batches of threes and fours, but in the short time at their disposal they put in considerable work. They were lucky too in that they had as their supervisors their great manager Mr Bill Struth a notable athlete in his day, and Arthur Dixon the trainer who was once a famous Rangers player himself. The work these two experts put in was not realised until after the match, but it was triumph of improvisation, for as events proved the part-time Rangers finished more strongly than their sternly disciplined opponents.

Perhaps the difference in the end was that Rangers really enjoyed their training. It was in amazing contrast to watch the grim Russians and then see the broad beams on the faces of the Scottish players as they joked and wise-cracked while they lapped and practised.

All the time the excitement over the match was mounting to fever pitch. Every ticket was sold but still disappointed enthusiasts offered as much as thirty pounds (around £1,300 today), for a single seat, money being much more plentiful than it had been in the austere days of the war.

Then on the eve of the match came a sensation, one of the most dramatic in football history.

Rangers had completed the signing of Jimmy Caskie from Everton. This little winger had played at Ibrox before he had gone south, and now he returned to Rangers and there was no doubt he was eligible to play against Dynamo. But Dynamo protested bitterly that he was really an Everton player and that Rangers had no right to play him. A terrific row broke out. All we could hear from the Russians was 'no', and they stood firm. There was panic as they threatened to pack their bags and return to London without playing the match. It looked as though an international incident couldn't be prevented. At a Glasgow Corporation dinner before the match Rangers brought in Sir George Graham the wise and diplomatic secretary of the Scottish Football Association, respected wherever football is played, to confer and try to convince the men of Moscow that they were mistaken and that Rangers weren't playing a capitalist trick. In vain the dour Russians shook their heads and simply announced again that they were going home and filed sombrely out of the city chambers.

What a situation; all the tickets had been sold. The city was in ferment, what could Rangers do? They were in the right, there was no doubt about that but finally in the spirit of diplomacy Rangers agreed to withdraw Caskie and this midnight decision was conveyed to the Russians who typically betrayed no emotion, as they won what to them must have been a great diplomatic victory. The line to Moscow buzzed that night.

Glasgow also buzzed with chat among the fans, and this significant victory cost the Dynamo considerable support and respect. Even on the alleged Red Clyde where football usually comes before politics and most of the workers were Rangers supporters – the Russians were condemned. The Dynamos who had been junketed royally, were taken for a sail down Glasgow's greatest river before the game. On many ships were painted slogans. A Russian official asked an interpreter to tell him what they were, and to his credit he grinned widely when he was told that one says 'Good old Rangers' the others ask 'who's afraid of Jimmy Caskie'.

So after finally relenting on the Caskie conundrum thoughts turned to what the Rangers' team would be for the big match with most speculating it would not be decided until the day of the game. Tom McKillop, Rangers half-back, was demobbed from the Royal Navy after five-and-a-half years' service. He was on the job the day before at Ibrox getting tuned up, so he was certainly in the frame.

Dynamo were also proving difficult in relation to a proposed final in the UK with an English FA XI at Villa Park, provisionally on Wednesday, 5 December. Aston Villa were having 70,000 tickets printed.

Press on the day before printed the police instructions for traffic around Ibrox Stadium, and directions for parking. The associated press and other interested onlookers, including Jock and Jimmy Smith watched the Dynamos putting in a spot of final training yesterday morning from the Directors' box. Did I say a spot of training? Actually it was more than 90 minutes the players were put through their paces. They were drilled for half an hour physically then an hour doing ball work under the eagle eye of their trainer. There was no slacking and one and all of the onlookers were open in their admiration of work they put in. There were few exclamations even at the initial limbering up work, and what admiration at the ability of the Dynamo forwards – hitting a running ball or dead ball.

All the preparation in the world was all very well but could this be translated into a competitive match; we would soon find out.

On the day of the match the atmosphere was tense. You could feel the electricity in the air. Football match? It had more the air of a battle. Indeed, I have never known such a palpitating day in soccer, and I have seen great matches in places as far away as Budapest, Belgrade and Vienna.

Football in Scotland had slumped. Heavy defeats by the brilliant wartime England team had affected morale, and Dynamo had been praised as the best football team to arrive in Britain for years. Could the part-time Rangers hold the mighty men of Moscow? At least they had all of Scotland behind them, and even Celtic supporters for probably the first and last times in their lives were there to cheer on their greatest rivals.

The waiting time before the teams came out was almost unbearable. Even in the tummies of hardened reporters in the lofty Ibrox press box there were butterflies. I know I have never felt more nervous before any match. For once even the wonderful view from the high press box, surely an artist delight, this entrancing bird's-eye glimpse of Glasgow embracing the dignity of the university, the bustle of the shipbuilding yards, symbolised by the great arenas and the majesty of the hills on the outskirts, failed to distract me. I smoked nervously. Suddenly there was a gasp from the seething crowd.

The Dynamo players had appeared 15 minutes before kick-off. Although continental teams who visited Glasgow later made the practice common place the intensive pre-match shooting session of the Dynamo in 1945 made us wonder at their thoroughness. There were 12 Russians with six footballs. They shot and passed, practised tactical moves. It was a real warm-up and a vivid contrast to the haphazard shooting-in with one ball indulged in by all Scottish sides at the time.

Just before the kick-off the Russians raced back to the pavilion and re-appeared a few minutes later in company with Rangers.

The anticipation was tangible, and it was a crisp sunny November day which saw 90,000 pack into Ibrox, with the preliminaries to the nerve wracked crowd seeming endless. The teams exchanged bouquets of flowers, the newly elected Lord Provost Hector McNeil was introduced, and the national anthems of both countries were played. Photographers fluttered around frantically trying to capture the best shots for the evening and daily papers. At last everything had been done, every courtesy exchanged, and referee Tommy Thomson from Leamington blew a sharp blast on his whistle, and the great game had begun.

This match was considered at the time to be the most serious friendly ever played but Rangers did no planning whatsoever. All Struth said in the dressing room before the match was, 'Let them play for 20 minutes so you will discover their style, then take it from there.' That was all very well in theory but, of course, by the time the style had been established the light blues were 2-0 down.

Jimmy Smith who was Rangers' rampaging centre-forward of the time recalled the match. 'I can remember that the first thing that surprised us was the support Dynamo received when they took the field. We later learned that 30,000 communists from all over Scotland had come to cheer on the Russians.

'The next thing I remember is how tough they were physically. We'd been told they were all good ice hockey players and it certainly looked that way from their style of body checking. It rattled some of our boys but I was over 6ft and 14 stone, so it didn't bother me too much.' Dynamo shocked Rangers with a goal after only three minutes, a flashing free kick from Kartsev, who was to add a second goal in the 25th minute.

'They were a clever team at times playing in little triangles. But we buckled down and didn't give them the space they wanted. We missed a penalty before they got their second goal, Willie Waddell's kick being saved by Khomich.'

Just before the interval Smith struck with a scrambled effort from inside the six-yard box.

'Watching the Russians in training before the game I noticed that every time Khomich came out to meet a cross he had his feet up high and into the chest of whoever was coming in with him for the ball. The boss Bill Struth asked me what I was going to do about that, and I simply said I would get in there first. And that's just what happened. I was supposed to draw back but I didn't. We both got hurt but I got the goal although I had to go off later in the game.'

Later George Young equalised with a penalty after Billy Williamson had been fouled. Afterwards the Russians said that Rangers were the 'finest athletes we have ever played against'. Big Jimmy Smith for years afterwards would get messages carried back to him from people who had visited Russia saying that Tiger Khomich was asking after him. 'I don't think he forgot about me in a hurry. At the big banquet after the game the girl interpreter told me that the big-shot from the Russian Embassy in London thought I kicked hard, since their big centre-half had to miss the function as he was resting up in bed.'

In keeping with the importance and prestige of the match the players got a very welcome £50 as a bonus payment.

The Moscow Dynamo clash was in Jock's view the only game that could compare with an Old Firm clash. 'That was a great game. We knew we had a right handful on our plates, and we were proved right. The crowd was fantastic that day. There were 90,000 but it was more like 190,000. I'll never forget the moment just after half-time when it was discovered they had 12 men on the park. One man had been injured but he wasn't off when another came on. It was Torry Gillick who counted them, I remember him saying "11 of them are hard enough to beat but 12…" Aye that was a great game all right.'

An interesting postscript to the game was that this match was also to generate a wee tribute to Tiger in song. The Russians had their giant of a keeper called Tiger Khomich but, while he was an impressive-enough character in the eyes of the Rangers support he did not quite match up to their version of the Tiger, and so they sang lustily, 'Oh the Russians came to boast about the Tiger, they said he was far abune them aw, but they surely came and saw a real defender, when they saw our own Wee Tiger Shaw.'

The last word on the Dynamos tour, though, should be left to the renowned author of *Animal Farm* and *1984,* George Orwell . In an essay entitled 'The Sporting Spirit' which appeared in *The Tribune* in 1945 he wrote, 'Now that the brief visit of the Dynamo football team has come to an end, it is possible to say publicly what many people were saying privately before the Dynamos ever arrived. That is, that sport is an unfailing cause of ill-will, and that if such a contest as this had any effect on Anglo-Soviet relations, it could only be to make them slightly worse than before.'

This game to all intents and purposes saw Jerry Dawson, the Prince of Goalkeepers, bow out as Rangers keeper after 15 years of loyal service. His last competitive game was at Fir Park in a 2-1 win against Motherwell on 24 November, and his final appearance was in a friendly against Celtic played at Petershill on 15 April 1946.

For the remainder of the season his place would be taken by Jock's namesake John Shaw, who held down the jersey until the summer arrival of Bobby Brown.

Post-war life in Scotland was difficult, particularly during the winter months, and any matches were generally played in bad light and poor weather in the days long before floodlights were introduced.

If you have not lived in an industrial city, such as Glasgow at that time, in the days before the introduction of the Clean Air Act in 1956, you have no idea how dense a real pea-souper of smog could be – a combination of smoke from domestic fires, industrial furnaces, exhaust fumes from vehicles and natural damp fog. Visibility was reduced to nil on occasions. In the densest fog, bus conductors were forced to walk in front of their buses to guide drivers and there were reports of domestic drivers following the tram lines in an effort to get home only to find themselves in the tram depot!

The atmosphere was very difficult and unpleasant to breathe for everyone and, even worse, life-threatening to many. It only took four days of continuous smog on the Forth-Clyde valley to fill the local hospitals, but the football had to go on.

On 15 December Rangers faced Kilmarnock at Ibrox with Willie Thornton making his first appearances for Rangers since 30 January 1943, when he had scored twice for Rangers in a 3-0 win against Hamilton at Douglas Park. The game was played naturally enough in a blanket of smog and play on the far side of the field could not be followed at all assuredly from the press box high up in the main stand. As the afternoon wore on the smog got worse and the players could barely be seen at all on the field of play. In the 25th minute the flight of the ball deceived Jenkinson in the Kilmarnock goal and Caskie ('probably', it was reported at the time) despatched it into the net. Officially he was credited with the goal. At half-time Rangers were leading 3-0 and, due to the conditions, the teams crossed over and restarted immediately. In the second half a Caskie cross was missed by the defence and Gillick scored. As none of the reporters saw the ball enter the net, they assumed he was the scorer by the handshakes he was being offered. The final score was 5-1 for Rangers.

Only two months before, Jock had had his first experience of travelling and indeed playing abroad when Rangers flew from Prestwick airport to Hanover, Germany, to take on a Combined Services XI on 17 October in front of 50,000 spectators, predominately servicemen. The light blues did not travel well, though, and went down 1-6 with Willie Waddell notching the only goal.

Strikers

On Sunday, 16 December 1945 a meeting was held in Glasgow attended by 94 of the 330 Southern League players to consider striking on 1 January 1946. At a meeting the previous month the players had formulated a demand for a minimum wage of £6 per week plus a £1 bonus per point for the current season. The Scottish League had rejected the demands, making a counter-offer of £4 per week plus a £1 bonus per point.

Since the start of the season each player in the Southern League had been contributing a shilling a week to a strike fund and the refusal of the Scottish League to meet the demands was as much an issue as the money itself.

The first thing the meeting did was express dissatisfaction with the existing committee for not representing the interests of the players robustly enough. As a consequence, Dougie Gray resigned from the committee along with several others. Jimmy Caskie was elected to the new committee along with Jock, Jimmy Delaney of Celtic and Robert Bolt (Third Lanark).

The decision taken at the meeting was to strike on 1 January. Following a night of reflection apparently, it was reported the following day that the Rangers players had decided against strike action so the question now was whether or not they had nevertheless to agree to abide by the majority decision at the Sunday meeting. The uncertainty arose because when the decision to strike was made the

Rangers players had remained and not left along with Dougie Gray, who had expressed disappointment at the decision, and Caskie and Jock had agreed to become part of the new committee.

Four days later Caskie announced that the Rangers players would not strike and he had resigned, to be swiftly followed by Jock. In a letter to the press, Caskie stated, 'Rangers players agreed to accept the League award during the transitional period (season 1945/46) but did not decide not to take part in the token strike. In that regard Rangers players were agreeable to abide by the majority decision.'

In any event the strike was called off after a meeting was held on 21 December between the Scottish League and the players' representatives (who by this time did not include the Ibrox contingent).

There are several interesting things to emerge from these confusing events. Why did Jock and Caskie resign from the committee so soon after joining? There is a suspicion that the influence of Bill Struth may have played a part as he believed his senior players should lead the others both on and off the field. To an extent he, of course, left the tactics and game management to them, so while quite happy to have Dougie Gray and Jock representing his players in the dispute, he was much less amenable to Caskie's involvement, having only very recently joined the club. Perhaps he thought he was too assertive in the matter of players' wages, appearing to support strike action, and told him as much. Perhaps that comes as no surprise as Caskie had only been at Ibrox just over a month at the time and did not want to blot his copy book too much in those early stages.

Rangers, as might be expected, were one club well able to afford to meet the wages the players were asking for. In the year to 30 April 1945, they made a profit of £2,766, which, when added to the balance brought forward, produced an overall balance in the profit and loss account of £4,124. This reflected a club in pretty rude health all things considered but Rangers were still some way behind English sides. For example, by way of comparison, the corresponding figures in the Everton balance sheet were £3,924 and £25,889 respectively.

At a subsequent meeting on Sunday, 30 December the players agreed to accept 'under protest' £4 a match plus £2 for a win and £1 a draw.

The league was also asked to produce the figures to verify their claim that 15 First Division clubs had lost an aggregate of £22,000 during the war.

In February 1945, the government had announced that war-service gratuities would be paid. For three years' service (none abroad) a private received £83 10s 2d, a sergeant £97 14s 2d and a lieutenant £117 1s 8d. These figures put the financial rewards for footballers firmly into perspective.

Following the succession of meetings, the issue of forming a players' union similar to that in England had been discussed but it was clear some of the more senior players were not keen on the idea. At yet another meeting in January, which was attended by the secretary of the English Players' Union, it was finally agreed in principle to form a union of Scottish players.

The attitude of the meeting was that top players should not be paid according to whether they had another job outside football. The Scottish League (whose president was Jimmy Bowie of Rangers), however, still believed that players should play football *and* work at the same time. Essentially, the belief being that football was a bonus to top up their main means of earning a living. The management committee of the Scottish Football Players' Union (SFPU) was set up in February 1946.

One of the first acts of the SFPU was to write to the SFA asking it for recognition as the only legitimate organisation of players in Scotland. In a carefully worded reply the SFA asked for a copy of the union's constitution and rules and assured the union that the association was always open to receiving considered requests from any organisation connected to the game.

Willie Telfer, who was at St Mirren at that time, speaking in 1987 gave a slightly different perspective on the events surrounding the proposed strike. 'The committee was dominated by Rangers men such as Dougie Gray, Jock Shaw and George Young and that suited us because Rangers were the biggest and most powerful team in the country. We all agreed to threaten a strike unless we were paid £6 a week, at which point the Rangers players got up and left the room. It turned out they were earning a lot more than £6 a week anyway so there was nothing a players' union could do for them. However, we were still a success in raising wages for players although it meant many were left to work out individual contracts with clubs.'

Rangers ended 1945 by beating Third Lanark 1-0, Clyde 3-1 and Falkirk 3-0. The points won against Clyde on Christmas Day (not then a public holiday in Scotland) meant that the Ibrox men needed only nine points from their next ten matches to secure the league title: one of those, of course, being the traditional Ne'er Day clash with Celtic at Celtic Park.

The crowd was restricted to an all-ticket limit of 75,000 which created a lot of complaints but in the end 70,000 attended what was a very tame affair on a frost-bound pitch which the players had great difficulty keeping their feet on. The only goal of the game came on 27 minutes, following a close passing movement between Gillick and Thornton, the latter of whom made the final pass to Gillick whose shot was blocked by Mallan in the Celtic goal but the rebound was gathered up by Thornton who drove the ball into the net. Thornton was certainly a man in a hurry to make up for the matches missed while serving on the front line.

In the second half Celtic bombarded the visitors' goal but failed to get the better of a defence in which Jock and Willie Woodburn were noted as being particularly resolute.

No time to rest on their laurels and the following day Rangers beat St Mirren 3-1 at Ibrox and the win all but gave Rangers the championship.

In the game at Shawfield on 5 January (their fourth in eight days) the left-wing combination of Williamson and Caskie outshone their right-wing compatriots, Waddell and Gillick (generally considered to normally be the key attacking components) thanks in part to the mastery of Symon in midfield and his intelligent prompting. They kept Rangers positively aggressive in a dour struggle, the winning goal coming from Thornton yet again with only eight minutes remaining.

The *Evening Times* described the game as a 'sair trauchle' for the Clyde defence, which was one way of saying they were kept very busy.

While Rangers headed to Pittodrie for their next match, Willie Thornton returned to his active unit in Italy. The match attracted a bumper crowd of 35,000, Aberdeen's highest gate for nine years, and saw the Dons thrash Rangers 4-1 with only a Willie Waddell spot kick to show for their efforts.

This was then followed by a 2-1 victory over Queen's Park, a 4-4 draw with Morton at Ibrox, then a 4-1 win over Hamilton Accies .

The penultimate match of the league season saw Rangers take leave of Ibrox, on league business at least, and they bowed out in no little style against Queen of the South. For the second successive week Rangers decisively defeated a club battling against demotion. While the result was never in doubt it was reported that Jimmy Caskie's cantrips saw to it that the Dumfries lads were constantly in turmoil and at times produced some lovely combinations which made the light blues step lively. Now I will confess I had to look up the meaning of the word cantrip but it actually is very fitting for the type of tricky player Caskie undoubtedly was. So cantrip is 'a mischievous or playful act; a trick'.

Maybe Queen's strip for the day, identical to England's, may have had something to do with it and it inspired Caskie and the light blues to take their performance levels up a notch, even though the league title was already secured. From goalkeeper to outside-left they kept up a non-stop tempo of attacking play all afternoon, though at times it did leave them a little exposed at the back but it was great entertainment for the assembled crowd of 12,000. The attendance clearly reflected the 'nothing to play for' status of the fixture.

After only four minutes Rangers were ahead through Waddell after keeper Townsend misjudged his lob towards goal. The lead did not last though and Law equalised on 12 minutes. Spurred into action Rangers then laid siege to the Queen's goal with Caskie blazing the trail with his trickery which delighted the crowd. One mazy run, in particular, saw him weaving past four defenders in the penalty area; he drew the keeper and crossed to Duncanson, but with an open goal he contrived to hit the bar and the ball rebounded back into the keeper's arms. Rangers, though, killed the game off as a contest with three further goals before the interval through Duncanson, Caskie and Williamson. They even had the luxury of Willie Waddell ballooning a penalty high over the bar onto the sparsely populated terracing behind the goal.

After the restart some of the urgency went out of the game and a few misplaced passes ended with a mistimed pass from Dougie Gray to Willie Woodburn being intercepted to allow Connor to pull a goal back on the hour. Rangers and Jimmy Caskie responded and he completed the scoring on the day six minutes later when he slipped after collecting a pass from Waddell but, while sat on the ground, he was able to poke the ball past keeper Townsend into the net. A comfortable day for Rangers and the star performer was noted as, of course, Caskie but ably supported by other light blues who pulled more than their weight: Jock Shaw, Woodburn, Duncanson and Williamson.

The league season concluded the following week with a 2-0 loss to Hearts at Tynecastle on 16 February.

The title was comfortably won by eight points, from second-placed Hibernian – an eighth successive title win in their various guises – but it was clear the Edinburgh side were emerging as serious challengers to Rangers' dominance.

Reconstruction

IN FEBRUARY, the Scottish League proposed that for the following season, 1946/47, there should be two leagues of 16 clubs with two up and two down in terms of promotion/relegation.

There would be no room, though, for Queen of the South, Hamilton or St Johnstone in the top division (all First Division clubs in 1939) but Morton, Queen's Park and Dundee from the 1939 Second Division would be 'promoted' on an election-type basis. These proposals were, however, rejected.

In April it was finally agreed that there would be three leagues – A, B and C.

There would be 16 clubs in A, 14 (possibly 16) in B and between eight and 12 in C, plus reserve teams from B and C.

The promotion/relegation arrangements would be two up/two down in A and B with one up from C to B.

The minimum annual wage for the teams in A would be set as £260, in B £156 and C £130. The match guarantee in A division would be £200, B £100 and C £70. The teams in Division A were the same that ended the season in the Southern League, to give some sense of continuity. But before the new league structure got up and running, there was a busy end to the 1945/6 season for the light blues as several cup competitions would reach their conclusion following the completion of the league season.

On 9 March Morton were the visitors to Ibrox in a Southern League Cup section tie. There was nothing like the eight-goal extravaganza of the league match six weeks previously, and with seven minutes to go the scores were level at 0-0. Then as the light blues pushed forward, Jimmy Smith flicked the ball on to Waddell and he sent a close-in drive crashing into the back of the net. No sooner had the ball hit the net than pandemonium broke out, and Morton surrounded the referee, and the rather unfortunately named Mr Blues, yielding to the violent appeals for offside, consulted a linesman. The consultation made no difference, however, and the goal stood. Morton's resentment was increased by the fact they'd had a similar sort of counter chalked off a few minutes earlier when McInnes had been the 'scorer'. The general view was that the referee was right both times, but both incidents were only in accord with a game that left a bad taste in the mouth. Finesse played second fiddle to brute strength. Practically every worthwhile move was brought to a close by a foul, many that could only merit the adjective 'vicious'. Left-back Fyfe of Morton, had his name taken at a time when a booking was relatively unusual, as the game itself was accepted to be much more agreeably physical. He could consider himself unlucky in so far as half a dozen others of both sides certainly offended as badly.

On the balance of play Rangers perhaps earned their win, but so unusually poor in match-winning ideas was the forward line, they were extremely fortunate to secure the two points. The absence of Gillick and Caskie could not be considered the prime reason as, while Torry was missed, Charlie Johnstone, who deputised for Caskie, was the best home forward.

Actually, the game was won by a Waddell-Smith switch just before the goal – ordered by trainer Arthur Dixon from the touchline. Big Jimmy had his share of chances but made little enough of them. Exempt from general blame were Scot Symon, Young and Jock Shaw. This trio were dominant throughout.

Just over a month later and Rangers were facing Queens again but this time at Palmerston in a Southern League Cup section tie. This, though, would be no stroll for the Gers, quite the opposite in fact. Jack Harkness in *The Sunday Post* described the action:

> There are some defeats more triumphant than victories. If I were a Queen of the South supporter that's how I would look on this Rangers visit. Because Queens can take as much credit as Rangers. Theirs was one of the biggest-hearted efforts I've ever seen. There wasn't two goals difference in actual play, but there were about 22 players difference in the class of the sides. That's where I give Queens their credit. They never gave in. They never pulled out the stop-'em-at-any-price stuff. They stooped to nothing shady. 'You play your game,' they seemed to say to the giants from Glasgow, 'and we'll play ours.' And may the deil tak' the hindmost. Difference in class maybe Queens the hindmost, but yet there were one or two occasions I felt like getting up from my seat in the stand and going and giving one or two of them a kick in the pants.
>
> I am thinking now of the tip-tap-tip-tap play of the inside-forwards. A diagram of Queens' play would look like a tree. A trunk reaching right up to a Rangers penalty area, then lashings of branches spreading out to the wings. If those goalposts had been out on the touchlines Queens would have won easily, because they could beat Rangers across the field, but Rangers know the goals are not the sides. Indeed, even without looking, they know exactly where the goals are, and their whole style of play is dedicated accordingly. The difference in the two goals was brought about by the difference between the strong, go-ahead play of Duncanson and Williamson compared with the criss-crossing of McQuade and Law.
>
> Not once did newcomer Matt Armstrong get the sort of passes Jimmy Smith was getting, yet Matt had one of those sorts of games that, without doing anything in particular, he seemed to do it extra well. Talking of newcomers, I was

greatly taken with the debut of Denmark, his exhibition of centre-half play was quite on par with that of Young's. And Young is about the best in the country these days. Rangers, too, had it at wing-half. Symon picked up endless balls from the branches of that tree, and placed every one to one of his colleagues up front.

I do hope Queens noticed how easy this game becomes if you can find your man, with the final pass. Let's hope Rangers' lesson wasn't lost on them. Not for one minute do I agree with those who said it was easy for Rangers, rather it was Rangers that made it look easy. Both goals were first-half affairs, scored too while Queens were on top. Smith opened up with a hard punching shot from 12 yards. A deceptive Waddell cross saw Black fist out. Smith took the ball on the drop, and well that was that. Second goal was the cleverest I've seen for years. Again, quick thinking made it look easy. Smith got the ball about midfield and trailed it to the left. Like a flash Johnstone took up big Jimmy's place in the middle. Over came a perfect pass, and Johnstone showed his appreciation by firing the ball home low and true.

In this game of skill, strength, and quick thinking versus honest endeavour, Jock Shaw was easily the outstanding performer. And the fact a Rangers defender was the star surely points to something. Savage also came in for defensive honours, and the pick of the forwards, apart from Rangers' inside pair, were Oakes, Armstrong, Johnstone, and Smith.

So Rangers comfortably qualified from their section, winning five and drawing one of their matches, scoring 15 times, while conceding only three in the process.

Dundee were despatched 3-1 in the quarter-final, which rather unusually was played at Hampden, and this took Rangers on to meet Hearts at the same venue on 27 April for a place in the final.

Rangers are more often than not expected to win; therefore, when they do, they get dashed little credit for it. This latest effort was no exception. At the close, it wasn't a case of 'Good old Rangers', but merely a nod of the head, same old Hearts, just up to their old tricks, seemed to hit the nail on the head.

Hearts got off to a dream start tearing Rangers apart with the finest move of the match, and crowning it by going ahead in the very first minute. Walker gave the ball to McCrae out wide, and the big inside-forward, instead of cutting in, went outside towards the corner flag, where a perfect swerve and sidestep wrong-footed Gray and Watkins. Walker came flying into the middle, over came the ball, Walker's header flashed into the net. That would be as good as it would get for the Jambos as it was all downhill from there and gradually their intensity and influence faded away. Rangers on the other hand steadied themselves, and gradually imposed themselves on the match, and in the end would run out worthy winners.

Early on, Hearts forwards showed what they were made of but eventually disintegrated into a disjointed collection of individuals. The main reason for this appeared to be that the service from the wing-halves faded, the fluidity of their play diminished and with it Hearts' chances. Compare and contrast that with how Watkins and Symon kept bringing up and playing those inviting balls forward. These passes simply made the Rangers forwards play. Waddell was perhaps the best man on the field, yet he was never required to go foraging, looking for the ball, as he had a ready-made supply from Watkins, Symon or Gillick. Off he would go, sand dancing his merry way past the Tynecastle defenders. Hearts had no one to rival Waddell, and just as importantly they had no one to compare with Thornton. When Hearts forward McCrae dropped out of the proceedings, Kelly was left as the only one likely to nick a goal, but the main barrier to that came in the shape of the formidable George Young. It became a case of everywhere Kelly went big George was sure to follow.

Rangers' equaliser in the 39th minute, if not so concerted as Hearts, was still brilliantly finished. Watkins lobbed a bouncing ball into the goalmouth where Thornton brought it down with his left foot, and on the turn, smacked it home with his right. A half-hook full-volley crashed knee-high into the net. Football at its balletic best.

It took extra time for Rangers to finally translate their advantage into goals. If Johnstone, out on the left, had taken his chances there definitely would have been no need for the additional time, but he had one of those sorts of days. Always he seemed to be caught on the wrong foot. Time and again the Waddell lob cleared everyone in the goal and landed at Johnstone's feet. Yet each time he seemed surprised. It just wasn't his day.

The winning goal, as so often happens in these big games, didn't come into the same class as the other two. A ground pass from Thornton saw Gillick jab in his foot. The ball hit the bottom of the upright and rolled back into the net.

While far from a classic, as is often the case in semi-finals, there were still some star performers for Rangers in the shape of Waddell and Young while yet again it was noted that 'Jock Shaw, too, was in Scotland form'.

Three days later the light blues took a break from competitive action as they headed across the water to Belfast on 30 April to play Everton in a testimonial match for Jack Price, the secretary of the Irish League, at Windsor Park in front of a really healthy crowd of 27,000.

Rangers were the better side in the first half but were not able to drive home their undoubted advantage against a very solid defence. After the interval Everton became more forceful and, in the end, deserved their 3-2 success. The Toffees' defence stood steadfast in the opening period, Humphreys proving a strong centre-half, and Greenhalgh and Jackson solid at full-back. The forwards were inconsistent but Boyes was really lively on the right flank and troubling the Rangers defence, and Catterick was a lively centre-forward. Watson gave the left wing able support. The first goal came on 37 minutes, through Watson, after neat work by Boyes and Catterick who moved into the outside-left position, and put across a centre, which Higgins headed into the net. There was some concern in the Rangers ranks that keeper Shaw (previously of Portadown) might have cut away the centre from which Everton scored.

Two minutes later, Symon, with a raking low drive from 25 yards, equalised. The scores remained level till midway through the second half when Boyes scored a superb goal for Everton, and then extended their lead on 72 minutes, when Higgins skipped past keeper Shaw who hauled him down for a clear penalty. Watson made no mistake from the spot and that appeared to seal the victory for Everton. Rangers, though, kept pressing, and seven minutes from the end Derek Arnison scored, but despite constant pressure they could not grab an equaliser.

It was no shame to lose to an Everton side who finished runners-up in the northern section of the regionalised English leagues.

The press commonly reported after the match that Tiger was the best back on show, and Scot Symon the most constructive half-back.

At the post-match reception Mr R. P. Tennant and his committee thanked Rangers and Everton for a thrilling contest, along with the Linfield officials who made the ground arrangements and contributed to the success of the match.

So it was on to Hampden and the Southern League Cup Final on 11 May 1946. This final would illustrate that, while success was expected and more often than not achieved down Ibrox way, it did not mean defeat was accepted in an unsportsmanlike manner. Perhaps the greatest exponent of these standards of dignity in defeat was the club captain Tiger Shaw – thankfully he was not tested too often, but always set the standard.

Rangers were classed as favourites, Aberdeen had performed well in the league and finished third, plus they had recently thrashed the light blues 4-1 at Pittodrie. So the stage was set for a fascinating final and 135,000 agreed as they packed the slopes at Hampden.

In the end the Dons came, saw and conquered despite some having reservations they would find the occasion and massive crowd too intimidating as they were a team who had never won a major honour before. However, if ever a team deserved to win one of the most sensational cup finals in history, it definitely was Aberdeen.

It was a game which in the end may have gone either way, but which fate decided should end in favour of the Dons.

Individually, constructively, even in decision-making, Aberdeen were ahead of Rangers. The biggest factor in their success was half-back power. As in the international against England in April, the standout performer was centre-half Frank Dunlop who was noted as holding the defence together, directing operations from the back, ensuring half-backs Cowie and Taylor supported the wing-backs Baird and Hamilton diligently going forward. When they were on the back foot and defence was the order of the day, there were the two inside men back working with the wing-halves. These four moved forwards and backwards so easily they might have been on rails. This seemed to be the rock Rangers' hopes crumbled upon.

Everyone knew the Ibrox team loved the open space to work in, and that the trademark Symon pass into that space preceded so many goals. Unfortunately, it just didn't occur here.

Not once did any part of the Dons' half of the field, which resembled Aberdeen on flag day, have any empty space and it was left with Rangers' wing-halves having to think of alternative moves.

On the day the Gers also met their match in terms of speed of thought as, on the park and in the head, Aberdeen prevailed. Aberdeen's day began with Jock Shaw winning the toss and putting the sun in Rangers' eyes, taking advantage of a slight breeze. This backfired spectacularly when barely a Rangers player had touched the ball. Straight from the kick-off Dons got cracking down the right, and Jock played the ball into touch. Cowie launched a long throw-in right into the heart of the penalty area. Hamilton ducked under the ball and did what no one expected him to do as he simply back-headed it. I should have said no one in a blue jersey knew what to expect, as Baird knew exactly what was coming and was in just the right spot to take Hamilton's flick on his forehead, and divert it low down past keeper Shaw. Cue raucous celebrations from the Aberdeen contingent; could this be their day?

There were some knowing glances exchanged in the press box: had Rangers not lost a first-minute goal in the semi-final against Hearts and still run out comfortable winners? Scribes sat back expecting a repeat.

They were to be disappointed as Aberdeen continued in the ascendancy and another strike was to follow on 18 minutes. Cowie raised an Aberdeen siege by thumping a clever telling ball away up the middle. Jock Shaw was worried by Kiddie, and uncharacteristically miskicked. Kiddie swooped like a panther on the loose ball and hooked it into the middle. In darted Williams, like a springbok, to toe-end the ball into the net. Quick thinking, and a just reward for pressing forwards and not sitting on the lead.

It was understanding in attack that made the Dons look so dangerous, especially in that devastating first half, when, as one hack was heard to say, 'they had as much magic in the front line as Betty Grable has in the waist-line'.

It certainly was Aberdeen's half but all the time there was the feeling Rangers' attack was relying too much on one man; 'Give it to Willie Waddell' was definitely the motto of the Ibrox supporters, and the players had a tendency to follow suit.

Soon Waddell was off on one of his runs, and the whole Aberdeen team seemed to be closing in on him. Picture a hare tearing along with five greyhounds after it, and it encapsulated the pursuit of Waddell.

It was a much better Rangers in the second half. A short rest from the worrying tactics of Williams, the flashes of Kiddie, and the upsetting square cross-field passes of Hamilton and Baird had done them good, as Rangers were worried. Here was a team playing better Rangers football than Rangers, and which had beaten them convincingly recently.

So, Rangers set about it as Rangers so often do.

Five minutes into the second half and during a goalmouth melee Arnison headed strongly at goal and Johnstone got his fingers to it. Cooper overstretched himself trying to get his head to it. In came Duncanson, who leapt head and shoulders over everyone else and headed strongly home. Was this the start? Was this the writing on the wall? Would Aberdeen fall the way of all flesh which opposes light blue jerseys?

They responded strongly. Kiddie smacked a beautiful shot right on to the face of the bar. Cowie shot through a crowd of players. His shot caught the foot of the post – and jumped up into the waiting arms of Shaw.

The excitement was at fever pitch; the next goal could prove decisive. Something was bound to happen. Something did, and Rangers equalised with the finest goal Hampden had seen scored for many years.

It was gratifying that there was such a huge crowd to witness this moment, and it was interesting to note at the time the comment that was made about an old-fashioned individual effort. Willie Thornton was the hero of the moment, and never had he scored a better goal. It wasn't just a case of beating the defence, he had them outstripped before they knew what was happening. On he went with everything under control, and slotted the ball home.

Ten minutes to go and now surely the momentum was with Rangers. Aberdeen were having none of it, though, and Cowie's shot hit the foot of the post and bounced into keeper Shaw's arms. They had a sense of destiny.

In the final minute came the final twist in this thrilling match when a drive by half-back Taylor from the edge of the box looked to be going wide and was left by everyone but inexplicably it hit the post, and bounced into the net to give the Dons the cup, as there was barely time to re-centre the ball when the referee blew for full time.

On reflection, the Dons probably deserved the win as on balance they were always ahead of Rangers in craft and spirit, with their half-backs kings of the day.

This was a historic moment as it was their first triumph in a major competition. Tremendous enthusiasm greeted the scoring of the last-minute goal by left-half Taylor, for Aberdeen had played themselves into the favour of the great majority of the 138,000 spectators at Hampden Park. Tribute to the greatness of the game was that scarcely a spectator left the park before the cup had been presented. There was a continuous roar of applause for fully ten minutes after the final whistle.

One of the first to congratulate the Aberdeen players in the dressing room was Alan Morton, Rangers' director. He told them the victory was well earned and that he was pleased to see the cup go north.

The views of the two captains were very positive. Frank Dunlop was breathless: 'It was, and is, wonderful.' While obviously disappointed, Jock showed true dignity in defeat by stating, 'One of the most gruelling games I've ever played. I congratulate a grand bunch of sportsmen.'

The teams were both congratulated by Lord Provost Thomas Mitchell, of Aberdeen. The cup was presented to Dunlop on the field by Provost David G. Gray (Airdrie), president of the SFA, and also in the official party were William Mitchell (Aberdeen chairman), James Bowie (Rangers) and William McAndrew (secretary of the Scottish League).

Most of Provost Gray's speech was lost in the roar of the crowd. As soon as he handed the cup to Dunlop, the skipper was chaired by team-mates Andy Cowie and George Johnstone. Amid the tumult and excitement the man who had been in charge of it all stole quietly away to do a job of work. He was William Webb, the referee. He had to go on the nightshift. Webb was a railway engine driver.

As soon as they were dressed, the Aberdeen players boarded a Largs-bound bus. They spent all week at the Ayrshire resort; in two days' time they were due to play Kilmarnock in a Victory Cup replay, and if they won that they would be back to Largs until Saturday, when they would meet Clyde at Shawfield.

One of the happiest of the Aberdeen party was 81-year-old Aberdeen director, William Philips. He said he had waited 55 years to see such a result.

Some 16,000 supporters travelled from the north to Glasgow by rail. Fifty casualties were dealt with at Hampden, all cases of fainting and minor injuries. Fifteen were removed to the Victoria Hospital for treatment.

A final postscript to the final dated back a number of years to Jock's Benburb days, as on the field at Hampden were four ex-Tinto Park boys. In the Aberdeen ranks were goalkeeper George Johnstone and man-of-the-match centre-half Frank Dunlop, while in light blue there was of course Jock and namesake goalkeeper John Shaw.

While Aberdeen had waited 43 years for their first major trophy success, they did not have the trophy in their possession for long. The cup which was struck and used for the Southern League Cup played for during the war years, after being presented to the Dons, was promptly handed over to the SFA to be used for its Victory Cup competition, the winners of which would get to become permanent owners of the trophy.

So, ironically, the very trophy Rangers had just failed to win, they could get their hands on within six weeks.

Rangers progressed to the quarter-final to face Falkirk by knocking out Stenhousmuir 8-2 on aggregate over two legs and Airdrie 4-0 in the second round. The tie against the Bairns was particularly interesting as it would feature Jerry Dawson in the opposing team after he had been transferred to Brockville only the month before.

The match was a tight niggly affair in which Dawson performed with all the poise and experience one may have expected to keep his old team-mates at bay, and the game finished 1-1. The replay took place on 25 May and this time there was no denying Rangers, who strolled through the tie comfortably 2-0 with goals from Gillick and Symon, to face Celtic in the semi-final at Hampden.

After a 0-0 draw, Celtic were also brushed aside 2-0 in a replay, with goals from Waddell and Young from the penalty spot, to take Rangers through to meet Hibernian in the final.

While the first semi-final game had been a bit of a nondescript affair for an Old Firm game, the replay was overflowing with controversy. Two Celtic men (captain Paterson and Mallan) received their marching orders and tried to get the rest of their colleagues to leave the field with them at one point. They didn't comply but another player was to leave the field limping and unable to carrying on, to leave them with only eight men to see out the 90 minutes. Rangers did not capitalise on this numerical advantage but were simply content to play out time. The Celtic support were another matter altogether. They were in fact apoplectic and a handful ran on to the pitch with one approaching the referee with a bottle and throwing it at him, just as the supporter was apprehended by the police. A further four men were arrested, linked to the disturbances, and the subsequent productions for the court proceedings made for interesting and horrific reading as they included nine bottles, three broken bottles, six large pieces of stone and one bread knife.

Perhaps our very own Tiger could have passed on some advice on how to take defeat with dignity.

So to the climax of the season and the last match under wartime playing arrangements – the aptly named Victory Cup Final. It was contested by clearly the top two sides in the country and was played on Saturday, 15 June at, of course, Hampden Park. This was an eagerly awaited contest as Hibs had finished second to Rangers in the league and an upset was distinctly possible.

They had each won one of the league contests, Rangers 3-2 at Ibrox, while Hibs triumphed 2-1 at Easter Road, so there seemed nothing to choose between the sides.

The big danger to Rangers was Gordon Smith on Hibs' right flank. He was widely acclaimed to be the best winger in Scotland at the time and Ibrox skipper Jock was warned, as if it were required, to expect a challenging afternoon.

Rangers, though, also had a powerful force on their right wing, of course, in the shape of Willie Waddell. Waddell was to Rangers what Smith was to Hibs, and coincidentally Waddell's direct opponent was Jock's brother Davie.

More than 88,000 packed into Hampden to see this momentous match and they were to witness some of the finest right-wing play ever as the sides battled for the silverware. It was Rangers, though, who were to display all the magic.

Waddell and Gillick tore the Hibs defence to shreds taking full advantage of some superb passing from right-half Charlie Watkins and constantly worrying the Edinburgh rearguard. At the opposite end of the field, it could not have been more different. Hibs' right-wing pair Smith and Peat were getting no change whatsoever from Jock, who had risen to the challenge of facing Smith, or indeed Scot Symon, so the Ibrox side seemed to be in complete control.

Despite being well on top, Rangers were not making their superiority pay and converting it into goals and Hibs keeper Kerr was not unduly troubled by the light blues' attacks. If this was Rangers in control, they appeared to have little to worry about.

Hibs, though, were soon to learn that the Ibrox men had one or two aces up their sleeves and they were about to play them.

In the 25th minute Jimmy Duncanson and Jimmy Caskie pressurised Hibs into giving away a corner. Caskie took the kick and he flighted it perfectly towards Willie Thornton who rose beautifully to meet the ball, but at the last second ducked to allow the ball to run through to Torry Gillick and Torry crashed it goalwards. In trying to block the shot a Hibs defender inadvertently deflected the ball, wrong-footing his keeper who could only watch helplessly as the ball flew into the net.

Now with the advantage Rangers really put the Hibees defence through the mill and Kerr was being put through the wringer and had to pull off several fine saves to keep Hibs in the game. Then just before half-time Hibs made Rangers pay for not making their superiority count.

Davie Shaw intercepted a pass meant for Waddell, and played the ball forward to winger Nutley who saw centre-forward Milne run wide and he sent a pass to that wing then raced to take up position in the middle. Milne and Nutley then worked a clever one-two, throwing the Rangers defence off balance, and as everyone expected Milne to cut the ball back he sent a great ball through to Aitkenhead who crashed a powerful shot past Bobby Brown for the equaliser. As the sides trooped off at the interval, Hibs could not believe their luck at being level.

That lucky feeling lasted all of one minute into the second half. Duncan sent Caskie away on the left and the winger showed Jock Govan a clean pair of heels before crossing the ball to Thornton. The Ibrox striker neatly back-heeled to Duncanson who raced in to thunder the ball behind Kerr to restore Rangers' lead.

It was a beautiful piece of football which brought the Hampden crowd to their feet and, from that moment on, Rangers retained complete control, and the cup only had one destination.

Hibs were in constant disarray but somehow Rangers found it hard to add to their lead, and as time wore on there were one or two signs from the Easter Road side that they were still in the contest.

Just after a Waddell effort was disallowed, Bobby Brown was called upon to look smart when Peat sent a fierce shot towards goal but Bobby saved comfortably and, just when the light blues support was starting to get jittery, in the final minute Duncanson netted his second goal to make the game safe. The 3-1 victory effectively brought the curtain down on wartime football and, taking into account Rangers' stranglehold of football over the past nine years, it was fitting that the last trophy of this period would be lifted proudly by Tiger.

The trophy sits proudly in the trophy cabinet at Ibrox to this day.

Changing world

SINCE THE budget the previous April there had been a run-in between the Chancellor Hugh Dalton and the Scottish Football League over admission prices for league games. In 1946 the ground admission price in Britain for football matches was 1s 6d, including entertainment tax. This meant that for every 1s 6d taken at the turnstile, the clubs kept 10½d, and the revenue 7½d.

Since before the war the football authorities had been asking for football to be included in the entertainments scheduled in the Finance Act as employing 'living human performers' and to be taxed at the reduced rate appropriate to this category. Eventually in 1946 the Revenue agreed to this request and the Chancellor intimated in his budget speech that in future football and other games would be classified as 'live entertainment' which meant the rate of revenue would be reduced by 5d to 2½d. He added that in return for this concession he expected ground admission to be reduced from 1s 6d to 1s 3d. His intention was that the 5d of tax given up by the revenue would be shared with the public. Instead of 10½d, the clubs would keep 1s ½d of the reduced admission price and so be better off by 2d, while the spectators would save 3d.

While Rangers basked in the glory of another trophy-laden season it was clear that a real challenge was emerging from the east coast in the shape of Hibernian, and indeed another Shaw at left-back, Jock's brother Davie, was playing a starring role. Soon to emerge were two of the most famous football combinations in the history of the Scottish game and that would lead to one of the most fiercely contested rivalries the game has known – the Iron Curtain v the Famous Five.

Hibs' 'Famous Five' began to form around 1946. The elegant Gordon Smith was the first to find a permanent place and then there was the powerful Eddie Turnbull and the smooth left-winger Willie Ormond. At centre-forward was Alex Linwood who was enormously skilful and masterly in the air. Between Smith and Linwood initially was Bobby Combe, a strong worker who latterly moved to the half–back line to support the line when Lawrie Reilly and Bobby Johnstone moved in. These five were immediately successful and they brought a new concept to Scottish football, for they did not stick rigidly to set positions. At that time a full-back played on the flank of the defence marking a winger who stayed on the wing, and he would be a reckless full-back who would stray beyond the centre line, a rash winger who would go inside.

Hibs altered that thinking, maybe because they had an inspiring and thoughtful manager whose influence is too often overlooked. Willie McCartney was a big, laughing, happy man who would have looked naked without a flower in his buttonhole. He had a magnificent presence with his special knowledge of football. His father had been manager of Hearts and so had he before switching to Hibs.

He gave an official sanction to the switching of positions of Hibs forwards during matches. He had Gordon Smith in his office one day to ask him why he had not stayed on his wing the previous Saturday. Smith told him that when he took the ball across field to the left wing, he left a space for somebody to move into and that others in the forward line were also prepared to do that and introduce an element of surprise.

Gordon Smith said of his manager, 'Mr McCartney was a big man but he was always prepared to listen. At other times he could shatter us without saying a word and just by his personality and presence. If things were not going well with us he would come down from the director's box and stand in the middle of the tunnel where he knew we would see him. I would say to myself, "Oh my God. We'll have to do something", and we generally did.'

Willie McCartney had the knack of switching players and although his team selections did at times look ridiculous, they usually came off and he had a spectacular result with switches during matches. He was a much-underrated manager. Gordon Smith remembers a train journey to a match in 1948 when Hibs were challenging for the league title. There were but a few players in the compartment along with Willie McCartney and Harry Swan. The manager was silent for a while then broke from his reverie to say, 'I'd love to win the league championship. If we could win this league, I would give every player £100.' Such a sum was a lot of money back then and Harry Swan quickly disassociated himself from such reckless enthusiasm.

The sad upshot was that Hibs did indeed clinch the title in April 1948, but sadly McCartney had died in February. He did not live to enjoy the team he built to bring pleasure to so many others.

Season 1946/47 and the Iron Curtain

THE RESUMPTION of football after the war saw a huge resurgence of interest in the game reflected in booming attendances.

It also saw Rangers take up where they had left off in 1939 and establish themselves as Scotland's top side. Two signings at the beginning of the season were to have a significant effect on Rangers for many years to come. Both Bobby Brown and Sammy Cox were snapped up from the amateur ranks by Bill Struth. They proved to be stars of the side as they battled with Hibernian over the title, and completed the area of the team to earn the name the Iron Curtain.

The Iron Curtain

'From Stettin in the Baltic to Trieste in the Adriatic an iron curtain has descended across the continent of Europe.'

With these words, in a speech delivered in Fulton, Missouri on 5 March 1946, Winston Churchill without intending to do so, of course, had given a name to the defensive line-up which was to be the foundation of Rangers' successes from 1946 to 1953. Fundamentally, the components of the Iron Curtain were Bobby Brown, George Young, Tiger, Ian McColl, Willie Woodburn and Sammy Cox. As Jock said to the forwards 'ye pit them in, we'll keep them oot'.

So then, who were the Iron Curtain?

Bobby Brown

Brown was born in Dunipace, Stirlingshire. He made his debut as a goalkeeper for Queen's Park in 1939, when he was still attending school. After leaving school, Brown attended Jordanhill College with the intention of becoming a physical education teacher. He went on to establish himself as the first-choice goalkeeper for Queen's Park in the next two seasons, but like many others at this time, his football career was interrupted by the Second World War. Brown joined the Fleet Air Arm of the Royal Navy, and he initially trained to be a navigator on a Fairey Swordfish torpedo plane. He was then transferred to the Navy's physical training department, where he worked as an instructor. This posting allowed him to play as a guest in the wartime leagues for Portsmouth, Chester, Chelsea and Plymouth Argyle.

Brown considered himself fortunate, as five of the six Jordanhill students who had joined the Fleet Air Arm with him died during the war.

He continued his teaching studies at Portsmouth College. In his last season with Queen's Park, in 1945/46, he shared the goalkeeper's jersey with another future Scottish international Ronnie Simpson.

It was Brown who was selected to play as the club won a rare trophy, the Glasgow Cup, during that campaign. Due to the wartime conditions, he made no official Scottish Football League or Scottish Cup appearances in his time with the Spiders, but did play 105 times for the first team.

At the end of the 1945/46 season Brown left Queen's Park for Rangers, where he played for ten years. During his time at Ibrox he played on a part-time basis while working as a teacher. Brown won three Scottish League championships, three Scottish Cups and two Scottish League Cups. He played in 296 matches in the three major competitions for Rangers, including 179 in succession, and also won the wartime 1946 Victory Cup and another two Glasgow Cups.

Brown's status as a part-time player subsequently caused difficulty with the Rangers manager Bill Struth, who wanted Brown to leave teaching and play football full-time. He was replaced by George Niven as first-choice goalkeeper in 1952, and only made a few appearances before leaving Rangers in 1956. Brown then moved to Falkirk, where he played for two years before he retired from playing.

Brown played in five wartime internationals for Scotland, with his first appearance coming at Villa Park in February 1945. His strong club form was rewarded with a full international call-up and, in January 1946, he made his Scotland debut in a Victory International friendly against Belgium: this was the first of five full international appearances for Brown, who remains the last amateur player to earn a full cap for Scotland and also the last to do so while a Queen's Park player. He also appeared eight times for the Scottish League between 1949 and 1952 while with Rangers.

After retiring as a player and leaving his teaching job in 1958, Brown became manager of St Johnstone.

The Perth club had finished 11th in the old Second Division in the 1957/58 season. Brown guided them to sixth place in his first season, and then promotion as champions in 1960. Saints were relegated in 1962, but Brown stayed on as manager and won promotion back to the top division in 1963 before stabilising them as a top-division club, finishing in mid-table in the next few seasons. In total he managed 393 games for St Johnstone.

Brown became the first full-time Scotland manager in 1967. He was also the first manager to be given full authority to pick the team, which had previously been controlled by a Scottish Football Association committee. His first international match as manager was a 3-2 victory over the 1966 world champions England at Wembley, which led to Scots declaring themselves as 'unofficial world champions'.

This game also saw Brown give his goalkeeping understudy from his Queen's Park days, Ronnie Simpson, his international debut at the age of 36. Brown continued as Scotland manager until 1971, but often found his squads depleted by club demands, and results suffered accordingly. He won nine of 28 games played, and the team did not qualify for either the 1968 European Championships or the 1970 FIFA World Cup.

Brown's only active involvement in football after leaving the Scotland job was to scout for Plymouth Argyle.

After finishing with Scotland in 1971 he turned to his business interests outside football. Brown and his wife Ruth settled in Helensburgh, where they ran a gift and coffee shop. Ruth died in 1983, aged 59, due to blood cancer. In 2017 Brown was retired and still lived in Helensburgh. He was inducted into the Rangers FC Hall of Fame and into the Scottish Football Hall of Fame in 2015. He passed away in 2020.

George Young

Born in Grangemouth, Young started his career with junior side Kirkintilloch Rob Roy before moving to Rangers in 1941. Although primarily considered a centre-back, he was often played at right-back during his 16 years in Govan, to accommodate Willie Woodburn.

Young won the league and the League Cup in 1946/47 and the Scottish Cup the following season, before Rangers became the first side to win all three trophies in the same season in 1948/49. Young himself scored twice from the penalty spot in the 4-1 Scottish Cup Final victory over Clyde which wrapped up the treble.

Young won further league titles in 1950, 1953, 1956 and 1957, also collecting Scottish Cup winner's medals in 1950 and 1953 to take his senior medal haul to 12. The 'lucky' Champagne cork he always carried earned him the nickname Corky. In total, Young had 458 appearances to his name, scoring 31 goals for the Ibrox club (not including 180 wartime games and 32 goals) when he departed in 1957.

Young was selected for a string of 34 consecutive senior Scotland matches between 1948 and 1953. His total of 54 caps made him the first member of the Scotland Football Hall of Fame. Young was selected as captain on 48 of those appearances. He was also the first player to appear for Scotland as a substitute, when he replaced Billy Campbell of Morton in a Victory International against Switzerland in May 1946. (The Scottish Football Association have since classified the match as a full international, but it is not recognised by FIFA.)

Young captained Scotland throughout the 1949/50 Home International tournament, which FIFA had decreed to be a British qualifying group for the 1950 FIFA World Cup in Brazil. The top two teams in the Home Internationals would qualify for Brazil, but the SFA decided Scotland would only travel if they were British Champions. England's 1-0 win at Hampden relegated the Scots to second place and they did not travel. Four years later, Scotland again qualified as second-placed country in the Home Internationals, and this time the SFA decided they would travel to Switzerland. Rangers, however, had arranged a tour of North America at the same time and refused to release their players, including Young.

In the qualifying tournament for the 1958 FIFA World Cup in Sweden, Scotland were placed in a group with Spain and Switzerland. The group began in May 1957, by which time Young had announced he would retire from playing at the end of that season. He led Scotland to a 4-2 victory over Spain in the opening game at Hampden on 8 May, and was again captain for their 2-1 victory over Switzerland, in Basle on 19 May. However, he sustained a thigh strain in that match and did not play in a 3-1 friendly win over then world champions West Germany in Stuttgart three days later. Young was not selected for the return match with Spain in Madrid on 26 May 1957, which Spain won 4-1, meaning his international career was over. Young also won 22 caps for the Scottish League XI between 1947 and 1956, the second-highest all-time total for the team.

After leaving Rangers, Young had a three-year spell as manager of Third Lanark between 1959 and 1962. Young was then a successful hotelier, and he passed away in January 1997 aged 74.

Ian McColl

Born in Alexandria, West Dunbartonshire, the grandson of Scotland international William McColl, McColl developed his footballing skills with Vale of Leven (Juniors), and joined Queen's Park in 1943 when he moved to Glasgow to study engineering at the University of Glasgow. He continued his studies after turning professional and later worked as a qualified engineer.

Rangers manager Bill Struth signed McColl in 1945. During his 15-year spell at Ibrox, he won six league championships, five Scottish Cups and two League Cups. He captained the club during the 1950s and his final appearance for Rangers was in the 1960 Scottish Cup Final, a 2-0 win against Kilmarnock. He made a total of 575 appearances for the Glasgow club in all competitions. He also won 14 caps for Scotland and represented the Scottish League XI.

After his playing career, he quickly went into management. He was appointed manager of Scotland in 1960 and enjoyed a winning start, beating Northern Ireland 5-2 at Hampden Park. Under McColl's managership, Scotland won the British Home Championships in 1962 and 1963. The team beat England 2-0 at Hampden and 2-1 at Wembley in the process. Other notable results under his tenure include a 6-2 win against Spain in Madrid, a 6-1 win over Northern Ireland in Belfast and a 6-1 win over Norway in Glasgow. He was in charge of Scotland for a total of 27 matches, winning 16 of them. This gave him a winning percentage of 59.3%, the second best of any Scotland manager.

McColl was appointed manager of Sunderland in 1965. Despite signing Jim Baxter, McColl was unable to make Sunderland into a successful side. He was sacked by Sunderland in 1968 and spent the rest of his working life as a civil engineer. He passed away in October 2008.

Willie Woodburn

Born in Edinburgh, he played for junior side Edinburgh Ashton before signing as a professional for Rangers in October 1937. He made his debut on 20 August 1938 in a 2-2 draw in the league against Motherwell and made 12 appearances as the club won the league title. After World War II he established himself in the Rangers side and won four Scottish League championships and four Scottish Cups. He appeared in the first Scottish League Cup Final in April 1947, when Rangers beat Aberdeen 4-0, and won it a second time two years later.

In 1947 he received a 14-day ban for a 'violent exchange' with Motherwell's Davie Mathie, then in 1953 he punched the Clyde striker Billy McPhail, which earned a 21-day ban. Later that year, Woodburn was sent off for retaliation in a match with Stirling Albion. The clubs met again the following season in a League Cup tie at Ibrox on 28 August 1954. Playing with a knee injury, Woodburn took exception to a bad foul and retaliated by head-butting a Stirling player. The Scottish Football Association convened a disciplinary hearing the following month, which lasted just four minutes, and Woodburn was suspended *sine die*. The England international Tom Finney, one of many well-known forwards Woodburn had encountered in his international career, described the ban as 'a grave injustice'. The SFA revoked their punishment three years later, but by then Woodburn was 37 and his playing career was over.

Woodburn won 24 international caps for Scotland between 1947 and 1952. He made his debut in a 1-1 draw with England at Wembley. Woodburn also appeared seven times for the Scottish League XI.

After his retirement from football Woodburn ran a garage business before becoming a sportswriter with the *News of the World*. He passed away in 2001.

Sammy Cox

Cox was born in Darvel, Ayrshire. He initially played for Queen's Park, Third Lanark and Dundee during World War II, joined Rangers in 1946 and played in the Scottish Football League when it recommenced play after the war.

Cox made his league debut for Rangers in a 4-2 win over Motherwell at the start of the 1946/47 season. He made a total of 13 league appearances in his first season, including a 4-1 win over Hamilton Academicals in the last match, as Rangers beat Hibernian to clinch the league title. In the following season, 1947/48, Cox was an ever-present as Rangers finished second to Hibs in the league, but won the Scottish Cup after a 1-0 replay win over Greenock Morton. Cox also netted his first goal during the season, scoring in a 2-1 win over Clyde at Ibrox.

In season 1948/49, Rangers became the first club in Scottish football history to win the treble and Cox played an important role, playing in 43 of the 44 matches. Rangers retained the league title in season 1949/50, and Cox was once again an ever-present as Hibernian were edged out by one point. Rangers also retained the Scottish Cup, beating East Fife 3-0 at Hampden.

The season 1950/51 was a disappointment for Rangers as they failed to register a trophy for the first time in five seasons. More disappointment followed as they were once again left trophyless in 1951/52; however, Cox continued to be an important member of both the Rangers and Scotland teams. In season 1952/53, Rangers returned to domestic success as they won the league and cup double with Cox featuring in 37 of the 48 matches; however, he missed out on the Scottish Cup Final win over Aberdeen.

Cox played in 44 games out of 47 in season 1953/54, but Rangers failed to win a trophy and finished a distant fourth in the league. Then 1954/55 was his last season at Rangers as he made only 15 first-team appearances. He played his final match for the club in a 2-1 defeat to Aberdeen on 19 February 1955. Cox made a total of 370 appearances for Rangers.

After his Rangers career, Cox had a spell with East Fife before emigrating to Canada in 1958. He played in the National Soccer League for Toronto Ulster United in 1958 and in that same year he served as a player-coach for Toronto Sparta, then for Stratford

Fischers in 1960. He also played for the Ontario All-Stars against West Bromwich Albion in 1959.

Cox won 25 caps for Scotland and 13 caps for the Scottish League XI. He made his international debut on 23 May 1948 in a 3-0 loss to France as a late replacement for Billy Campbell, whose boots had broken. Due to the unexpected change, some records incorrectly attributed this to Charlie Cox, a distant relative who also played at a high standard but never appeared at international level.

In 1954 Cox played his last match for Scotland; he captained the team at Hampden in a 4-2 defeat by England in front of 134,544 spectators.

He was also related to Jackie Cox (who served Hamilton Academical, among others, as both player and manager). He passed away in 2015.

In the past it was common for Rangers to hold a public trial match at the beginning of the season to let Supporters view new signings and at which the traditional team group photo would be taken. Donald Caskie described that and Rangers opening to the season in his Possilpark to Ibrox Book 'For Rangers' public trial at the start of the season on 5 August 1946 (a regular event many years ago) the Blues were: Brown, Cox, Shaw, Watkins, Young, Symon, Waddell, Gillick, Thornton, Duncanson and Caskie. The stripes, who won 3-2 were Shaw, Gray, Lindsay, Laurie, Woodburn, McColl, McIntyre, Johnson, Arnison, McIndewar and Johnstone.

If they were all fit the Blues' forward line represented the Gers' first-choice attack. The trial game attracted a reasonable crowd of 15,000 with £257 raised for charity.

The public trial match died out in the 1960's and only other occassion it has taken place since was prior to the ill-fated 1997/98 season.

The first league game was against Motherwell at Fir Park which resulted in a 4-2 win. On 14 August, in only the second league match of the season, there were 61,000 at Ibrox eagerly anticipating the match with close rivals Hibernian. Within two minutes of kick-off one half of the Shaw family was happy as a sand boy, while the other in depths of despair when David was adjudged to have handled a Gillick shot deliberately and Young gave the Gers the lead from the penalty spot – a dream start. Despite Rangers being in the ascendancy, Hibs settled down into the match, regained a foothold and equalised just before the interval. Shortly after the restart Gordon Smith beat Jock on the inside just over the half-way line, and with his left foot sent a magnificent cross-field pass over the heads of the Rangers defence to Aikenhead on the left and he in turn centred to Weir to notch what turned out to be the winning goal. Despite having over half an hour of the match left Hibs defied everything Rangers could throw at them and Kerr in goal was inspired. At full-time he was given a standing ovation and Jock was recorded, in true sporting fashion running the length of the pitch to congratulate him on his performance – sporting integrity of the highest order, in spite of crushing personal disappointment.'

The first Old Firm game of the season was set for Celtic Park on 7 September. The Rangers Supporters' Association had been formed in 1946 with Jimmy Caskie's brother Richard as its first general secretary, and announced on the Monday prior to the match that its 6,000 members would boycott the all-ticket game to show their disapproval of the increased admission prices being charged for the game. Celtic at the time had 4,000 stand seats and 7s 6d was being charged instead of the usual 3s – a pretty excessive increase to say the least. The Celtic Supporters Association, in a show of solidarity, also said their members would boycott the stand but watch from the terracing. The capacity limit for the game was 70,000 but only 60,000 tickets were printed and, in the end, only 28,000 were actually sold. Heavy rain in the lead-up to kick-off did nothing to help, and an hour before the scheduled start the police gave permission for cash to be taken at the turnstiles, but by this late stage it added little to the attendance.

Oldest known picture of the Shaw
brothers, Jock on left

Meg and Tiger Golden Wedding 1998

Young David and Margaret playing on
beach in Aberdeen while Tiger has a
snooze

Tiger and Meg with Super Ally

Son David celebrating Rangers title success in 1999

A Rangers scarf made from Tiger's last Rangers jersey

Tiger and David outside Hampden 1963

Rangers August 1948 – The treble winning squad

Tiger with Sandy, Bill Struth's dog in 1953

Willie Woodburn's 70th birthday party. Amongst guests Tiger, Ian McColl, Willie Waddell, Joe Craven and Johnny Haynes

A happy Campbell family group. Son-in-law Hugh, Margaret and grand-daughters Elaine and Lorna. Tiger in background on rhythm guitar

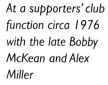

At a supporters' club function circa 1976 with the late Bobby McKean and Alex Miller

Margaret, Meg and Tiger post-match at the St Enoch Hotel, after the Scottish Cup Final against Celtic, 1963

Is there a prouder moment for a Scotsman leading the team out at Wembley 1947

Glenboig's favourite Santa

Tiger with friend Telford and Maureen Mullan in the Wee Shop, Glenboig

Tiger and brother David along with Frank Brennan visiting old work colleagues at Bedlay pit the day before they faced England at Hampden 1946

ATURDAY, APRIL 13, 1946.

THE AIRDRIE AND COATBRIDGE ADVE

ANNATHILL'S 'NATIONAL TRIO

THEY CAUSED FOOTBALL SENSATION.—Here you see Frank Brennan towering above Davie Shaw on his right and "Jock" Shaw on his left, with proud and happy Bedlay villagers surrounding them. This small mining village created a minor sensation in the football world when it was known that these three lads would all play in the Scottish team to-day.

Bedlay Juniors with Tiger's father David in centre of front row

Tiger reading daughter Margaret a story 5 April 1946

An Iron Curtain reunion in 1994. Tiger and Ian McColl at back and George Young, Bobby Brown and Sammy Cox at front

Tiger and Meg officially open the extension to Luton Rangers Supporters' Club 10 December 1981

Tiger pictured with Jim Forrest and Denis Trail along with some of the groundsmen circa 1960

Proud grandparents with Elaine and Lorna

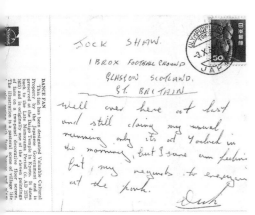

The postcard sent by boxer Dick McTaggart from Olympics in Tokyo, Japan to Tiger

Tiger and Alex Willoughby interred side by side behind the Copland Road goal at Ibrox

Takings were said to be only £1,800 compared to what should have been at least double that. To the match itself. Despite being without Waddell and Thornton, Rangers triumphed through goals from Jimmy Duncanson with a double and Jimmy Parlane (Derek's father).

On 28 September in a League Cup sectional tie Rangers met Queen's Park at Hampden before 30,000, winning 4-2. This match was notable for the fact three balls had to be used. The first gave out after five minutes, the replacement hung around for a further 25 minutes before being replaced again and the third thankfully made it to the end of the 90 minutes.

October saw Rangers entertain foreign visitors once again, this time from Czechoslovakia in the shape of Sparta Prague. The Czech side were, like Moscow Dynamo, making a short tour of the UK. En route, though, they had to survive a scare at Cologne airport when their Junkers collided with another aircraft on the runway.

In stark contrast to the protracted shenanigans with Dynamo the year before, this was a much more relaxed affair. In fact, before the game there was a loudspeaker call for squad players Laurie and Williamson to stand by as it had been agreed substitutes would be permitted and Sparta had three players sitting on chairs at the side of the track already. Before 50,000 spectators the light blues would win 3-1 with goals from Arnison, Caskie and Gillick. It was reported that the Czechs required a lot of space and time to trap the ball and pass the ball which the crowd found wearisome, while in contrast Rangers were always alert and on the move. Further reports went on to speculate that the game again demonstrated that there still appeared to be a big difference in quality between the top British and top continental sides. There is still a difference between the top Scottish and the top continental sides but sadly it has to be said that the better quality is usually played by the continentals.

Official club matchday programmes first appeared in this season. A subject very dear to my heart, but which causes my wife Yvonne angst, the match programme was properly introduced on 1 January 1947 for the clash with Celtic, and recorded as issue number one. Today, typically, you would expect to pay around £800 to purchase this coveted piece of Rangers memorabilia. The size of the publication was most probably influenced by paper shortages after the war. Inside there were pen pictures of the players for both teams. Rather bizarrely the half-time scoreboard, very much in evidence in all match programmes of the era, included the attendant match itself. Perhaps this was to help remind those who had over-indulged a little over Hogmanay how proceedings were going. The scores were announced over the loudspeaker while the match was in progress.

To the match itself: this survived another boycott by both supporters' associations, this time in protest at Rangers' admission charges, which ranged from a controversially expensive 7s 6d, to the very low but equally controversial 1s 6d. The fans wanted uniform charges of 3s 0d for the stand and, like the Chancellor of the Exchequer, 1s 3d for the terracing. The Celtic Supporters Association said they would only boycott the stand and enclosure but the attendance of 85,000 suggested the boycott had been less than successful.

The match ended in a 1-1 draw; Hazlett opening the scoring for Celtic while Waddell equalised for the light blues. It's fair to say a draw was probably about the right result though the match never really reached any great heights of excitement as it was punctuated by fouls and interruptions, with 34 free kicks awarded to Celtic and 16 to Rangers. The view of the assembled press was that Rangers and Celtic were destroying the good of the game, in particular in respect of off-the-field behaviour among spectators.

January and February 1947 produced some of the worst weather ever recorded. The freezing temperatures and heavy snowfalls produced chaos on the roads, on rail and fuel shortages along with power cuts. Coal stocks piled up at the pits and the electricity and gas companies struggled to maintain minimal supplies of power.

Despite the nationalisation of the coal industry on 1 January 1947 there was still massive absenteeism in the pits and fuel rationing had to be introduced.

Other rationing, including clothes, bread, milk, sugar, potatoes and meat also arrived. In addition, a ban on what was referred to as pleasure motoring, coupled with petrol rationing, had remained in force after the war as the country was compelled to 'tighten its belt', but football carried on.

Many grounds at the beginning of the year were in very poor condition but all games scheduled to take place at Ibrox went ahead. The match against Partick Thistle on 11 January was played in a downpour in front of only 18,000, with pools of water all over the pitch. Rangers experimented with Waddell at outside-left in three games but the forward line appeared disjointed. The considered wisdom was that Gillick was Waddell's partner and no one else, and it would lead to huge problems if they persisted with this outside-left experiment. On the day, Rangers did run out comfortable 4-0 victors through goals from Waddell, Thornton, Gillick and a George Young penalty.

On 1 February a poor gas supply resulted in there being no hot water at Hampden so Rangers changed at Ibrox and travelled across the Southside to Mount Florida in private cars for the league match with Queen's Park which ended in a 0-0 draw.

That same week the club were censured by the SFA for not having ensured selected players joined the Scottish side on the stipulated day, before the match against Ireland the previous November. The delay was caused by players attending the annual Rangers dinner dance the previous evening, a black-tie function for all those connected with the club.

Later that month Rangers met Hibernian at Ibrox in the Scottish Cup in horrendous underfoot conditions. It seemed the rivals would contest the destination of every trophy. A crowd of 95,000 attended as the Edinburgh side continued to be the light blues' closest challengers so fireworks were expected. The pitch had small patches of dull grass in the corners but otherwise it was a tapestry of sand interlaced with uncleaned snow.

The absence of any protection for the pitch, such as might have been provided by straw, meant that, without the benefit of undersoil heating, pitches were frozen hard when the temperatures fell below zero and had to be covered in up to 30 tons of sand, to make them playable. The match had the stage set and 95,000 packed the slopes of the ground eagerly anticipating this clash of the titans. Jack Harkness in *The Sunday Post* reported as follows:

> Never have I seen such full-backs. Any game in which not a solitary goal was scored, yet which could keep 95,000 folk shouting their heads off till the final whistle, definitely has something. After this I'm convinced nothing could possibly be drab or dismal when Hibs don their battle order to challenge the supremacy of Rangers. And here the stakes, maybe the Scottish Cup itself, just couldn't be higher.
>
> There's no doubt Rangers had worked like Trojans to get this ground in condition. It was playable all right, but playable for the first-time kicker, the slick tackle and the lads who think out positional moves. Not playable for the artistes, the boys with the delicate touches, the lads who dribble, swerve, trap, and sand dance their merry way past bewildered opponents. So what did we find? As play progressed along the lines of speeded-up film, the big men of the match sorted themselves out. And the four who stood head and shoulders above the rest were David Shaw, Jock Shaw, Alec Young, and Jock Govan. All full-backs. I can truthfully say that never before have I seen full-back play made to look like a highly-developed art.
>
> A continuance of this sort of stuff and these two teams will just never be separated. One minute the Ibrox crowd were cheering Jock Shaw for besting Gordon Smith. Next

minute they saw their own idol, Willie Waddell bending his knee to Davie Shaw. Not only did each full-back do his own job to perfection, but they were also here, there, and everywhere, sensing slips by their colleagues in front. Yes, 'twas a defenders' day at Ibrox all right.

While it was generally agreed a draw was pretty fair, I have a feeling a boxing referee would have given a points verdict to Hibs. They always seemed to be putting more into it than Rangers. More cunning, more construction, more enterprise. For instance, the joyous abandon of Kean, the studied Alec James, the long passes of Finnigan, and the darting raids of young Turnbull. All touches which suggested Hibs had a plan. A concerted action. A something which the Rangers hadn't.

You can't get nearer to scoring than have two balls cleared from under the bar with the goalkeeper away from home. Hibs had that galling experience. A Finnigan scoring shot in the first half was kneed for a corner by Jock Shaw. Had the footing been softer, too, Willie would have clanged that one home. Then there was Turnbull beating Brown to a jump, his header just sailing into the net when up bobbed the head of George Young. The accountants quickly calculated the potential gate at the replay, and got the true value of that goal-saving header.

There was some re-arrangement of Rangers' attack near the close of the match – Thornton centre, Arnison on the wing, and Duncanson inside, and this move coincided with Rangers' brightest patch of the game. Their storming of Hibs' goal was an inspiration. But a totally wrong reflection on the whole show for the customers who had come in for the last ten. However even Rangers' rousing finish did not compare with Hibs' midway second-half spell of superiority. Here saw them at their brightest and best. And when you add that only the finest defence in the land could have survived it, Rangers will get what I mean. The goalkeeping was also grand. Hibs had a pull wing-half, and Aird was every bit as effective as Woodburn.

It was not a forwards' day, but the best were Turnbull, Gillick, Ormond, and Duncanson. If players occasionally lost their balance, one man continually kept his head. Referee Benzie was efficiency personified.

Onward now to Easter Road. And the team which decides to shoot the opposing backs first will go forward to the next round. That's the impression this game left, anyway.

In the circumstances a no-scoring draw was unsurprising, and the match was a perfect example of how closely matched the sides were. Hibs would win the replay a fortnight later at Easter Road in front of 48,816 spectators, 2-0. This reinforced Hibs as Rangers' bogey team that season as, in four games up to the cup exit, they had drawn two and lost two to the Hibees, and for a long time Hibs looked favourites to land the league flag. However, in the closing weeks of the season Rangers proved to be more consistent and eventually took the title by two points.

The exit from the cup also meant this was the first time in many, many years neither Old Firm side was in the third-round draw.

Some revenge was to follow in the semi-final of the League Cup when Rangers ran out 3-1 winners.

For their part, Hibs were immediately installed as favourites to lift the trophy and marched into the semi-final of the Scottish Cup against Motherwell, and the 'play to a finish' rules meant that the tie took 142 minutes to decide before they emerged victorious 2-1. Interestingly, due to playing five full ten-minute periods of extra time, with the winning goal arriving two minutes into the sixth period, the teams had to change ends seven times; the goalkeepers' heads must have been spinning!

Hibernian could not clinch the trophy, though, and were beaten 2-1 by Aberdeen in the final.

The league flag was clinched at Ibrox when Hamilton Accies were defeated by 4-1 before a disappointingly small crowd of only 8,000.

SFL v SFA

While the Scottish League was content to allow corner kicks to decide drawn games, which was something not stipulated in the laws of the game, the SFA insisted drawn cup ties must be replayed. They further insisted those replays took place on a Saturday to avoid playing midweek and interrupting industrial production, an initiative not taken in England until sometime later.

In addition, it was laid down that replayed games were to be played to a finish; if necessary, extra time of two periods of ten minutes each and then, if still tied, further period of ten minutes until a deciding goal was scored – a precursor to the golden goal of the 1990s. These exceptional rules were set due to the difficulties the country was facing thanks to unprecedented bad weather. The Scottish League for their part resented the attitude of SFA in allowing extra time to be played at the end of the first tie, but instead insisted on replays on a Saturday – the day traditionally set aside for league games. Some member clubs felt the league was entitled to establish some authority in the game and to exercise that authority in view of the commitment of league clubs to the game in Scotland. The dispute eventually fizzled out when the changeover to British summertime arrived and better weather allowed evening kick-offs.

February 1947 was quite a month as, on 8 February, 250,000 folk watched Charlton Athletic play Blackburn Rovers in an FA Cup tie at the Valley. This match was to be the first televised since 1939. It was reported that enough was seen to indicate that, given good weather, the 'tele viewer', aided by three cameras giving long-shots and close-ups may get a better view than spectators. As it was, the glare from the snow-bound pitch made for a poor picture experience and the

31,000 who shivered at the game did in fact get a better view on this occasion. For the record, Charlton won 1-0, and would go on to win the cup at Wembley for the very first time having been runners-up the previous season to Derby. This time they beat Burnley 1-0 after extra time.

As for the Iron Curtain, what was surprising was that, unlike today when teams work on shape and press and all the current buzz words, possibly the most famous and effective component of any Rangers side did no work outside of a matchday to hone their effectiveness.

They were made up of two quite separate entities: those who were part-time (McColl, Brown and Cox) and the full-timers (Jock, Young and Woodburn). They would only ever meet up on matchday. As Ian McColl recalled, 'We never played to any great tactics. We just went out there and played.' The reason for their great success was very simple: every man could play and they were a testimony to Struth's shrewd recruitment and team selection.

Talking about the Iron Curtain, Willie Woodburn recalled, 'We just seemed to knit so well, but we had a good blend. Two big fellows, George Young and myself, helped for a start. Then Ian McColl and Sammy Cox could play football. Ian was quite an artist really. If he was in a tight situation, you could be sure he would come out with the ball. Sammy was versatile. He could win the ball and had the ability to play it away well. And then there was Jock Shaw. At left-back he was a right tearaway. Like I say it was a good blend. In fact, that whole team was a good blend.'

He also added, speaking in 1988, 'Some games I have seen recently see defenders moving up to the halfway line to try and play offside. In those days we would never have contemplated trying to play a team offside. Also, the centre-half was the beacon in the middle of the defence; there was no sweeper or whatever. Passing back to the goalkeeper was something we hardly ever did. If you did give the ball back to Jerry Dawson, he would tell you he didn't want it and get it up the park. Football is a really simple game and it shouldn't be complicated too much.'

Almost every game in which they played brought goalmouth interventions or saves from Jock, Jerry Dawson or Dougie Gray; those saves were not accidents. The trio had a working arrangement. Anything in the six-yard box was Dawson's. If he had to leave that box, the backs fell into place on the goal line. Jock said, 'Best of it is that no one ever said thanks, it was just part of the job.'

George Young also said, 'We were hard to beat, but we had great forwards as well. We could have defended as much as we liked, but we still needed the likes of Willie Waddell and Willie Thornton to get the goals to win the games.'

A feature of Rangers' play during this period were Young's huge upfield clearances, sometimes as far as 60 yards. He said, 'They were not aimless bootings as some people would suggest. I practised for hours on end so that the ball went onto a space, just where I wanted, like the modern golfers who practise the same thing.'

Bobby Brown was the final component to the famed Iron Curtain but speaking in 1972 he said in his early days he did have it tough and was not sure if he ever enjoyed the greatest of relationships with his mates on the field. If they ever let anything through and Bobby was caught out, they let him know all about it.

'We became good friends off the field, and I still see a lot of those lads.'

They were too dumbstruck to roast him, though, when he made his biggest error. As Bobby recalls, 'It was in the 1948 Cup Final against Morton. There was a bit of a wind blowing and before the game I had been told to come out for everything because that Hampden wind can play funny tricks. At least my interpretation of the order was to come for everything. In the very first minute Jimmy Whyte of Morton hit the ball from far out. I came to catch it on the edge of the box when all of a sudden, the wind whisked the ball right over my head. There I was lying on my back helpless.

There was a terrible silence at the Rangers end of the ground. I knew it was a goal and I remember thinking 40 minutes to go this half – how much more can go wrong. Not a word was said by my team-mates. They just looked at me in stony silence. Even at half-time not a mention.'

* * *

The world was still a volatile place following the end of the Second World War, and while the population was slowly becoming accustomed to a return to some form of normality, the Cold War between East and West was beginning, bringing with it the ever-present threat of nuclear war. Post-war depression was rife and those home-coming soldiers were once again in the front line, with few outlets for their frustration. Football was, though, a welcome escape, and crowds grew to record levels.

The interest in those post-war years was such that a new cup competition was introduced this season – the Scottish League Cup, to follow a similar format to the wartime Southern League Cup.

In the early days folk were sceptical about the effect it would have on the game: to some a welcome inclusion, to others a hindrance and a distraction from the League Championship and Scottish Cup.

Rangers and Tiger in particular wanted to win every trophy, and they agreed this cup was no exception. The press, though, gave it their own name of the Egg Cup due to its considered unusual appearance.

In the 1946/47 season Rangers were drawn with Queen's Park, St Mirren and Morton in the new section format for the tournament and qualified easily, winning every match, scoring 18 goals and only conceding two in the process.

Dundee United were despatched in the two-legged quarter-final by an aggregate of 3-2, and the pretenders to their supremacy, Hibernian, were beaten 3-1 at Hampden in the semi-final before 125,154 spectators with goals from Gillick, Thornton and Waddell.

This propelled Rangers to their first-ever League Cup Final where they would meet Aberdeen and revenge was on the light blues' minds after the previous season's Hampden defeat.

The aforementioned spectator boom saw all 137,000 of the issued tickets snapped up and the final took place on 5 April 1947. Horrendous weather on the day of the final limited the actual attendance in the ground to 82,000.

Aberdeen supporters chartered buses and trains to take them to Glasgow, while the team prepared once again at their lucky Largs venue.

Rangers came to Hampden fit, confident and determined to be the first name etched on the trophy. The final, it was decreed by then league president John McKenzie, would be played to a finish on the day.

Rather uniquely, when the two teams lined up prior to kick-off for the national anthem, as Russian MPs were in attendance the Soviet anthem was also played – surely a once-in-a-lifetime occurrence. The Russian delegation under the leadership of M. Kuznetsov, chairman of the Supremo Soviet Union of the USSR, arrived in Edinburgh on the Friday evening for a short Scottish tour.

On arrival at Waverley station by special train they were piped to their hotel by Edinburgh City Police Pipe Band. They later attended a reception organised by the Scottish Soviet Society. On the morning of the final they visited Edinburgh Castle. Finally, on Sunday they were to be taken on a tour of the Highlands including visits to two of the new hydro-electric schemes.

The referee for the final was the well-kent figure of Bobby Calder, who two years later would go on to become chief scout for Aberdeen, a role he would fill with great distinction until 1981.

Prior to kick-off, upon invitation from Mr Struth, Tiger's instructions to his team-mates were unambiguous: 'Go out and win that cup and make sure we do it.' Aberdeen won the toss and elected to kick into the stiff breeze. Despite an apparent huge disadvantage of the weather conditions the Dons took the game to Rangers and had them pinned back for the first 20 minutes, and missed at least three gilt-edged chances to take the lead. As is the way though, they did not make their superiority count and were hit with a sucker punch.

In the 24th minute Willie Thornton collected the ball wide on the right and moved infield, racing towards goal. It looked like he was going to try and swerve a shot into the net. Instead, he cut the ball beautifully back to Duncanson who chipped it perfectly over the heads of the onrushing defenders to Torry Gillick who headed home with the ball spinning off the hands of keeper Johnstone.

Aberdeen were stunned and tried to hit back right away. Harris was the main thorn in Rangers' side and he twice came close to equalising with only the agility of Bobby Brown denying him. Then there was a further hammer blow to the Dons when on 30 minutes Rangers extended their lead.

Eddie Rutherford bore down the right wing and then crossed for Gillick to hit the ball at knee height towards goal. The Dons keeper managed to leap across and palm the ball away but he fell into a puddle and Billy Williamson was on hand to lash the ball home.

Aberdeen were now two goals behind, despite dominating the match. They were stunned and they began to reel under a continued light-blue onslaught. Rutherford, who was playing in place of Willie Waddell, was causing all sorts of problems to the Dons defence.

The more Aberdeen tried to get back into the game the more exposed they left themselves and Rangers duly capitalised. Torry Gillick broke quickly out of defence and passed to Billy Williamson who was heavily covered but Williamson smartly passed to Duncanson who for a moment looked offside, but there was no whistle. Dunky ran a few yards forward and slipped the ball under the advancing Johnstone.

Half-time came and remarkably Rangers were three ahead, and the match all but beyond the Dons.

Aberdeen had the advantage of the breeze after the interval but Rangers were in no mood to surrender their advantage. Harris and Hamilton buzzed around the Rangers goalmouth in the opening minutes of the second half. Jock and Willie Woodburn commanded the defence and made sure no one broke through, but on the few occasions the Dons did penetrate, they met the solid brick wall of Shaw and Woodburn while Bobby Brown was as safe as ever.

On 56 minutes a fourth was added. Williams picked up a long kick-out from Brown and he sent it on to Duncanson who casually chipped it past the keeper for number four.

As the final whistle blew, the Ibrox side turned to receive the acclaim from their fans who had stood bravely in the pouring rain.

Ibrox chairman Jimmy Bowie was presented with the trophy in the dressing room by Sir Hector McNeil and they did indeed get the honour of being the first name inscribed on the trophy. After the match Tiger said, 'Give us a three-goal lead, and the entire British Army won't beat us.' How very true.

Jousting with The Hibees

IN MID-AUGUST 1947, Rangers manager Struth was reported as calling the Rangers playing staff together. He advised them the club were placing a ban on players accepting gifts or testimonials from Rangers Supporters' Club branches. This was not because Mr Struth had anything against the supporters' clubs, nor was he against his star players being figureheads such as honorary presidents and vice-presidents. However, when it came to these being accompanied by presentations of silver tea services, gold watches, companion sets and other expensive gifts, the Ibrox boss considered he must draw the line. The practice had reached what he considered astonishing proportions. Rarely a week passed but one or other of the Ibrox supporters' organisations held an installation and presentation.

This may seem a curious turn of events but Mr Struth was concerned at the level of what he considered to be one-upmanship going on and it was apparent branches were competing for the distinction of handing over the most valuable gifts. In Struth's mind the contributions towards these gifts from many supporters was creating issues. Hard-earned cash, which could be better used for domestic purposes, was going towards the presentation funds. A pair of shoes for a bairn may be sacrificed so that the present may gain in value. It just had to come to an end.

At the time, the view was that the players too welcomed this development. During the recent continental tour Jock had told reporters that the presentations were sometimes pretty embarrassing, but 'you just didn't like to refuse'.

Mr Struth therefore recommended that henceforth a parchment or certificate should be the limit of the gift, a suggestion it was believed would be favourably received by all reasonably minded players and supporters.

That month there was also chat about that perennial topic, a British League. The initial unofficial talks about the concept were considering membership on merit only to decide its composition, and there would be promotion and relegation. The thinking at the time was four top teams each from Scotland and England, plus a couple from Ireland would compete. League placings in the parent domestic leagues would be the gateway to joining. It was being emphasised, though, that clubs would remain members of their parent associations, playing in cup competitions, and soon, and that there was definitely no suggestion of any breakaway. As one prominent English legislator put it, 'This is just a logical extension of the present football set-up.' What the national associations thought of the idea was not recorded but it is safe to assume they would not embrace the concept.

On 13 September 1947, Rangers visited Dens Park for their final League Cup sectional game. The Ibrox team were already certain qualifiers by then. They'd beaten Dundee 3-0 in Glasgow earlier in the campaign, and west of Scotland opinion was that the dark blues stood little chance of success. The Dens Parkers worthily earned a draw, however, and were a shade unlucky not to send Rangers away pointless.

It was the fourth game of the season and the pretender to the Rangers crown, Hibernian, rolled into town. This was a chance for the light blues to put the Hibees in their place.

In the end, though, the match simply did not live up to the hype and there were just two things wrong with this battle of the giants – there was precious little battle and too few giants. The chief reasons for the game failing to qualify for a place among the previous classics were (a) the terrific strain the importance of the match placed on each player; and (b) the slippery, greasy surface of Ibrox. The combination of these two factors meant all sorts of strange things were going on amongst the normally well-controlled legs of the best of players. For every near thing around Hibs' goal, there were half a dozen around Rangers'. Yet, on careful reflection, it is the considered wisdom that Rangers just about deserved victory.

They had an uncertain start with George Young floundering; McColl and Cox were toe-ending balls to the forwards when a pass-and-move approach would have been much more successful. Up front, the light blue right wing was forever tying itself in little knots, and on that side of the park Hibs were having greatest impact. Wing-halves Buchanan and Kean were playing the sort of passes which made you think Hibs had an extra man on the field. And Combe and Turnbull were accepting these in such a manner as to make friend and foe alike proud to acclaim this high standard of inside-forwards in Scottish football.

Highlights in a disappointing game lacking in all-round brilliance were the tackling of Jock Shaw and his mastery of Gordon Smith; the delicate touches of Combe and the rollicking, thunderbolt shots of Turnbull; the steadiness of Woodburn and the full-back play of Jock Govan. How galling it must have been for a Rangers supporter to see a fellow with a name like that do so much to thwart them! But Hibs can take consolation from the fact that, for a team composed mostly of Scotland's reserves, against a team composed mostly of Scotland players, they definitely put up a darn good show! Rangers team was: Brown; Young, Shaw; McColl, Woodburn, Cox; Rutherford, Paton, Williamson, Thornton, Duncanson. Hibernian's was: Brown; Govan, Shaw; Buchanan, Aird, Kean; Smith, Combe, Reilly, Turnbull, Ormond. The referee was T. Shirley, of Troon.

The opening goal came as no surprise. Gordon Smith was in full flow through the centre when he was fouled just outside the box. He took the free kick himself, and slammed the ball against a wall of

Rangers. It squirmed out of the ruck, ran clear for a few yards and Combe pounced to smack past Bobby Brown. Hibs might have had one or two others but for some immaculate work by Rangers' keeper. Particularly notable was his handling of the greasy ball that showed Brown was right at his best, and succeeded in doing to Hibs what Kerr had done to Rangers in the same match the previous season. Rangers gradually turned the corner. Returning confidence was fully evidenced by the equaliser. In a goalward raid, Williamson made to lunge forward. Instead, he cutely back-heeled to Paton. The Hibs defence was somewhat spreadeagled and the unmarked Paton's crisp shot sizzled past outdriving Jock Brown.

Any ideas about Hibs romping home to victory were blown sky-high within a minute of the interval. Rutherford raced down the wing and slung over a curling centre. In dashed Williamson, running in a sort of semi-circle, to hook the ball past the advancing Brown; a smartly taken goal, even though it needed the aid of an upright to convey the ball into the net. That was all that was needed to give Rangers the victory scent. Gers' raids were now full-blooded, concerted affairs, instead of tip-tap, hoping-for-the-best stuff. The forwards, roused from their early lethargy, developed sufficient power to push back Hibs' wing-halves. And young Woodburn and Shaw, with Brown behind them, looked as if they now had each and every Hibs raid well and truly under control.

It took until December for Rangers to ascend to the top of the table and then they were purring along nicely after an indifferent start to the league campaign. There had been some adjustment to the team, and in turn the form of the key performers had been taken to a different level. The chat among supporters was that George Young had never played better, Sammy Cox was excelling at right-back and Eddie Rutherford had reached a standard of consistency which was at least the equal of the until-now peerless Willie Waddell. Of the more mature team members such as Gillick and Duncanson they were said to provide a certain style and poise to the inside-forward positions.

As for Jock, now aged 35, and most assuredly in what would be termed the veteran category, there had been some grumblings about his personal early-season form and the understandable questions pondering if age was catching up on him. However, the whole team's form had been poor and, for Jock, age was simply a number, and if anything, he was quite possibly just about the fittest member of the entire squad.

As the team improved so did the perception of Jock Shaw's performances and it was noted that he was well and truly answering his critics by serving up some immaculate displays, ably supported by Jimmy Caskie, who was once again his tricky effervescent self.

It is perhaps also worth emphasising that the Rangers side was pretty much unchanged from that which had been operating very successfully for the previous few seasons, with perhaps one exception – Rutherford replacing Waddell in attack. Right-winger Eddie Rutherford had caused Rangers fans to almost forget the absence of injured Willie Waddell as, like Waddell, he had a terrific turn of speed and lacked none of the internationalist's ball control. At the season's start, newcomers joining the first-team squad included Paton from Kirkintilloch Rob Roy and Willie Findlay from Albion Rovers in an attempt by Bill Struth to freshen up the side. Both were given the chance to make the inside berths their own, but lacked consistency and Rangers reverted to the tried and trusted old Gillick, Thornton, Duncanson trio.

This was the season too when Scot Symon was setting in place the foundations which would lead him to become a manager at the top level and atop the marble staircase. Starting his managerial journey at East Fife, Symon knew he still had a lot to learn and as part of his learning he reported to the SFA offices at Carlton Place, put himself in the hands of George Graham, and asked to be shown all the snags and pitfalls liable to crop up in signing, registering and retaining players. This was an invaluable session as in one day the new Methil boss had learned more than he would have picked up in two or three years, finding out things for himself through bitter experience. It is perhaps worth noting that the Methil board were so delighted with the recapture of Symon as their manager they immediately considered the possibility of installing floodlights to enable the club to play midweek games.

It was also reported that ex-Rangers legend Jimmy Simpson had an attractive offer to coach one of the top Dutch clubs; while flattered, Simpson was looking for something closer to home as the Dutch league was not considered to be of any great significance back then and the thought of uprooting to play in a nondescript league could not have been appealing. While asking for more time to consider, he was offered the job at Alloa Athletic which he plumped for as it was obviously closer to home.

At the beginning of December, Rangers headed to Tynecastle, traditionally a tough venue. Despite not quite firing on all cylinders Rangers were led on the park by a man who ensured they were a well-organised unit. That was the difference ultimately in this encounter; while not everything came off for them there was a plan which was plain for all onlookers to see.

In the early stages the light blues were taken a little aback by Hearts' forcefulness, and Rutherford, Thornton and Caskie would drive forward only to find themselves thwarted, by Mathieson and McKenzie in particular. This stout defence, linked to some probing attacking by Hearts, had the Jambos believing this may be their day. However, it soon dawned on them that all the enthusiasm, all the strong tackling, all the efforts of the Hearts players were failing to knock any dents in Rangers' defence. When it came to anything which looked remotely ominous, Tiger and Cox were always there, ever clever in their anticipation and cutting out the final pass. A marvellous description from one Hearts player being, 'Some say Jock Shaw is roon the corner, as he uses his head to think that far ahead,' as he did here, 'he will still be a good player when he's 90.' Which was one way of saying, despite his advancing years, the Tiger still had plenty left in the tank.

The real difference on the day would prove to be the forwards and their almost telepathic understanding. The inside-forwards would look for Caskie and find him, then send searching passes away across towards Rutherford, and he was there. Gillick was an even more striking example. Without looking up at all, Torry could smash that ball away up into the empty space and again, of course, a Ranger was darting in. Rangers' opening goal in 32 minutes was a glorious instance of quick thinking. The ball was running to the left when Gillick quickly stepped in and pushed down the right, Rutherford swung it goalwards. Thornton rose and headed it nearer and Duncanson flashed in a header past Brown. 'Goal' could have been written on the ball from the moment it left Gillick's foot. So Rangers led at the interval.

Upon the restart Rangers came flying out the traps. Before the echo of the referee's whistle had come back off the Pentlands, the light blues were two up. Duncanson and Caskie weaved their way up the left. Suddenly Duncanson swerved goalwards; as the defence closed in, he simply passed the ball to Rutherford and the winger would never have scored an easier-looking goal.

This seemed to settle the contest and the next half hour or so was played out like a pre-season friendly with Rangers seemingly happy with what they had and Hearts apparently without the will to try and get back into the game.

Towards the end, Sloan and Kelly of Hearts changed places, and there was an almost instant complete transformation of proceedings, and suddenly the Jambos came to life again. The Tynecastle crowd sensed a revival, and Sloan got in and smashed a beautiful shot past Brown. Ding-dong it went, right to the end, but the Iron Curtain stood strong and tall.

It probably took until December for Rangers to really hit top form and they brushed the Dons aside easily to win 4-0, and to lead the league on goal average with three games in hand over nearest challengers from the east coast, Hibernian. Their next game was against Third Lanark and was played at Hampden as Cathkin was undergoing reconstruction, and the work had not yet been completed. The points were secured with a single goal from Torry Gillick. A Duncanson hat-trick won two more points at Dens Park on Christmas Day, principally due to the seasonal spirit of the Dundee defence who too often relied upon an offside trap they were incapable of executing effectively. Two days later at Ibrox on a pitch which cut up very badly Rangers beat Partick Thistle 2-1.

So the scene was set for the traditional Ne'er Day encounter with Celtic at Parkhead. Unfortunately, the pitch was unplayable on account of surface water and an hour before kick-off the match was called off and postponed for 24 hours. Those 24 hours only delayed the inevitable as Rangers consolidated their position at the top of the league by thrashing Celtic 4-0. The defence was watertight, and their speed and sharpness in the forward areas was something Celtic simply could not cope with and Gers were three up by half-time through McColl, Thornton and Rutherford. Jimmy Duncanson added a fourth in the second half as the light blues won at the proverbial canter.

It was reported that the bravest man at Celtic Park post-match was the vendor of a colour Celtic team-group photograph for a shilling, still trying to ply his wares with zero to purchase.

On 3 January 1948 Dundee were at Ibrox and another 2-1 win followed. Next up for Rangers was a trip to Brockville on 10 January. The light blues were, of course, neck and neck with Hibs at the top of the league so it was imperative the Ibrox men picked up both points. The home side, though, didn't show any sign of fearing their illustrious opponents.

Indeed, the early stages saw Falkirk look the more aggressive outfit. They pressed forward relentlessly, but faced by the famous Iron Curtain defence the Bairns just couldn't cash in on their outfield superiority.

All too often the hamsters created scoring chances only to be thwarted by the timely intervention of big George Young or Willie

Woodburn. As so often is the case, that failure to convert chances proved to be fatal.

With half an hour played, a Ranger rarely seen as an attacking force, Sammy Cox, picked up the ball on the left touchline and edged forward looking for support from his forwards. He caught sight of the seemingly disinterested Torry Gillick lying free just outside the Falkirk penalty box and promptly swung the ball towards the inside-forward.

Torry didn't waste a second in showing what he could do. He took the ball on his chest, wheeled round and cracked it viciously into the net under the crossbar of former Ranger Jerry Dawson.

Falkirk's reaction was to hit back fiercely but again the redoubtable Iron Curtain stood in their way. A superb Ian McColl tackle on inside-forward Aikman as he took possession in a dangerous position and a fine save by Brown from an Inglis shot maintained Rangers' lead.

Then as the half-time interval approached, the light blues floored the Brockville men with a double-barrelled blast.

In the 42nd minute Jimmy Caskie sent Jimmy Duncanson clear and Duncanson beautifully eluded a tackle from full-back Whyte before chipping in a superb cross which left Gillick with the easiest of chances in heading home. Two minutes later, with Falkirk still reeling, Willie Waddell cut inside and fired in a fierce shot which was blocked by keeper Dawson but the keeper couldn't hold the ball and Jimmy Duncanson followed up to net the rebound.

The game ended as a contest at that point, but to Falkirk's credit they kept plugging away in the hope against all hope that Rangers would throw them a lifeline. It never happened; the light blues were not the sort of side to throw games away lightly and they monotonously broke down the home side's offensive and set up their own counter-attacks. It was from one such counter that the Ibrox men went further ahead in the 65th minute.

A hefty George Young clearance was picked up by Jimmy Duncanson and, with the Falkirk defence paying more attention to the presence of Willie Thornton in the middle, Duncanson strode forward unchallenged and crashed the ball into the net from the edge of the box.

Falkirk still kept fighting pluckily and they were rewarded with a consolation goal in the 74th minute when Inglis beat Bobby Brown to a Henderson cross to head home. They couldn't stop the rampant Rangers and five minutes from time the Bairns centre-half Fiddes dallied on the ball and was dispossessed by Willie Waddell who sprinted clear to slot home the light blues' fifth goal.

So, Rangers ran out 5-1 winners, but as the 20,000 crowd made their exits the main talking point was the efficiency of the Ibrox side which had turned an even battle into a landslide win. Efficiency was a trademark of that Rangers team, however; many sides had fallen to the light blues for the same reason after threatening to put one over Bill Struth's men.

Next up were Motherwell who were easily swept aside 2-0. The famed football correspondent of the time, Alan Breck, opined that Waddell, Gillick, Thornton, Duncanson and Caskie was a forward line for getting things done. He likened it to something akin to 'The Rangers Dance, featuring the Waddell Wallop, the Gillick Glide, the Thornton Two-Step, the Duncanson Daudle and Caskie Cantrips.' I think it was a saying for the times which meant this was poetry in motion.

The rhythm blended well once all the players got tuned in, and Breck thought Caskie in particular, despite being 33, was playing more delightfully and usefully than ever and could stand fair comparison to the new star of the left wing, Willie Ormond of Hibernian.

In the first round of the Scottish Cup against Stranraer at Stair Park the home side held out until 70 minutes when Gillick popped up to net the only goal of the game.

On 31 January a huge crowd of 52,750 congregated at Easter Road for the top-of-the-table clash with Hibernian – this would undoubtedly be the match of the season so far.

Both defences were on top despite the attacking talent on show for both sides but, with only a minute left, and the match seemingly destined for a goalless draw, there were scenes of unbridled joy and no little euphoria in Leith when Jock Cuthbertson netted the winner.

Understandably the celebrations were particularly raucous, in no small part down to the fact that Hibernian's manager Willie McCartney had died of a heart attack at the end of their cup tie against Albion Rovers the previous week. Sadness cast its dark shadow over Ibrox too as that same week Torry Gillick's young daughter had passed away the night before the game – quite how he had the strength of character to turn out as he did and play the match, goodness alone knows.

The Tiger and the Pig

AFTER THE disappointment of the Hibs defeat, Rangers would have time to lick their wounds for a few days as they were heading for sunnier climes, and their destination was Portugal.

So it was then that 10 February 1948 saw Rangers embark on one of their most memorable adventures oversees when they travelled to play Benfica.

Nowadays, the Eagles are one of the most renowned names in European football, having won the European Cup in 1960/61 and 1961/62, and been Portuguese Champions on 37 occasions.

In the immediate post-war years though, Portugal was something of a footballing backwater, so in a bid to spark interest in the sport the local teams would regularly invite foreign teams from mainland Europe for friendlies.

Such visits did not have the desired effect, though, and the lack of success prompted local paper *O Seculo* to cast the net wider and bid for leading British sides to visit the Iberian nation, and they reckoned the team all Portugal wanted to see was Rangers.

So Rangers flew out to Lisbon and such was the esteem in which Rangers were held, 5,000 Portuguese fans turned up at the airport to welcome them. This was to prove an eventful trip to say the least.

Rangers' first team and three reserves (all insured for £400,000) travelled in a twin-engine Dakota and the journey, which today would take around two and a half hours, lasted an energy-sapping 11 hours. So, it was a leg-weary party which finally arrived in Portugal after a refuelling stop in Bordeaux, France (this was as far as planes could go back then on one load).

The players found the flight a bit of a chore with one notable exception in the shape of Willie Waddell who was to meet his future wife on the flight as she was one of the air hostesses on duty.

Warm and sunny Lisbon could not have been in more stark contrast with the cold and snowy Scotland the players had left behind. They were put up in a luxury hotel and were royally entertained. Players would still have been used to post-war rationing and it must have been a fabulous treat to have more meat served at one meal than they normally got in one month's ration. It was also reasonable to assume that the players were smokers, as Jock certainly was, and they were presented with handsome cigarette cases.

The warm reception continued throughout the trip with several thousand turning out just to watch Rangers train. There was something of a shock in store when Bill Struth asked their hosts to water the pitch to take some of the fire out of it. No sooner had the request been made than a group of groundsmen appeared with hoses, but the visitors were taken aback to see the supervisor in charge of this operation watching his workers down the barrel of a rifle. It wasn't until later that Rangers were told the groundsmen were in fact convicts from a local prison who had earned the privilege of treating the park.

It is worth noting that the pitch had been laid down with imported Cumberland turf and carefully nurtured into immaculate condition. In Jock's opinion only Wembley was better.

The game took place in front of an expectant 60,000 in the Estoril stadium on Tuesday, 10 February 1948, and so little was known about the Portuguese by the Scottish press that they referred to the opposition as 'Bonifica'.

Officials of the Lisbon club soon saw the error and ensured it was corrected but while they taught some journalists how to spell, their players taught Rangers absolutely nothing about playing football.

Neat ball work, short passes and an almost suicidal insistence of carrying the ball too far were the features of Benfica's play and the light blues with their Iron Curtain defence were obviously a class above the local side.

The swirling wind and the bumpy surface did not suit Rangers and the Portuguese side had plenty of possession but the Ibrox players were quite prepared to let the home side do all the work so long as they didn't threaten to score. And that's exactly what transpired.

Benfica, with winger Melao particularly worthy of attention, set up camp in the Rangers half of the field, but when it came to getting shots at goal, the Eagles of Lisbon just couldn't make any impression on the Ibrox rearguard.

What efforts eluded the defence were confidently dealt with by Bobby Brown and it was no surprise when Rangers punished the home side's lack of the killer touch by showing them just how it should be done.

A superb through ball from Willie Waddell sent Thornton clear and despite a brave attempt by keeper Machado to save at the Ranger's feet, Thornton shot the light blues into the lead. The silence which greeted that goal was a combination of disappointment and healthy respect for the Ibrox men's professional ruthlessness.

The score remained unchanged for the greater part of the game and the pattern of play was similar to that in the early stages, although a young inside-forward called Mario Coluna was making telling passes which would have troubled lesser defences than the Ibrox Curtain.

Coluna was just starting a career that would span more than 20 years and would see him appearing in all five of Benfica's subsequent European Cup finals. There were some glimpses in this match of what was to come.

With 85 minutes played Torry Gillick foxed the Benfica defence with a lovely dummy, Jimmy Duncanson raced on to the ball and shot into the net from 12 yards.

While the Portuguese were still harbouring some feelings of injustice having had so much of the ball, Rangers then rubbed salt into the wound when Duncanson grabbed a third.

A 3-0 win over Benfica would have the whole of football talking now, but back in 1948 few noticed the result and what attention was focused on the match reckoned the scoreline had flattered Rangers. That opinion is a little unfair because the object of the trip was to show the locals how the game was played at the highest level. Having scored three goals, despite allowing Benfica to do all the pressing, Rangers showed up the Portuguese side's failing in that department and in turn taught them some harsh lessons.

It was a lesson the Eagles would use to their advantage in the years ahead, but despite all their conquests, when the Portuguese champions came over to Ibrox for a friendly seven years later in 1955, they fared only a little better and were on the end of another defeat, this time 3-1.

After the match the Benfica president presented the club with a beautiful model of a 'carvel'– a ship used by sailors from bygone days of yore. The model, which sits resplendent in one of the cabinets in the trophy room today, is a gilt and enamel figure which rests on a walnut pedestal and is accompanied by a richly embroidered banner suitably commemorating the visit. Each of the players, as already mentioned, received a handsome cigarette case.

The trip also featured the introduction of Willie Woodburn's nickname of 'Ben'. At the post-match reception, he kept toasting the Portuguese with the words 'Viva Benfica' over and over again. So 'Ben' it was to be forever more.

Now we come to the very special gift in store for the Tiger. It may have been some form of tradition but the captain was singled out for a special memento of the occasion in the shape of a live pig. It may sound like a strange gift but at the time it was viewed as a great thing because rationing was still very much in place. The only problem was Jock was 1,800 miles from home. The Benfica president duly presented the pig to Jock, adorned with a blue ribbon and dog lead. Jock then takes up the story. 'I couldn't believe it but apparently it was a great honour, but this pig on a lead with a blue ribbon was too much. However, I couldn't even take it back to Scotland because of the quarantine regulations so unfortunately, I had to leave it behind, but I guess it was a nice thought.'

Upon their return to Scotland, suitably refreshed, Rangers beat St Mirren 3-2 in their next league game and then saw off Partick Thistle 3-0 in the third round of the cup. The following week Queen of the South were in town and were expected to be easily despatched. What transpired was the biggest shock result of the season. Ten years previously the Dumfries side had faced relegation and won 3-2 at Ibrox to secure their safety. History very sadly for Rangers almost exactly repeated itself with the Doonhamers triumphing 3-2 and again going on to survive in the top flight, finishing ahead of Morton, Airdrie and Queen's Park. For the light blues this was another blow to their title hopes and the loss saw Hibs leapfrog Rangers to the summit of the league by a single point.

Next up was a clash with an old friend in Scot Symon and his Second Division East Fife side. The public interest around the Symon aspect was such that the clash attracted an unusually massive crowd of 90,000 who paid £5,400 in gate receipts. Rangers were rapid in attack but it took them until a couple of minutes from the interval to take the lead, when Duncanson netted from a Rutherford cross. There was a turnaround in more ways than one after the interval as East Fife dictated the play for long periods but could not capitalise on the openings they created and Rangers saw the game through to record a narrow victory. The down side was a knee injury to left-winger Jimmy Caskie.

For the next game in Greenock an unchanged XI was expected but Caskie had not recovered in time and Waddell was again deployed to the right wing, with Eddie Rutherford moving to the left wing. Rangers won a tense clash by a single goal from Thornton but the following week crashed 1-2 at home to Queen's Park – not title-winning form – and Rangers' stranglehold on the league flag was loosening.

The main issue appeared to be in attack and the forward line was considered not to be functioning at all well, and the left-wing berth in particular was considered a real issue. Jimmy Caskie was now 34 and succumbing more and more to injury, so could not be relied upon for the longer term and therefore the search for a replacement had been going on for months in preparation for the next season.

Despite their indifferent form, Rangers went into the Scottish Cup semi-final with Hibernian in determined and confident mood. Hibs had been matching them if not bettering them in recent clashes but, as the motto on Mr Struth's desk said, 'Cometh the hour, cometh the man.'

The weekend of 27 March 1948 was a remarkable one in Scottish Football history – perhaps only ever equalled since by 19 April 1972 when Glasgow hosted two European semi-finals on the same night. Back though to 1948 and this was semi-final day in the Scottish Cup with Celtic facing Morton at Ibrox, while Rangers were facing up to their arch foes of the period in Hibernian. An astonishing total of 223,000 spectators were in attendance, a record which is unlikely to ever be equalled in British football history.

A crowd of 82,000 were at Ibrox to see Morton despatch Celtic by a single goal after extra time. By far the biggest crowd was at Hampden though, where 143,570 were in attendance, paying record gate receipts for the time of £9,300, and it is estimated that at least another 5,000 were turned away at the gate. Some of the statistics associated with the match are staggering.

More than 100,000 queued in Central Station to be transported in 17 special trains to Mount Florida. Others either walked, went by tram or hitched a lift. During the match there was the astonishing sight of young boys being passed over the heads of the crowd to get to the walls at the front of the terracing for a better view. The police eventually allowed some to sit around the track and it was later claimed over 400 left the ground as they could not see a thing.

On the day there were 300 police in attendance but not a single arrest. There is some footage of the match available via YouTube and it's worth viewing to get a true sense of the mass of humanity present at Hampden on the day. Jock is very clearly featured, jousting with Gordon Smith.

The scene was set for a classic confrontation as these were the kingpins of Scottish Football at the time – it's worth noting that of the first seven championships contested after the war, Rangers won four while Hibernian won three and there were the Shaw brothers in the midst of this – Jock and his younger brother Davie.

The teams were, of course, also neck and neck in the title race and Rangers were determined to make up for the aberration of the previous week when they lost out to a late goal from Queen's Park in the 2-1 defeat.

In glorious sunny weather and with the huge crowd packing the terraces this created an electric atmosphere. The game kicked off to a frantic start with the great Gordon Smith spurning two gilt-edged chances for the men from Leith, yet Hibs continued to dominate. However, the Ibrox rearguard of Jock, Willie Woodburn and George Young stood firm, having the intuition to read the play and break up their opponents' moves as they reached the danger zone. The Rangers support was hushed, as despite outnumbering their rivals two to one, they knew their favourites were under the cosh.

Willie Thornton many years later recalled the game: 'Hibs were a very good side at that time. They were a few years off the time when their "Famous Five" attack was really earning their reputation, and we knew we would have a hard time. The other thing was that although everyone remembers the Hibs attack of that time, I don't think enough credit was given to their defence that every side found difficult to get past. In fact, they were a good all-round team, and they showed it that day. The semi-final was a great game and I would have to admit that overall Hibs probably had the edge on us in terms of outfield superiority and chances created, but the main thing was that there was a lot of good football played throughout by both sides and plenty of entertainment was provided.'

All that was to change, though, as in a rare attacking move Rangers took the lead in the 30th minute. Young cleared high and long from inside his own half and Willie Waddell tore after it, pursued by Jock's younger brother Davie. As they reached the corner flag, Waddell put his foot on the ball and dragged it back a few feet while Shaw slid past. Waddell steadied himself and crossed the ball and keeper Farm came to his near post to apparently safely clutch the cross, only to inexplicably drop it at Thornton's feet and he duly hooked the ball into the goal.

Thornton recalled the moment vividly speaking in 1975: 'Over came the cross and I went running for it; I realised however that George Farm in Hibs' goal was going to get it before me, so I didn't jump with him. Whether George was expecting me to jump, I couldn't say but something went wrong for him. He seemed to have the ball in his grasp then suddenly it slipped out of his hand straight in front of me. I just had to tap it into the empty net. It was by no means the greatest goal Hampden had ever seen but it was good enough for me that day. It was into the goal at the traditional Rangers end of Hampden too, so you can imagine the roar that went up.'

Hibs were stunned as the goal had come against the run of play but were not downcast; they dusted themselves down and proceeded to pound Rangers' rearguard who held firm till half-time.

After the interval the pattern appeared to be repeated but events which straddled the 47th minute had a huge bearing on the eventual outcome. Firstly, Young appeared to handle the ball at the front post and there were loud appeals for a penalty but referee Jack Mowat waved play-on. Still fuming, Hibs were fit to burst when a minute later Tiger sent Alex Linwood sprawling to the turf but play was again waved on.

The apparent injustice seemed to galvanise Hibs even more, and Rangers had keeper Bobby Brown to thank for keeping them in the game time and again.

Overall, though, the Iron Curtain was at its best here, standing uncompromising and strong to counter the effervescent Hibs onslaught and seeing the game out until the final whistle, which took Rangers through to the final to face Morton.

The holders Aberdeen incidentally returned the cup to the SFA wrapped up neatly in a brown paper parcel for the presentation on final day – changed times with today when replica versions are used for the lap of honour and so on.

Although it was a disappointing outcome on the day, Hibs would go on to break Rangers' dominance and win the league by two points. Historically this was the first time ten in a row was stopped, not 1975.

So to cup final day on 17 April, where Rangers were due to face Morton. Rangers were hot favourites as Morton were struggling at the foot of the table and would only escape relegation by three points. A crowd of 131,975 turned up at Hampden to watch the action.

Bobby Brown reminisced about the match, speaking in 1987: 'I can laugh at it now, but at the time believe me it was far from funny. We were up against a big strong Morton team and in the pre-match talk in the old St Enoch Hotel manager Bill Struth spoke about the wind, which is always a problem when it blows at Hampden. He said he wanted me to come out and go for everything, not just in the immediate goal area but in the penalty box. He was certain that if they got the wind in their favour Morton would try to rattle us with that tactic. Morton won the toss and sure enough they took the wind and the game was not even a minute old when a high ball was thumped through the middle. I started coming out for it and then suddenly realised I had misjudged its flight on the wind and that I had gone too far. The ball flew over me, bounced twice and I watched in horror as it rolled into the net. At half-time I was a pretty miserable picture in the dressing room. I was isolated and nobody would talk to me and I couldn't look at anyone.'

His colleagues though dug him out of the hole he created, when ten minutes later Jimmy Duncanson swung over a cross from the left, Willie Thornton rose above Miller to nod the ball down sweetly into the path of Torry Gillick who gave keeper Cowan no chance with a first-time shot from about six yards out. Morton were on top for the remainder of the first half, and they passed up a great chance to go back in front. Murdoch and Hepburn were both left unmarked as a Colin Liddell cross came over from the left but they got in each other's way in the excitement of the chance and the danger was gone.

The second half belonged to Rangers but they simply could not find the net. Jimmy Cowan made an astonishing save after 74 minutes when Willie Thornton rose to head an Eddie Rutherford corner goalwards. Billy Williamson then shot over a minute later. The 90-minute mark came and went with the scores still tied, and so it was to be extra time.

Neither side, though, could find that spark of inspiration that was required to break the deadlock, and it was Morton who probably came closest when a thunderbolt of an effort from Murphy beat Bobby Brown but Tiger was on hand to bravely block the ball with his stomach on the goal line. It winded Jock severely but it was all in the line of duty and he was made of stern stuff, this son of Annathill. The match ended all square so fast forward to Wednesday for the replay.

When the players gathered at the St Enoch Hotel pre-match for the replay, amongst those in attendance, but not for a second believing he would play, was Billy Williamson. In fact, the day before he had turned out in a Staff v Pupils match at Lenzie Academy where he was a teacher. However, while leaving the hotel Mr Struth pulled him aside to alert him there was a very strong chance he would be playing. In those days there were no team talks of any great strategic significance or player pools; the team was normally announced just before kick-off. When they got to Hampden and Williamson was named in the team he could scarcely believe it and it took a while to sink in, even after the 'heads up' from Mr Struth.

Rangers started the match much more positively this time and had Morton under the cosh with only some squandering of chances created and good goalkeeping by Jimmy Cowan keeping the light blues at bay. As the game wore on, the urgency ebbed away, to be replaced by some nerves, as the match was still so finely balanced and the tie slipped over into an extra 30 minutes for the second time.

The closeness of the two games was especially surprising to many observers as Morton finished the season third bottom of the league. However, Rangers had struggled against them in the two league encounters, winning 1-0 and drawing 1-1.

There was one unusual talking point during extra time. These were the days before floodlights and the gloom was descending across the cavernous Hampden bowl with less and less people being able to clearly see the action. The referee had to stop play and ask photographers to stop taking flashlight pictures as they were distracting the Morton keeper.

Then with dusk really setting in came the pivotal moment. Eddie Rutherford picked up a throw-in wide on the right-hand side of the pitch, and Jimmy Cowan, expecting a deep cross, positioned himself towards the back of the goal. When the cross came, though, it was low and towards the near post where Williamson met it and directed it into the net for the only goal and another winner's medal for Tiger.

After the match the team got a police escort back to the St Enoch Hotel for a celebratory dinner.

It is worth noting that the two games were watched by 265,000 spectators.

The gate receipts from the two games amounted to £38,287, equivalent to £1.4m today. From the gross receipts, £8,925 was destined for entertainment tax and £5,335 to Queen's Park for use of the stadium. The two finalists then had the remainder split evenly. While there was no limit on bonuses which could be paid for a Scottish Cup tie, it was reported as a matter of public record that Rangers' players received a £1 bonus for the first drawn game and £8 for the success of lifting the cup – the same money as paid in 1939.

Before he passed away, I visited Bobby Brown at his home in Helensburgh to talk about Tiger, and he was so helpful, even coming to collect me from the train station. We had a long chat and he was very fond of Tiger, particularly as he had looked after him so well when he joined the club. He relayed a story about the 1948 cup final that saw Tiger fall foul of Mr Struth. 'Before the final we had heard that Morton were on £200 a head bonus to win the cup. Today that seems very little, but then it was a lot of money [£7,300 today]. That made some of our team think we should be on a similar bonus, as ours was a lot less. Jock, as our captain, was persuaded to go up the marble staircase and speak to Mr Struth about it. Suffice to say he came back with his tail between his legs. Struth apparently said, "Now John, have a seat and tell me what's on your mind." Once he had done so, he was reminded in a straightforward fashion how well-paid Rangers players were, win or lose, and that we were in finals regularly, whereas Morton didn't reach many finals. And "John" was left in no doubt there would be no increase in our win bonus.'

In the league, three 1-1 draws against Aberdeen, Falkirk and Motherwell along with a 2-1 defeat at Ibrox against Hearts in the last game of the season sounded the death knell on Rangers' title bid and Hibernian were worthy champions by two points. This was to be Gordon Smith's first league title but by no means his last. He would go on to lift another two with Hibernian (1950/51 and 1951/52) while also collecting winner's medals with Hearts in 1959/60 and Dundee in 1961/62. A remarkable achievement considering that none of these victories were while playing for one of the Old Firm. It is a feat I can say with almost a 99.9% degree of certainty will never be repeated.

The Rangers aficionados were firmly of the view it was in attack where the light blues had issues and that was the principal reason for their failure to clinch a tenth successive title. In particular, Willie Waddell's absences due to injury hit the side hard and he featured in only 12 of 30 league games.

For Tiger this was the completion of his tenth season as a Ranger, and the first he did not finish as a champion. At 35, though, he missed only three league games and, in addition to the Scottish Cup he added winner's medals in the Glasgow and Charity Cups to his collection.

One end-of-season review paid tribute: 'Under Jock Shaw, Rangers have again been successful in lifting the Scottish Cup, and were just pipped at the post by Hibs for the coveted double. Tiger's steady play and enthusiasm at left-back had a grand influence on his colleagues.'

During the close season in England, they decided that television would be detrimental to football and laid down that only the FA Cup Final could be televised. The charging rule was also changed: 'A player shall be penalised if he charges fairly, i.e. with shoulder, when the ball is not within playing distance of the players concerned and they are definitely not attempting to play it.' It would take serious injuries to goalkeepers in the 1957 and 1958 FA Cup finals as a result of charging, plus pressure from the rest of Europe, before the keeper was finally given complete protection. In 1957 Manchester United keeper Ray Wood was left unconscious with a broken cheekbone, while in 1958 United were again the victims when Harry Gregg was bundled over the line in the process of Bolton scoring their second goal.

Developments in Scotland included the Scottish League increasing the guarantee to visiting sides to £200, plus half of any gate money over £400. The home club retained the drawings from the stand, including season ticket money, though they did also stipulate only 1,000 season tickets could be issued, a real drawback to a club like Rangers whose main stand had a 10,000 capacity. In England, however, it was agreed that the whole stand could be reserved for season ticket holders. The visiting clubs then received 20% of the gate money less tax and expenses, plus 2d for anyone entitled to attend as season ticket holder. It would be some years before Scotland followed this example.

That August, the Seventh Rangers Sports attracted 40,000 – a tribute to Bill Struth's enthusiasm for athletics and talent as an organiser.

Season 1948/49 – The First Treble

WARTIME RESTRICTIONS were still very much in place and, for example, there was a huge waiting list to get a new car. The system had not reckoned on Mr Struth though, who was about to come up trumps. Bobby Brown takes up the story: 'One day after training, it was during the school holidays, as I was full-time by then, Jimmy Smith told me, Willie Waddell, Sammy Cox and Jock Shaw that the Boss wanted to see us in his office. I can tell you we went up the marble staircase rather nervously in some trepidation, as naturally our first thought was we were in some sort of trouble. He opened the door to us as immaculately dressed as ever, looked us up and down as usual, then told us to take a seat. He then asked us individually if we would like a car. Everyone of course said "Yes", till he reached me and I had to tell him I couldn't drive. To which he replied, "It's high time you did." At this time post-war there was a five-year waiting list for cars but somehow he had managed to bypass that and arrange for those Austin A40s to be made available for us through Carlaws motor dealers. I started taking lessons and arranged to sit my test in Stirling in an old Armstrong Saddley which was not the easiest to drive, as it required double de-clutching. Having slipped back during a hill start, which caused a passing workman to slip on the icy road scattering his tools everywhere, I asked the examiner "tongue in cheek" if I had passed, to which the answer was a resounding "no". Thankfully I passed on the second attempt, driving the Austin, which was an easier car to drive.'

As Rangers commenced a season that was to have a momentous conclusion, they were supremely confident and desperate to wrestle the league title back from chief rivals Hibernian. As David Leggat observed, speaking about Tiger, 'In Jock, Struth had a man out there as his captain who was in line with the way the manager thought. A skipper who always ensured everyone always gave of their best and that was all the Rangers manager had ever asked of his boys.'

Jock himself summed up the outlook: 'It was easy for me, as we had a team who were all wholehearted players. You didn't have to gee up players like Ian McColl, Willie Woodburn and Sammy Cox. They always played with their sleeves rolled up, and sweated for Rangers and with them in the team we never knew when we were beaten. But I remember we did not play too well in the first weeks of the season and seemed to take a wee while to get into our stride.'

Jock was spot on. Of their opening eight league games the light blues only won three, and the final match in that opening sequence was a comprehensive 4-2 defeat to Hibs at Ibrox. The signs were not looking good.

On the positive side there were a couple of victories over Celtic to savour. On 21 August, Rangers travelled to Celtic Park. While the final scoreline recorded a narrow margin of victory by 1-0 thanks to Willie Findlay, it did not accurately reflect Rangers' dominance or the fact the Celtic attack was so insipid. This would be the third league game in a row Celtic had failed to score in. There was a lot of chat about how Celtic's play was very easy on the eye but their attempts at goalscoring by contrast were lamentable. During the match they had 14 corners yet barely threatened the Rangers goal.

The only goal must have been a real body blow, coming after only six minutes, and must have been the strangest, softest goal ever conceded by the Parkhead club.

From 35 yards Findlay shot, foolishly and harshly most in the ground thought at the time, and the ball was sailing harmlessly past the right-hand post. Keeper Willie Miller left his goal, then decided to save the ball boys a run, by halting the ball's progress himself. However, while trying to stop the ball crossing the touchline, all Miller succeeded in doing was mishandling the ball and deflecting it into the net. Everyone in the ground was astonished, even Findlay, but what a start. Rangers graciously accepted this gift goal and they immediately trimmed their sails to suit the breeze. They concentrated, as only Rangers could, by holding on to their slender lead with an iron grip.

Celtic, though, were presented with a chance to level. While Tiger was off the field injured from 15 minutes into the second half, Rangers became a little disorganised. Woodburn was just inside the penalty area when he handled a ball that bounced up sharply in front of him. Mallan took the kick and, in keeping with Celtic's efforts at goal throughout, his weak attempt was easily saved by Brown.

Tiger's injury was the result of a tackle with Tommy Docherty. As Jock was being carried off by stretcher it was feared he could have a broken leg, but it was only a cartilage displaced and a quarter of an hour later he was back, full of vim and vigour once more.

For a Rangers-Celtic match it was considered a most uninspiring, thrill-less affair, but this Rangers defence was like a sponge. Celtic didn't punch a dent in it; they just hadn't the ability to find a gap and the Young, Shaw, McColl, Woodburn, Cox set-up was simply watertight. During the second half Torry Gillick received a head-knock and was obviously dazed. Tiger balanced him on his feet facing the touchline, and pointed to the left-wing position. Gillick walked away, and walked right off the field into the arms of a police inspector. The inspector guided Torry to the tunnel entrance and walked him right inside.

On 16 October the final League Cup section game against Celtic at Ibrox attracted a remarkable 105,000 spectators, one of whom was Eamon de Valera who had been deposed as Irish President in February. I think it's safe to assume his choice of scarf would not have been Royal blue. He had been detained at a luncheon engagement rather longer than he had expected, and only arrived at Ibrox just before half-time. His thoughts on seeing Celtic lose 2-1, with goals from Williamson and Waddell, were not recorded. At an Irish Anti-Partition league meeting which he addressed in St Andrews Hall, Charing Cross on the day after the game, a motion was passed thanking Rangers Football Club for the courtesy, hospitality and extremely dignified way in which they had received Mr de Valera at Ibrox the day before. Surely no surprise to all friends of Rangers due to the standards the club set but nonetheless it must have been extremely gratifying for the Rangers directors.

The match itself was noteworthy for one unusual incident; it was reported that this was the first time ever that forward Thornton had charged an opposing goalkeeper while they were in possession of the ball.

So back to league business and Rangers' deep-rooted left-wing problems were continuing and, following the defeat at Ibrox to Hibs on 6 November, they had dropped seven points out of a possible 16, losing two consecutive league games to Hearts and Hibs respectively.

On 13 November St Mirren were beaten 2-0 at Love Street which was the catalyst to an upturn in Rangers' fortunes as they proceeded to win five matches in a row and drew with Falkirk leading up to the New Year clash with Celtic.

One of the games in that sequence was against Clyde at Shawfield on 4 December. One spectacular 15-minute spell 'made' this match. In that time all four goals were scored and there were more goalmouth thrills than are usual in an entire game. Clyde from the outset did not appear to have the guile required to really truly trouble Rangers and after opening the scoring on ten minutes through Thornton's header from a McColl lob into the box, Rangers were in regal mood. Up front Rutherford, Thornton and Paton were sand dancing to their hearts' content, along with Duncanson rampaging along the left wing, and generally firing panic in the Shawfield rearguard. Behind them was a half-back line simply effusing offensive spirit. Cox and Woodburn dominated and McColl, with the hardest job controlling live wire Archie Wright, was equally effective. Sensing the home side's trepidation, Rangers pressed home their superiority. Paton crashed an 18-yarder home from a Duncanson pass, after Rutherford had weaved past several hapless defenders on 19 minutes. Then a minute later Thornton headed number three from a Paton chip. On 25 minutes Wright whacked home Ackerman's pass from the edge of the box but it was merely a consolation even at that early stage. The second half was notable only for what was described as a Gilbertian duel by Jock Shaw and Alf Ackerman, who challenged each other, pace for pace, over half the field, the winner being, of course, our very own Tiger. Overall, a very comfortable afternoon.

As a prelude to the Ne'er Day game Rangers then went to Brockville, which would be a real test of their title credentials as Falkirk were doing well in the league, and would eventually finish fifth, one point ahead of Celtic.

A crowd of 21,000 packed into Brockville in expectant mood on Christmas Day 1948. The conditions were not great underfoot and the icy covering on the pitch made play at times a little farcical but nevertheless it was entertaining fare for the big crowd.

Falkirk opened the scoring on seven minutes, a fierce Anderson drive from an Aikman rebound. The equaliser was as a result of a snappy bit of opportunism by Paton when Findlay mishit a drive. And Rangers' second, on 49 minutes, was a Willie Waddell affair in the very best Waddell tradition of solo endeavour. We then had Aikman, Inglis and Cox all hitting the post as play raged from end to end. The star of the show was to be Falkirk striker Archie Aikman though. By day a schoolmaster but at the weekend a strong, strapping striker who it was reported beat Woodburn more in the air than had ever been see before.

With two minutes to go Alison had clipped a loose ball down the middle, Aikman trapped and swerved in one sweet move to beat both

Woodburn and Young, and then side-footed the ball past Brown for a deserved equaliser.

This was a well-earned point for the Gers, particularly as they lost Willie Findlay, who had been having a fine match, with a knee injury. No doubt a major cause would have been the difficult conditions and Rangers had to play the majority of the second half with ten men. Again, setting the standards was Tiger, who was noted as being sure-footed and inspiring in the tricky conditions.

So it was on to the Celtic match, and in front of 95,000 an early goal from Thornton set the tone and Rangers then went on to completely dominate their opponents with a hat-trick from Jimmy Duncanson which took them back to the summit of the league, a point ahead of closest challengers Dundee.

However, inconsistency crept back in and five dropped points in January saw them slip to third place behind Hibernian and Dundee.

The approach to matches back then was much different to what we see now. Bobby Brown was able to describe the match-day experience. 'On home match days, his [Struth's] routine never varied. If it were a particularly important game or cup tie, we might gather at the stadium where we had to report by 1.30pm for the then normal 3pm kick-off. Punctuality was important to him, and being late was not a good idea. Players would start their warm-up routines, which then were done indoors, in the gym and running area beneath the main stand. Once I had done some running to loosen up, I would go into the gym and practise my handling and do some shot-stopping.

'By just after 2pm, we were all back in the dressing room. At 2.15pm on the dot, Titch [a ground staff member] would carry in Mr Strut's swivel chair and position it in the centre of the room, the signal that he was on his way. Once he came in, always impeccably dressed and carrying his walking stick, the hubbub of noise and chat would die away as the manager would look around the dressing room, eyeing us, taking everything in. He didn't have to say a word for it to go quiet. His presence really was amazing. He would usually say a little about how he wanted us to play that day in general terms and ask the captain, Jock Shaw, to contribute, with others chipping in occasionally. There was no tactics board or any sophisticated briefing such as nowadays. He would speak individually to players, reminding them of their role and encouraging them.

'Your white shorts were always last to be put on before going out on to the pitch to ensure they were spotlessly clean. As with everything, Mr Struth was a stickler for his team turning out immaculately and would check their kit. Finally, just as we were about to leave the dressing room, he would add, "And don't forget you're playing for your ham and eggs." With that he would throw the ball to Jock Shaw and say "Take them out captain."'

The Scottish Cup that season produced more public disagreements between the Scottish Fuel Efficiency Committee (which was campaigning for a ban on midweek sport in the interests of the national economy) and the SFA (which was acting in the interests of its members). The SFA believed there was no substantive evidence that midweek games had much impact on absenteeism in industry, using the English example, where midweek games and horse-racing meets took place.

The SFA subsequently decided that second-round ties played on 5 February would be replayed in midweek in the event of a draw, but to show some level of compromise and to take some of the heat out of the situation, they stipulated that extra time of 30 minutes would be played in the first game of the third-round ties. That there was a danger of absenteeism when midweek games were played was underlined when the Blythswood shipyard at Scotstoun told their men there would be no Sunday overtime for anyone who had been absent from work the previous Wednesday afternoon to watch the League International at Ibrox against the English League. As Sunday work was double rates, any men involved could have lost £3 – a high price to pay for the privilege of watching the English triumph 3-0.

Rangers' next home match at Ibrox on 8 January was of some significance to Jock as it was widely reported that he was the star of this particular show as Rangers won 2-0 with goals by Paton and Thornton. The story in *The Sunday Post* focused on the tale of the wonderful veteran.

John Shaw, already an internationalist, left Airdrie for Ibrox. Since then, he's played over 400 games in light blue. He's been his country's hero. He has taken all the honours there are. He was now unashamedly a veteran but, judged by his latest showing still one of the greatest backs in all Britain. It wasn't that he was asked to do so much. But how superbly he did what little there was. And how strong was the contrast to the performance of the majority in a game packed with big names, but with almost nothing else to recommend it. Jock Shaw always won in the tackle. He always placed the ball to an unmarked mate. He was always in the right spot at the right moment. And all the time he was calling, encouraging, exhorting as a good captain should. The response was poor, but for his peace of mind, it was somewhat better than the best Motherwell could offer.

For me, at least and, I think, for a goodly portion of Ibrox's 50,000 this was the season's biggest disappointment. Because we expected so much and because there was no possible excuse as conditions were perfect. Here were two teams on past performances among the best we have in technique and ball play. And yet in 90 minutes they could scarce raise a thrill among them, scarce produce a solitary sweet move to make the memory brighter. Rangers, for instance, took 44 minutes to get a lead against a side that had pivot Paton missing for 20 minutes. Even then it wasn't convincing, a close-in Paton drive after his namesake had missed a cross soon after returning from the pavilion. The second half was of a different standard, thank goodness. Thornton ducked under a cross, this deceived Paton and Shaw, he then crashed a raging shot past Johnston. The solitary example of what many had paid to see. I remember Aitkenhead and McColl shooting over when reasonably well placed. I can think of no other instances when Motherwell worried Brown. I left with the impression Rangers had played as if they knew they must win, and Motherwell as if they knew they hadn't a chance.

Best ball worker on the field was another Ranger, Rutherford. The casual Eddie is beginning to wear a Wembley look, an opinion I'm sure Kilmarnock will endorse. McColl was the best wing-half in what was the most disappointing department. Aitkenhead was the success of the Motherwell attack, showing surprising ability to take the ball up to and go past a George Young not in his usual form. Johnston made one miracle save, and was blameless for the goals. But the difference was in team work. Rangers, even with their individuals failing, were flawless with defensive covering, instinctively in the open space when moving to attack.

Rangers' clash against Aberdeen at Ibrox had a significant bearing on the relegation battle as the Dons gained a welcome if unexpected point. It was too early yet to say whether it would be the means of saving them from relegation, but the 1-1 draw with Rangers did show that the Dons still had the ability to rise to the big occasion and would certainly do them more harm than good. There was no fluke about the result. Rangers had the bulk of the second-half pressure, but taking the match as a whole it was difficult to believe that there was such a gulf between the teams in the league standing. Aberdeen's forwards faded out once Rangers had equalised, but they played better in the first half than they had done for weeks (Aberdeen raising their game against Rangers, was it always thus?). The difference seemed to be the inside-forwards, being much more positive, were having a shot at goal, and there might have been a different story to tell had Emery not shot too hurriedly after a miskick by Woodburn had left the road to goal wide open. On the other hand, Rangers had so much pressure in the second half that they didn't deserve to lose.

It was during this period that the Dons' defence was up against it, and they responded gallantly. Every man played his part, but keeper Curran deserved a special mention. He had luck on his side at times, but this was offset by a succession of brilliant saves. The goalkeeper inspired confidence with his clean punching when the agile Thornton was on the spot for Waddell's dangerous crosses. Almost equally effective was Roy at centre-half. He could proudly claim to have prevented Scotland's four outstanding headers from scoring, and it was unfortunate that he should mar an otherwise fine display by a slip which gave Rangers their goal.

Both Ancell and McKenna stuck grimly to the task of holding the dangerous wingers, and were on par with Young and Shaw, although Scotland's captain often turned defence into attack with his tremendous array of long-range passing. Aberdeen's defensive set-up was completed by Stenhouse and Waddell, whose destructive qualities almost completely snuffed out Duncanson and Paton. In attack they were not as effective as McColl and Cox, the Rangers' pair, who often started attacks with well-judged passes. Rangers had a definite advantage on the wings, with both Rutherford and Waddell showing willingness to press in the final third with the ball. Winger Pearson was rather easily subdued by Jock, it was reported. On the other flank, though, it was the left-winger who got the Dons' first goal in four matches after 17 minutes. Williams neatly tricked Tiger and smacked the ball against the bar, and it rebounded to Mather, and the Englishman shot hard into the far corner of the net.

A header from Thornton, which hit a post, and Emery's shot on the run were other efforts of note before half-time. In the second half Rangers piled on the pressure and brought the best out of Curran. Then, 17 minutes after the restart came the fatal slip. Roy had plenty of time to get rid of a loose ball. Attempting to pass back to Curran, he only half hit the ball and Duncanson came racing in to shoot past the helpless goalkeeper.

The first major trophy of the season was the League Cup, now in its third season of existence. The competition kicked off on 11 September. A tough section was navigated through, winning 2-1 against Celtic, then losing 3-1, Hibs were defeated 1-0 at Ibrox and the sides shared the spoils at Easter Road 0-0, while Clyde drew 1-1 at Ibrox before being beaten 3-1 at Shawfield.

In the quarter-finals, St Mirren were despatched 1-0 through a Thornton goal before a strong Dundee were defeated 4-1 in a Hampden semi-final. Gers had to wait almost four months for the final at Hampden. This would be against Raith Rovers from the Second Division. Raith were a decent side who would go on to gain promotion as champions, and while they made Rangers fight all the way there was never any real danger of an upset and the light blues lifted the season's first honours with a 2-0 win with goals by Gillick and Paton.

The Scottish Cup was the next trophy up for grabs and Rangers, as holders, were keen to hang on to the trophy won for the second successive year. Elgin City were despatched in the opening round 6-1 at Ibrox. There then followed a trip to Fir Park where Motherwell were convincingly beaten 3-0. In the quarter-final Partick Thistle were soundly thrashed 4-0 at Ibrox.

Next up were East Fife at Hampden in the semi-final before a remarkable crowd of 104,958. Rangers had Willie Waddell in their ranks, newly returned from honeymoon, but it was his team-mate Willie Thornton whose day it was, with an individual performance of skilful play at speed, and flying bullet headers.

Rangers were breathtaking in the opening ten minutes with Thornton three times releasing Duncanson, Waddell and Paton – only for Niven to foil them each time – but the opener came as early as the sixth minute, when Waddell sped away down the right wing, cracking over a fast cross touched on by Duncanson for Thornton to net with a flying header from beyond the far post.

East Fife were all at sea, and after 32 minutes Rangers added a second when a McColl/Waddell/Paton move saw the Ibrox inside-forward whip over a fast cross for Willie Thornton's diving header to find the net. Four minutes later Bobby Brown blocked a vicious David Duncan drive with his knees. It knocked the goalkeeper right over and into the net, but any Fife hopes of a comeback were sunk immediately after the interval when that man Thornton controlled a ball with his right foot, flicked it on to Waddell who hit a first-time cross and Thornton rose with a miraculous spring to head home. East Fife had class but lacked punch, their final high ball being meat and drink to George Young and Willie Woodburn.

Three headers, three goals, Rangers were triumphant, marching on to glory.

Tiger recalled that semi-final in particular. 'There was a special feeling for that match as East Fife were, of course, managed by Scot Symon and he and old Struth had been very close when Scot played at Ibrox, or at least as close as any player got to the old man. But we were good that day and Willie Thornton got a hat-trick and we won 3-0.'

So to the cup final and Bill Struth was only too acutely aware of the significance of the occasion as Jock describes: 'During that spell we had been dominating and we had so many really great players in the team that it was natural for us to think that we could go and win everything going. But it was only in the week before the Scottish Cup Final that we realised we could now do something which had never been done before. Struth made it clear to us a few days before the game at Hampden when he spoke about the opportunity we had to make history and we had all seen stuff in the newspapers going on about the triple crown.'

The cup at this stage would only form the second part of that triple crown. Unlike today, the cup final was played before the league season had been completed.

By this time Bill Struth was 73 years old, and in 1949 this would not just have been considered old, but very old, based on the fact that life expectancy at that time for a male was around 66 years of age. So, the fact he was still actively involved in football was quite remarkable. Like most males of his generation, he kept his thoughts very much to himself, but he must have thought his career was coming to an end and, in turn, his opportunities to become the first manager to make a clean sweep of all the national trophies. Tiger had his own views on his longevity: 'To us the old man was indestructible, and would go on for ever.'

The final was to be against Clyde (a club with a special place in Struth's affections) who had struggled in the league, sitting third bottom on 23 April, and in real peril of dropping out of the division. It was rather ironic that Clyde had finished their league fixtures and their top-flight status depended on Rangers. If Rangers defeated Morton in their penultimate league fixture Clyde would be safe. If Morton won, then Clyde would be consigned to the drop along with Albion Rovers.

Despite their lowly league status Bully Wee put up a stern fight in front of 120,162 inside Hampden. Clyde obviously realised they had nothing to lose and it was the Rangers defence which was busiest in the early stages. Centre-forward Alec Linwood was the man giving the Iron Curtain most problems but the defence stood strong.

Five minutes from half-time came the turning point when Rangers were awarded a penalty after Billy Williamson was brought down by a despairing and poorly timed tackle from behind by Milligan. Clyde keeper Gullan hardly had time to move as George Young's spot kick sped past him into the corner of the net.

Clyde were clearly stunned after so much early pressure and Rangers rubbed salt in the wound when they made it 2-0 only three minutes later. Billy Williamson had become a hero the season before when he scored the only goal in the replay to lift the cup. This final was again to be the only match he had played in the Scottish Cup all season but he was playing a pivotal role and he netted again. This time Willie Waddell made the byeline on the left wing with a mazy run and his first-time cross was met by the head of Williamson flying through the air – again giving keeper Gullan not a chance.

Rangers started the second half seemingly in complete control but Clyde were not for throwing in the towel and three minutes into the second half they pulled a goal back. A Campbell free kick from around 30 yards out eluded the Rangers defence and Galletly squeezed his way through the 'curtain' to shoot past Bobby Brown.

The goal rejuvenated Clyde and a couple of minutes later they were almost level as a shot from Galletly hit the post with Brown well beaten.

The resurgence was not to last as on 54 minutes Rangers re-asserted their authority.

Ian McColl flighted a free kick into the Clyde goalmouth and Willie Thornton rose to meet it. He was set to pounce when Milligan pushed him in the back for another stone-wall penalty. Young once again stepped up, placed the ball calmly on the spot, then with the minimum of fuss despatched the ball into the net.

The destination of the cup was no longer in any doubt and there seemed to be an air of resignation and defeat about Clyde for the rest of the match. Six minutes from time the light blues scored again through Jimmy Duncanson to give a slightly flattering look to the scoreline, which did not fully reflect Clyde's efforts.

Clyde had fought gallantly, without much luck, including being denied a potential penalty and giving two away themselves. The general consensus at Hampden, though, was that man of the match was Jock, which reflected very well how tough a battle this had been for the Gers.

Tiger later said, 'The final was against a Clyde side which had struggled near the bottom of the table and which just managed to avoid relegation, but they raised their game against us and we had one of those days when everything we did was just a wee bit off.' This was the final which spawned one of the iconic Rangers pictures where Tiger is hoisted atop the shoulder of his team-mates clutching the trophy. It may be an iconic image but Meg hated the photo as Tiger did not have his teeth in and had rather a gumsy smile.

There was at least some good news for Clyde as Rangers defeated Morton 1-0 to send them down to Division Two and save Clyde.

So fast forward to 30 April. It's not often the destination of the league title is decided on the final day of the season but that was the tense and exciting scenario which had unfolded for the concluding day of the 1948/49 season.

To win the league Rangers had to beat Albion Rovers at Cliftonhill, but if Dundee beat Falkirk the title was theirs. The odds were against Rangers pulling it off for it is never an ideal situation having to rely on another's misfortune. In addition, Dundee were a point ahead, and had lost only one of their last eight games while Falkirk had lost their last four matches. The one hope down Ibrox way was based on that Christmas Day battle they had had at Brockville: if only the Bairns could raise their game one last time.

On the day, the stars would align for the light blues as Falkirk somehow beat Dundee while Rangers triumphed easily against the Wee Rovers by 4-1, which included a Willie Thornton hat-trick, lifted the title and in turn completed a glorious first-ever treble.

It was ironic that after the final whistle the light blues had trudged from the field fully expecting to be told Dundee had won. However, a quick phone call to Falkirk and the joyous news was relayed – Falkirk 4-1 Dundee.

In the dressing room the players hugged each other with delight and there was a triumphant air until the players' gaze was drawn to one man, manager Bill Struth. Struth, who had guided the club to a multitude of honours over his 30-year tenure, was sitting on a bench with tears of joy streaming down his cheeks. It was only then that the players truly appreciated the magnitude of what they had achieved.

Jock played in 27 of the 30 league matches, and Celtic finished a dismal sixth.

During June, Jock attended the annual end-of-season dance and presentation of prizes of the Coatbridge and District Amateur Football League held in the Good Templars' Hall, Coatdyke.

While he presented the trophies and prizes won in the Senior Section competitions, Jimmy Mitchell handed over the awards to the Junior Section leaders and the runners-up. Gartsherrie United, it was, who carried all before them. For the time, they went down in local amateur football history as the side that just couldn't be beaten, winning the league championship and also carrying off all the competitive trophies: a feat hitherto unachieved by any team. As secretary William McWhinnie proudly said, this had been a great achievement, and one of which Gartsherrie could feel proud.

This view was supported by Jock, who echoed Mr McWhinnie's feeling of pride. Jock also voiced his suspicion that United's players had been in at Broomfield getting a few tips. He had to compliment the team on their achievements, and it was further to their credit that all through the league and other competitions they had played the game, and not one player had been reported or sent off the field. Commenting on his own role that night, in presenting the cups and other prizes, Jock pointed out it was an unusual position for him, as he 'was usually at the receiving end at functions', the senior season just ended with the treble being a prime example. Jock also had some advice for the fledgling stars of Gartsherrie United. 'Watch what you are doing,' he counselled. 'This is my 19th season in football and I know. Think what you are doing when you sign a professional form.'

The End Is Nigh

THE SANDS of time were marching on, and this season would be the last one when Jock could be considered a Rangers first-team regular.

There was no time for rest and it was recognised that the captain's job is not an easy one to every player. There are many who go off their game because they feel the responsibility too heavily. Others seem born for the job; a shining example of the latter type was Scotland's captain, George Young, the big Ranger, in good times and bad, being an inspiration to his team-mates. He was quick to integrate newcomers to the international fold, and encourage them on the field.

Rangers were in a unique position as they had two captains on the field – not only the international team's captain but their own club captain, Tiger. Teams were out to beat Rangers, making most games into 'cup ties', and Tiger got plenty of opportunities to make his presence felt. He was always quick to rally his mates when things were going against his team, and to these inspirational powers must go a lot of the credit for many a Rangers' fightback.

The summer break also saw the recruitment of the eventual solution to the Rangers left-wing conundrum in the shape of Johnny Hubbard, though it would take him three seasons to fully establish himself in the first team.

This was to prove another memorable season for Rangers as they lifted their 27th league title and completed a hat-trick of Scottish Cup successes, and also annexed the Glasgow Cup.

The race for the First Division title was once again a tight affair between the light blues and Hibernian.

Rangers got the season off to a flying start in the league, winning their first five league games, which included an encounter with Celtic on 24 September. To the Rangers support this counted as a couple of valuable points, and it was smashing to win the match, but it was expected.

To onlookers there appeared something phoney about this whole show. Temporarily, the atmosphere which supplied the edge in this game had been removed, leaving the occasion as something which only bore a passing resemblance to past encounters. Firstly, there was the Celtic supporters' boycott of Ibrox, which most reasonable-minded commentators viewed as being carried too far. (And, in a show of solidarity, the Celtic forwards decided to stay away from Bobby Brown.) The boycott meant the loss of £2,400 in gate drawings. Instead of 95,000 people, there were only 60,000 present. And, with the banners and the bottles removed, the players accepting the referee's decisions and everyone concerned generally wary, there was an unreal atmosphere about the whole business. Then, when Celtic took the field without Tully, Weir and Macaulay, the result was a foregone conclusion.

Maybe the introduction of so many youngsters had something to do with it, but rarely has such hapless finishing crowned so much promising lead-up play. The finishing was just unreal and reflected the general atmosphere. 'Twas a strange spectacle indeed. The terracing behind the east goal was packed in all its glory with a happy, seething mass of Rangers supporters. What a contrast to the Celtic end, where occasional thin green lines were strewn along the crush barriers. It must have been a weird experience for the players. A goal or a good bit of work by a Ranger was the signal for all sorts of outbursts of cheering from the Rangers support, but there was barely a Celt who got any acknowledgement for any promising play – and then it was akin to something from the Whispering Gallery. So, if encouragement goes for anything, Rangers had this game in their pocket from the moment the first turnstile started to click. The 4-0 score was a little flattering to the Ibrox men, with goals coming from Rutherford (six minutes), Finlay (42 minutes), Waddell (penalty 86 minutes) and Williamson (88 minutes).

With the score 2-0 up till four minutes to go, there was a feeling that, if Celtic did get a goal, then anything might have happened. What was it then that Rangers had which Celtic hadn't? Firstly, they had Woodburn and an overall defensive set-up in which, when one player made a mistake, there was always another ready to cover up. Despite quite a few mistakes, too, they still looked a solid bunch. Up front Rangers had Waddell. When it came to bursting open defences, you felt one Waddell was equal to five Celtic forwards. With more experience under their belts, Collins, Taylor, Haughney and young Rennet might have tried various subtle moves in the defence-opening business. But here the master man was Waddell.

With two goals tucked away by the interval, Rangers pulled their inside-forwards back and concentrated on defence. That more or less finished the game as a spectacle. So much so that, during the turgid second half, it could be argued that those who boycotted were also psychic.

Rutherford's opening goal on six minutes was a masterpiece of anticipation. Even before Finlay had played a long, angular ball goalwards, Rutherford was off his mark like a rocket. He arrived at the far-away post in time to smash the ball into the net. Number two was a perfect shot from a peach of a pass from Waddell. The third was a penalty. McGuire charged Jock Shaw, who was hobbling at outside-left, having returned to the field following an injury, and Mr Mann had no hesitation in giving a penalty. How odd it was to see a penalty kick being awarded for a foul on a left-back. Waddell had no hesitation in slotting the ball home. A beautiful Waddell cross saw Williamson head home after a text-book counter in the closing minutes.

Mr Mann was a most efficient referee, although the players certainly did their bit to make it easy for him, therein perhaps lies the reason why his games were so tame, and one-sided.

Raith Rovers proved thrawn opponents over the course of the season and the match on 19 November at Stark's Park was no exception.

If ever a goal took a team out of a tight corner, restored lost confidence and put them back on the rails, it was Billy Williamson's first counter. For a solid 40 minutes Rangers' defence had taken a terrible pummelling. Pressure was eased momentarily, and Johnston slipped through a pass which found the burly centre 25 yards out. Williamson carefully took aim and smashed a glorious right-footer past the bewildered McGregor.

Just prior to this there had been some controversy around the Rangers' goal. A confident and loud Raith appeal came when Joyner's shot got stuck in the mud with Brown beaten, and they claimed it was over the line. A mis-header flew past the post, and then came an appeal for a penalty, with some justification, it appeared, for handball. Then a Colville 20-yarder shook the rigging with Brown looking on helplessly but the referee had blown for an infringement a split second previously. The light blues' contribution during this spell was exactly two shots and one goal, thank you very much.

Into the second half and a last-ditch Young clearance with Brown out of position meant Rangers were still riding a storm. Yet, for all the chances, Rovers had nothing to show and still trailed, but the fact the chances were squandered was not Rangers' fault. Again, Rangers' heroes were at the back: Bobby Brown was faultless while Tiger Shaw stopped many of the first-half defensive leaks in particular. Thornton with his intricate footwork and Williamson for his enthusiasm and endeavour were the Rangers forwards who mattered most.

Williamson claimed Rangers' third goal when he rose to meet a Rutherford cross and headed accurately into the net. Thornton sandwiched one in between when he wound his way through Raith's defence and scored from close in. Maule helped himself to a well-placed shot and netted Raith's one crumb of comfort in front of a frenzied crowd of 25,000.

December produced one of the matches of the season in the shape of a clash with Clyde, perhaps unlikely protagonists. On 3 December Clyde came to Ibrox without a league victory there for 35 years, and Rangers had only conceded four goals in their preceding nine games that season. So, the visitors were reckoned to have a less than slim chance of getting a result that day.

The Bully Wee, however, soon made their presence felt.

Their right-winger Ackerman raced down the flank and sent over a dangerous cross which keeper Bobby Brown couldn't hold and striker Linwood followed up to put the visitors ahead with only eight minutes on the clock.

Two minutes later Rangers got the equaliser when Joe Johnson cracked home a great shot after good lead-up work from Eddie Rutherford, and now the fans sat back in anticipation of a light blues' goal rush, but Clyde refused to be overawed and came back to give the light blues another shock. In the 21st minute, inside-forward Dealing picked up the ball 25 yards from goal and let fly with a great left-foot shot which beat Brown all ends up.

If Rangers doubted they had a fight on their hands, Deakin's goal confirmed that point and the light blues hit Clyde with everything.

A great run by winger Willie McCulloch left the Clyde defence trailing and he drew Hawkins from his line before cheekily slipping the ball through the keeper's legs, but Willie's joy was short-lived as the ball rebounded from the post and was scrambled clear.

Justice was done in the 34th minute, however. McCulloch sent a great cross into the goal area where Willie Thornton met the ball with his ever-so reliable head to tie the scores at two goals each.

Would this destroy the heart of the visitors? Don't you believe it.

Three minutes after Willie's equaliser, Clyde winger Barclay ran down the left and his neat cross was headed into the net by

Linwood, and that's how the first half ended, and Rangers left the field somewhat bewildered at the thought of having conceded three goals in the course of the first 45 minutes.

The Ibrox men set about retrieving the situation immediately after the restart and, following some near things in the Clyde goalmouth, Thornton equalised from an acute angle.

Once more, incredibly, Clyde hit back. Only six minutes later Barclay made great progress on the wing and his inch-perfect cross was nodded home by Deakin, the inside-left heading over Brown as the keeper raced from his line to cut out the cross.

At this point Rangers must have felt jinxed. On each occasion they'd come back from being a goal behind, Clyde simply went up the park to restore their lead, and if the Shawfield side had been playing a lesser team than the light blues they would undoubtedly have come out victorious. This is where the great Ibrox spirit paid dividends and it was the almost unheard-of goalscoring skills of Sammy Cox which were to save Rangers.

Sammy's blistering left-foot drive from 25 yards out made it 4-4 in the 75th minute and one could have been forgiven for expecting Clyde to hit back with a fifth goal immediately. However, before the visitors could contemplate mounting another attack, Rangers struck once more through Cox.

He met a loose ball some 20 yards out and unleashed a first-time rocket which almost uprooted the net and that proved to be the decisive goal, the Ibrox team playing out the remaining ten minutes to emerge 5-4 winners.

Post-match the press enthused about the quality of play from both teams in what were far from ideal conditions and the great tragedy of it all was that only 25,000 saw the match. The Rangers defence of that era was usually watertight and few teams could score one goal against the light blues, never mind four.

Holding a 4-3 lead with 15 minutes to go, Clyde had looked a good bet for a win, but unsurprisingly did not legislate for Cox.

Sammy's late double shattered the visitors and it would be fair to say surprised a few Rangers fans, expecting him to stick to his usual rearguard role. No one complained about his ventures up field in this epic match.

At Bayview on 7 January there were eight internationalists in the two teams but the football was never of a high standard. Too often the long punt upfield was used. Two young Rangers forwards had been hitting the headlines in recent weeks, outside-right McCulloch and inside-left Johnson, but only McCulloch lived up to his reputation. He gave Sammy Stewart an uncomfortable time and came out on top at the end of the 90 minutes, which not many wingers were able to do. Johnson was overshadowed by Alan Brown, his opposite number in the East Fife team.

In the first half Brown kept the home attack going and gave McColl a roasting. Just before the interval, when Willie Laird was injured, Brown went to right-half and played out the second half in this position, where he completely subdued Johnson. He finished up by being the best inside-forward in the first half and the best half-back in the second. As long as Brown was in the attack, East Fife were dangerous. With the forward line rearranged they never looked like overcoming Rangers' defence. Rangers, on the other hand, could always produce something 'out of the bag'. Their opening goal was typical. A free kick was taken by McColl from the right. And as soon as the ball was kicked, Williamson was rushing into the goalmouth to meet it with his head. Until the ball was in the back of the net the entire home defence seemed mesmerised. That was the only time Williamson got out of Finlay's grip. The centre-half was on a par with Scotland's Woodburn. Philip defended stoutly when he moved back to take Laird's place and Jock was noted as being deserving of a pat on the back for the canny way he dealt with the tricky Laird. The points were clinched with a second goal from Rutherford.

To the return league encounter with Raith Rovers on 25 February. Willie McNaught and Tiger were the respective left-backs on show.

The former was a relative newcomer to big-time football, in comparison to Tiger, but one thing they did have in common was football skill and cunning. A total of 35,000 light blue fans came along to see the one and only Willie Waddell play his first home game for 13 weeks. They expected to see something out of the ordinary. They got it, but hardly in the way they imagined. Apart from a few dangerous crosses, Waddell was never in the game; his long lay-off clearly had had an impact. However, McNaught also played a part and every time Waddell got the ball, the Raith stalwart played a waiting game, choosing the right moment to pounce. So effective were these interventions, Waddell seemed to realise he'd met his master for the day and started to roam the field in search of more scope for his talents. As luck would have it, McNaught was to blame when Rangers scored their second goal, and it was Waddell who took full advantage. It was here Tiger entered the picture. He collected a ball midway inside his own half, survived tackles by three Raith players before sending a ball away into the Raith goalmouth, right at McNaught's feet; however, McNaught failed to control the cross, the ball broke loose, and quick as a flash Waddell was on it and had it buried behind Johnstone in jig time. As well as making this goal, Shaw was the man who, time and again, thwarted Raith's attack – he simply wouldn't budge.

After Williamson had opened Rangers' account with a rather soft goal, Raith went all out to draw level. When they found Penman, he was more or less subdued by Young, so they concentrated then on the right wing. Here again, they had to bow the knee, thanks to Tiger; even after Rangers had increased their lead Raith still kept hammering away but still Jock wouldn't budge. He even found time to clear a Collins shot off the line, which all goes to show that, on the whole, the apprentice (McNaught) was very much in the shadow of the master (Tiger).

Rangers went through their fixtures suffering only two defeats: a narrow 1-0 loss to Hibs, plus a shock 4-0 defeat at Fir Park against Motherwell.

Hibs visited Ibrox for their last fixture of the season on 29 April with only three defeats behind them. Rangers were level on points with the Edinburgh side but had another match against Third Lanark at Cathkin to play the following midweek. Hibs had to win at Ibrox, therefore, to take the title as their goal average was vastly superior to Rangers'.

A crowd of 101,000 turned up at Ibrox for what proved to be a tension-riddled affair. The atmosphere was electric as the teams took to the field and the players were well aware this was to all intents and purposes a title decider.

The tension was obvious in the play straight from the kick-off as the ball was heaved around the pitch with little creativity. Hibs centre-half Johnny Paterson (father of future Hibs and Rangers centre-back Craig) quickly stamped his authority on the game with some elegant play to control the Rangers attacks. He was ably assisted by Cairns who was giving Rangers right-winger Rutherford a rough time. This was proving frustrating to Ian McColl who sent the winger through several passes with slide-rule precision which could not be capitalised on.

At the other end the Famous Five were continually frustrated by the resolute Ibrox defence. Hibs' Gordon Smith was known for his forays on the right wing but Jock tracked him really well and left Smith in no doubt where he got his Tiger nickname from.

Lawrie Reilly and Willie Ormond rarely got involved in the play and equally Willie Thornton got next to no service. The best chance of the match fell to Ormond in the second half with a snap shot from six yards that slipped narrowly past the post. Although there were few chances in the match it was nonetheless a nail-biting afternoon as the dour midfield battle unfolded, and essentially both sides were cancelling each other out.

While Hibs knew victory would secure the title, they also knew that any other result would leave matters out of their hands. George Young and Willie Woodburn and Jock stood firm as the seconds ticked away. When the referee blew the final whistle with no score, the Edinburgh side knew deep down their chance had gone, while Rangers knew a draw in midweek at Cathkin would retain the title.

Thirds had been battling relegation but were now safe, so either the edge would be taken out of their play or they would be relaxed and play with no pressure, potentially making them more dangerous. Interestingly the Thirds' keeper on the day was Andy Goram's father Louis, of course, an ex-Hibee.

There was a massive crowd present of 32,800 and additional police were on duty to try and control it as Cathkin Park was bursting at the seams.

This match was of such importance to the Ibrox men that Ian McColl, who was due to be married that day, postponed his wedding.

Rangers started at lightning speed and were soon two ahead through Williamson and Paton. Thirds hit back, though, to recover the deficit and equalise and then missed a penalty which could have turned the whole season on its head. The tension was palpable; nails were being bitten to the quick.

As the end neared, Bobby Brown asked photographers behind his goal how long there was to go, to be told 15 minutes. At the end he said those 15 minutes felt like 15 hours, but in the final analysis Rangers were champions yet again and it was an 11th title success for Tiger.

On 6 May 1950 Rangers were at Hampden to take on Celtic in the Charity Cup Final.

Pre-match there was a bit of razzmatazz with the appearance of a very special guest in actor Danny Kaye. A massive Hampden roar (of laughter) greeted him when he pranced on to the field. He clapped his hands to his ears in mock alarm. Then he swooped on the ball. No footwork for Danny. He clutched it tight, and sped towards the goal with referee Davidson on his heel, and boy could he move. He arrived alone before the empty goal, and smacked the ball with great force, high, wide and handsome. This delighted the crowd, and they yelled for more. It duly came when Danny was presented to the players. He chose that moment to show Tiger a few tricks in ball control that even trained seals wouldn't know. Then Danny's eye alighted on the Glasgow Police Pipe Band. One moment Pipe Major Kaye was strutting along with a busby crammed on his head, then it disappeared. The band spluttered rather than played 'Hielan' Laddie'.

In the midst of the pandemonium referee Davidson blew his whistle and Thornton kicked off for Rangers and the crowd, in a rare good mood, turned their attention to the business. Sadly, there was no happy ending on this occasion as Celtic got a consolation prize for an awful season, winning 3-2.

The Scottish Cup this season proved to be a bit of a marathon as it took eight games, plus a bye in the third round, before the light blues finally secured the trophy. On their road to the final, Rangers disposed of Motherwell, Cowdenbeath, Raith Rovers (after three games) and Queen of the South, after a semi-final replay.

Victory over East Fife in the final made it three cup triumphs in a row. This resulted in Rangers arranging to strike a memento to mark the occasion for each player, in the shape of a special medal, known as the three-in-one medal.

The first round was a tricky start away to Motherwell at Fir Park. There was increased significance around this match as in December the Well had thrashed the light blues 4-0 at the same venue. Normal service was resumed, though, as Rangers came out winners by 4-2.

For Cowdenbeath's visit to Ibrox they were cheered on by two special trainloads of fans and by champagne at the interval. Rangers, though, were without Tiger who suffered an injury to his back in his paper shop in the week leading up to the game. His place was taken by Lindsay at left-back, a more than useful player and Rangers' defence was not significantly impacted, and the champagne bubbles would have helped dull the pain of the 8-0 defeat for the travelling away support.

After a 1-1 draw with Raith Rovers at Ibrox, Rangers headed to Stark's Park for the replay, where a new ground-record crowd of 26,000 people packed the stadium on a Wednesday afternoon, and those who thought Raith had much of a chance must have been few and far between.

This replay was the cup tie that had everything: thrilling goals, neck or nothing clearances, flashes of brilliance, tackling which made you close your eyes as the opponents clashed together, plus the treat of an additional 30 minutes' extra time. All in all, it was a terrific battle between the accepted giants and the acknowledged underdogs.

Raith had the better of the play and many more chances but when you make the chances then refuse to take them it's not bad luck, and you certainly can't place any blame on the other team. The only time Raith looked unlucky was in the 70th minute when they were already a goal down. A ball from the right beat Brown at the far post and Urquhart collected and his shot looked destined for the net when it caught George Young's wrist and squirmed round the post for a corner. It certainly looked a very definite penalty but referee Mowat didn't give it and admitted at the finish he just didn't see the incident.

The real highlights of the game were, of course, the goals. Rangers scored the perfect machine-like goal, while Raith's was a classic individual effort.

The Ibrox side dominated during the first 20 minutes without creating too many clear-cut chances. Then in a flash Rangers pulled a decisive concerted move, the finest of the whole game, right out of the bag.

Tiger scrambled a ball clear, and Cox picked it up; driving upfield he passed on to Thornton. In a twinkling, Thornton transferred to Duncanson, who slickly pushed the ball back into the middle, and there was Williamson, all on his lonesome, who smacked a first-class first-timer past Johnstone. This was Rangers at their best, but it was a lead they held only briefly. The Raith front line was mostly a struggling set of individuals, players of high reputation who could make no headway against a resolute, quick-tackling set of defenders.

The second half was well on its way, and it looked as if Raith had carved a name for themselves as the season's gallant losers. Then came an equaliser which will go down in history as one of Stark's Park's greatest goals ever. Joe McLaughlin, standing around the centre circle, collected a clearance from one of his full-backs. McLaughlin noticed that, for once, Rangers' defence was spread pretty wide open. He powered forward, driving deep into the Rangers half like lightning, with the ball completely under control. About 18 yards from goal the whole Rangers' defence seemed to be about to converge on him, and with perfect timing he shot and the ball sped into the net. The noise which greeted this stunning strike split the evening sky.

The extra time was played at a much slower pace; many hard knocks had been freely given and taken. Quite a number of players were on their last legs as the final whistle sounded. It was just that sort of a cup tie.

At the end the Raith team were all heroes; over the course of the match they thoroughly deserved their draw, and, in fact, it was Raith who looked more like a real footballing team than at any other time. Once again Rangers had to thank their defence, with Tiger simply immense, giving his usual sterling, inspirational performance, which was described in *The Sunday Post* as, 'Jock Shaw playing a real skipper's part putting the hems on Black.'

Alongside him Bobby Brown was brilliant in the goal and Young's powerful clearances made sure there was no such thing as any continuous pressure. McColl and Cox were also good defenders, and were kept so busy in this department that they were allowed no time to show their attacking prowess to any great extent as they were constantly being harassed into make some misplaced passes while in possession. Williamson, in addition to his smartly taken goal, was the most dangerous player. Woodburn had a better game against

Penman than in the first match on the Saturday, but, even then, was still troubled.

Arrangements were made for the second replay when the directors of Raith Rovers and Rangers met in the Station Hotel after the match. On the toss of a coin Rangers called correctly and it was on to Ibrox for the third attempt, which Rangers won.

Following the defeat of Raith, Rangers then cleared a path to the final by defeating Queen of the South 3-0 in a Hampden replay, following a 1-1 draw.

So, the scene was set for a final against East Fife who had knocked the light blues out of the League Cup earlier in the season 2-1 in the semi-final.

As Rangers went into the final on 22 April, they were level with arch rivals Hibernian at the top of the league with a match in hand and looking to retain their title. However, the main aim was to beat East Fife to win the cup for the 13th time along with lifting the trophy for a third year in a row, the second time they would have achieved that feat.

Another bumper crowd of 120,015 turned up at Hampden and, although Rangers were favourites, a close tie was expected as the Fifers had gone on to lift the League Cup and were sitting fourth in the league (where they would eventually finish two points ahead of fifth-placed Celtic) for the second year in a row. One dominating figure not present, however, was Rangers manager Bill Struth, due to ill health. His best wishes' telegram to captain Tiger was pinned up and displayed in the Rangers dressing room.

The gentlemen of the press were denied their customary facilities for this final, the press box having recently been burnt out, although whether this was in response to a journalist's words of wisdom is unclear.

On the day, though, the Methil men were no match for Rangers, who produced probably their best display of the season. East Fife's early attacks were constantly stifled by the Iron Curtain and they were never truly able to recover from Rangers' opening goal by Willie Findlay after only 30 seconds.

From kick-off the ball was passed to Eddie Rutherford on the right wing, who beat East Fife full-back Sammy Stewart and cut the ball low across the face of the penalty area. As everyone else hesitated, Findlay propelled himself through the air no more than three feet above the turf to send a diving header past bewildered keeper Easson, whose first touch of the ball was picking it out of the net.

It was the perfect start for Rangers, and a real sickener for East Fife. However, it was the Bayview men who enjoyed the lion's share of possession for the remainder of the half without truly threatening to equalise. They fought back with all the heart they had but here was more guts than guile. Always there was that fatal hesitancy to have a go on sight. How the fans sighed for Fleming and Brown in their real sharp-shooting form.

For ten minutes in the first half, they pinned Rangers back. Duncan cut the ball back to Brown, Fleming or Morris to deliver a scoring shot but Woodburn, Young and Tiger were impregnable and repeatedly got in the way of the delayed attempts to score. Fife's nearest came from a Morris header towards goal which Alan Brown followed up. Bobby Brown caught the ball but dropped it when charged by the Fifer. Brown recovered and smothered the ball on the ground.

They did look to have a good penalty claim turned down a few minutes from the interval when Willie Woodburn clashed with centre-forward Morris inside the box. Referee Mowat, though, waved play-on and Rangers reached the interval one goal to the good.

The second half was a different story and totally belonged to Rangers. George Young was quite majestic and he was well supported by Tiger, Willie Thornton, Sammy Cox and Willie Findlay.

The Ibrox men put themselves two ahead in 63 minutes with a goal to savour.

Ian McColl played the ball forward from defence to Eddie Rutherford, who once again skinned Stewart on the right wing.

This time the cross was a high one to the near post and it was made in majestic style by Thornton whose header blazed past Easson.

Only two minutes later and it was three. Rutherford played the ball forward to Willie Findlay on the byeline. The striker was met by a diving challenge by Easson but he managed to flick the ball over the East Fife keeper's head into the middle and there Thornton was again, in the right place to rise and nod the ball home.

With Rangers in complete control, they saw the game out as comfortable winners. Rangers' forward play was a revelation to some English football people who spoke to ex-Rangers striker Andy Cunningham and told him they had expected to see the best defence in Scotland and the worst forward line but, as he said in his speech at the celebration dinner afterwards, the Rangers forwards gave an exhibition such as he had not seen since before the war.

Straight after the match, chairman John Wilson called Bill Struth to let him know the cup had been secured. Mr Struth was delighted to have the news confirming his belief that Rangers would win. Post-match, a jubilant Jock commented, 'We went out there to win the cup and give the boss a tonic. We have done that in fine style.'

The cup was presented on the field to Tiger by Lord McGowan, after which the players of both sides were presented to the ICI chief.

As a postscript, Willie Thornton's disallowed goal denied him the record of being the first and, at the time, only Ranger to achieve a hat-trick in a Scottish Cup Final. Gordon Durie, of course, achieved that feat in 1996 against Hearts in the Laudrup Final.

Outside of football, Food Minister Maurice Webb announced changes in points rationing. All canned meats, canned milk, canned beans and shredded suet came off the scheme, which was some relief to the struggling households of post-war Britain.

Planning for the future

IT WAS becoming clear to Jock that he was nearer the end of his playing career than the beginning, and he started to think about the future. To that end he rented a small newspaper shop in nearby Glenboig and after many happy years in Coatbridge moved to Glenboig in 1950. The shop was an annexe to a small cottage in the village, and Tiger arranged a complete refurbishment of it. In later years, after the business closed, the site of the shop was converted into an additional bedroom. Tiger also bought another premises, a confectioner's in the centre of the village at the Oval. A chemist's now sits on the site of that shop.

Glenboig was only two miles from Annathill so Tiger was a little closer to home, and it was, at that time, a thriving village much like Annathill. In the late 1800s it had become the leading manufacturer of firebricks in the world. These bricks were used to build the furnaces that fuelled the industrial revolution. By 1876 there were four different works – Garnqueen, Old Works, Gartsherrie Fireclay and Star Works. The village grew in population from 261 in 1861 to over 3,000 by the beginning of the 20th century.

Glenboig bricks were exported all over the world to countries such as France, Holland, Russia, India and the United States. Even now it's interesting to see social media posts from far-flung corners of the globe where a Glenboig brick has been spotted.

The Glenboig Old Works ceased production in 1958, and by 1976 production had ceased at the Star Works; it was the end of an era, but Glenboig remains proud of its reputation as the home to the largest and best brickworks in the world.

The closure of these factories along with Bedlay Pit and nearby Gartcosh and Ravenscraig Steelworks had a devastating impact on the community, along with the closure of the train station.

The community has rallied though, and started to rebuild. Almost £2m was raised to redevelop the Community Centre with a large new hall, post office, shop, training kitchen, café and gym. Building is underway to construct 750 new houses, and the Glenboig Neighbourhood House, which is at the forefront of this regeneration, now employs over 20 people.

The renowned football commentator Archie MacPherson hailed from nearby Coatbridge and started his working life as a school teacher in Glenboig. In his excellent autobiography, *A Game of Two Halves*, he describes the experience.

They were still mining in the clay pits when I arrived in the small community of Glenboig in August 1957, in my first official teaching post. With post-war estates on the fringes, it was too sprawling to be called a village although at the heart of it was the main street, the centre of the old village before the expansion of housing. About a couple of miles away to the east was Annathill, the coal-mining village for the Bedlay coal pit. Very famously, one terraced row in that village produced the core of the defence for Scotland in their triumph over England at Hampden in the Victory International in 1946. Jock Shaw and his brother David, and the big man who eventually became a folk hero in Newcastle, Frank Brennan. Even from a rival area the folk in Glenboig spoke with pride of Annathill's favourite sons, and indeed one of them, Jock, the captain of Rangers in the days of the Iron Curtain defence in the forties, had established a shop in Glenboig main street. He was a popular man in a community where Protestants and Catholics still live amicably side by side but in distinct awareness of each other's tribal associations.

There were no outrageous, massive displays of bigotry. It was a commendable area of honest working-class people, most of whom in sociological jargon would have been considered upwardly mobile, and indeed some of my pupils, who came from homes where they had to scrape together to make ends meet to ensure their offspring got the best out of life, ended up achieving very successful professional lives.

There were three focal points – two schools and a pub. It would be difficult to assess which of the three made the greatest impact on the generations of Glenboig folk, for the social affirmations of the pub and the mulling over of values at a bar can never be overestimated. But the schools and the pub had something inflexibly in common. They both practised separatism. In the pub there were two entrances. Protestants used one, Catholics used the other. Not just sometimes but always. Regulars simply did not breach that code. As Tevye sang in *Fiddler on the Roof* to justify the intransigence of particular ways of life, 'Tradition, tradition!' It was nothing of the kind. It was just a reflection of the way two strands wished to co-exist; peacefully, but steadfastly refusing to merge identity. If there was such a thing as benign tolerance, then it was practised here. And they were proud of it. They boasted about it. They were never slow to tell you about the separate doors. To a civilised outsider this seemed absurd. But equally it was prudent to hold your tongue on the issue and certainly not mock it.

But they didn't mock the even more preposterous situation of this small area having separate schools. The white-painted public primary school stood prominently on a hill to the south and nearer the centre of the village was the Catholic school. This was the norm. The ethos was simply Shettleston all over again, but with fewer people. I despised the religious indoctrination, of course, if it had to be at school at all, and should not be actively promoted as the only system of belief. There is now more discussion on segregated schools than there has ever been before, but in the sixties if you dared bring the matter up professionally, amongst teachers of the different faith, you were summarily dismissed as something of a bigot.

So here, in a village that more accurately could have been Ballyglenboig, was a reflection of many of the divisions across the Irish Sea. Depending on which door you went through at the pub, or which playground you frequented, you could have a Protestant lager or a Catholic long-division sum. I was learning in this superficially harmonious community that people go to great lengths to make life more complex than it really ought to be. Which door of the pub did I go in? I didn't. I drank elsewhere. As the local teacher I had summed up the perils of association-by-door fairly quickly so all my information of that place came second hand. But my whole experience of Glenboig was to focus, as I had never before, on the deep splits in our society and especially on those fomented by segregated schools.

In 1957 the primary school was small, with only five classes. The headmaster George McFadzean, was a meticulous man who carried himself with great authority, and who was eventually to lead Scotland's teachers as the president of the Educational Institute of Scotland, the teacher's union. He was not only a brilliant teacher but also a man with the common touch. In keeping with what I have already said about the pervasive influence of the Old Firm, he travelled every week with the local Rangers supporters' bus all around the country wearing the colours and occasionally could be seen weaving his way woozily home of a Saturday night eating a fish supper out of a newspaper wrapping. But by Monday morning, this spruce man would appear, ready for the teaching fray, as if all had been done at the weekend was the *Glasgow Herald* crossword.

The great loves of his life were family and Jim Baxter, the Ranger with genius in his left leg. We would discuss games before the nine o'clock bell. After that it was action stations, as he ran the school with a military precision and nothing escaped his notice, particularly my late-coming. When you missed the requisite bus at Coatbridge you had problems, and the bus timetable to Glenboig would bear unfavourable comparison with the rate of camel traffic on the silk route to Samarkand. You had to depend on Good Samaritans giving you a lift, amongst which were a baker's van, an AA patrol vehicle, a tractor, a coal lorry, a police van and on one occasion a hearse (empty it has to be said). The journey was awkward but worthwhile. For it was in that village that my whole life blossomed, first when I met my prospective wife and second when I witnessed something very briefly one afternoon which was to change my life utterly. One warm sultry afternoon I spied something which caused me to write a short story. I simply put it in a drawer not knowing what it had in store for me.

During the close season Tiger was always a willing participant in the summer sports days and associated football tournaments. It served a useful purpose in that it helped keep him fit and playing football.

On a warm summer's day, Hearts, Rangers, St Mirren, Partick Thistle, Queen's Park, Clyde, Third Lanark and Celtic were all taking part in a five-a-side tournament at Helenvale Park. The players certainly played at a pace to reflect the heat, and the material of jersey in those days did not lend itself to the temperature of the mercury.

Rangers performed the amazing feat of getting into the final without one of their players scoring a goal. In the first round they beat Hearts 2-1, through own goals by Arthur Dixon and Willie McFarlane. In the semi-final Rangers and Third Lanark played out a scoreless draw, and with no penalty deciders in those days it was a toss of the coin to decide the winners. The omens did not look good, as twice already Jock had called heads and won choice of ends, at kick-off and prior to extra time. What were the odds of winning again? This time Jock called tails, and lo and behold the penny turned tails up and Rangers were into the final. The luck ran out though and Thistle comfortably beat Rangers to take the trophy; it would kinda sum up how the season would unfold.

Further evidence that it was going to be a difficult season came when Rangers, for the first time, failed to qualify from the League Cup section, losing twice to Aberdeen home and away.

There were glimpses of some good form, in particular when Clyde came to Ibrox on 19 August. Clyde had barely put up any resistance and the sum total of their efforts at Ibrox in front of 45,000 fans were shots from Davies and McPhail which Rangers' keeper Brown dealt with confidently, along with a Barclay header that hit the bar. It's worth noting that these efforts occurred only once Rangers were three ahead and coasting. Rangers just freewheeled to the winning post, playing much that was brilliant. So much were Rangers on top that there were regular forays into the danger zone by George Young, Tiger and Willie Woodburn around the Clyde goal, and they also contrived to miss what appeared to be open goals through Waddell, once, and then Paton twice. Man of the match by a country mile was Clyde keeper Willie Miller who gave an outstanding display to keep the scoreline respectable, and showed why he had six Scotland caps. Those in the 45,000 crowd who'd come in expectation of Clyde's usual fireworks against Rangers were left disappointed this time – the previous season for example, they had participated in a rip-snorting 5-4 Rangers victory at Ibrox.

Clyde, though, were second best in every department with the exception of keeper Miller. Rangers moved like a well-oiled machine. While Findlay and Paton were still developing as players, they had McColl and Cox ably supporting them with subtle prompting. It was, though, in attack where Rangers excelled. Waddell, injury-free and running and moving more easily than for a long time, was more like his old self, with a particularly impressive first half. Thornton's leading of the line merited his hat-trick. After 15 minutes Willie's header converted a Cox free kick and 11 minutes later the centre took advantage of a Paton slip to fire home from 16 yards. Seven minutes from time Thornton completed his hat-trick beating Miller, after Cox and Findlay had had shots blocked. The other goal came when Joe Dunn hooked a glorious ball past his own keeper.

This was to be a rare day of celebration in a season which was to prove the most disappointing in many years. Rangers lost nine league games, the most they had lost since 1925/26. The league was surrendered to Hibernian, who won the title by ten points.

In addition to an early exit from the League Cup, they did not fare much better in the Scottish Cup, knocked out in the second round by Hibernian 3-2 at Ibrox. The only minor consolation was a Charity Cup success, beating Partick Thistle 2-0 in the final. Clearly all was not well, one of the main issues being an ageing team, along with a manager in his mid-seventies whose health was deteriorating. In early August Mr Struth was hospitalised and Tiger would spend many a Friday afternoon at his bedside giving him the latest news on the team and the club they both loved.

Despite their trials and tribulations on the park, Rangers were still a class apart off it. A good example of this was at Cappielow on the opening day of the season on 12 August; ex-Morton and Scotland stalwart Billy Campbell was a guest of the club and he went into the home dressing room to wish them luck. When Jock and the Rangers players heard this, they promptly left their own dressing room to go out into the corridor and shake the hand of someone they had the utmost respect for and who had also been a team-mate in a Scotland jersey.

The signs were there too for Tiger that time was catching up with him, with his appearances for the first time seriously impacted by recurring injury. He only played in 18 out of 30 league games, though he still managed to pick up a Charity Cup winner's medal.

On 16 September Jock Shaw suffered an injury in the 0-0 draw against Dundee which was more serious than was first thought. Jock turned up at Ibrox with his foot encased in plaster, as an X-ray had shown that a bone in his ankle had been chipped. The Rangers fans were far from happy, not just with news of Tiger's injury but the poor form of the team in general, and the toothless display of their team against Dundee did not help. Perhaps the Rangers legions had been spoiled. Used to success for year after year, this downturn in form was not something they were happy with. In addition, they were not used to others being in the limelight.

During September and October Jock missed six weeks, and Rangers lost three of five league games in that time, along with a Glasgow Cup semi-final replay to Partick Thistle.

During this period, he reflected upon his role as club captain: 'Some people take the view captaincy doesn't mean a thing, that the team would play just the same if there wasn't any. By contrast I have heard an international player say of a team-mate who is also a captain, "So long as he is on the field I would never give up, even if we were half a dozen goals behind."'

His manager, the most successful in Scottish Football history, knew the pivotal role the captain played. Mr Struth was a master at recruitment and identifying leaders. As is well documented, Struth was not a tactician but relied upon his generals on the park to organise the matches. In the mid 1930s he had identified Tiger to be made of the right stuff and a future leader, and it is fair say that decision was yet another masterstroke.

With the injury healed, Jock played his way back to fitness with the reserves. One of these matches was to feature the introduction to the club of a future legend, Billy Simpson, who made his first appearance in the reserves against Queen's Park Strollers on 22 October.

An £11,500 capture from Linfield, Simpson's presence swelled the crowd to over 12,000. In the early stages, fans were a little disgruntled with the slowness of Gillick and Findlay to capitalise on the chances Simpson provided with head and foot flicks. After 51 minutes the crowd got what they wanted when Simpson gave Rangers a 2-1 lead with a left-foot drive, then followed that up after 77 minutes when he got his third with a Thornton-like header from a McCulloch cross to the delight of the crowd. A superb Ramsay save prevented any further score. The general feeling after the match from supporters was that Simpson looked ideal for the inside-forward role. His flicks and delicately stroked passes suggested that should be his position. Rangers won comfortably with Tiger giving his own ever-dependable performance and looking like he was almost ready for a first-team return. It was also noted that Johnny Hubbard had an excellent match.

As always Jock was keen to support local events in North Lanarkshire, and on 24 November he took the chair as guest of honour at a Friday night event at Airdrie Public Baths, presiding over what was described as a Trophy Night, when six championship cups were competed for.

Not only were injuries starting to feature but having previously only very rarely been cautioned, Jock's exemplary disciplinary record was marred with two cautions in one season. The first came at Dens Park on 30 December when frustration set in during a 2-0 defeat, and then apparently against Hearts at Ibrox on 20 January. I use the word 'apparently' as Jock appealed the caution to the SFA because he was not aware that he had been cautioned during the match, and was only made aware upon production of the match report. Needless to say, the appeal failed.

Shortly after this, Jock picked up another injury, on 17 February against St Mirren at Ibrox, and this time would be out for eight weeks. He was now 38 and the reality was starting to set in that he could not go on for ever.

Jock continued to champion local events, and his presence was always a welcome sight. He took up a new pasttime in June 1951, presiding as referee for the Carluke Rovers fundraising sports day at Loch Park for local charities. Lanark United, Forth Wanderers, Wishaw Juniors and Carluke Rovers took part and it was reported they were well marshalled by Tiger; they would not have dared step out of line though, would they?

The Last Hurrah

OVER THE next three seasons Jock would make only three league appearances for Rangers. During this time the team would win the league title only once, in 1952/53 in a final hurrah for the ailing Mr Struth. Many players and indeed club legends were coming to the end of their careers and the manager himself would soon step aside.

Despite Tiger's appearances in the first team now being sporadic, clubs sounded him out about prospective moves, as even at the age of almost 40, teams recognised his fitness and ability. *The Yorkshire Post* of 18 July 1952, for example, noted that Jock had been recommended to Huddersfield Town but unfortunately would not be joining as he has signed once more for Rangers.

Jock's experience was to be used to good effect playing in the reserves. He was not yet quite ready to be hanging up his boots so was keen to school the emerging talent in what it took to be a Rangers player.

In August 1952 he played in a Second XI cup tie and, in front of a 7,000 crowd, Celtic A defeated Rangers A 3-2 in the first round. The crowd was swelled by Fifer Jimmy Walsh making his first appearance since he re-signed for Celtic; however, at outside-right, he was reported to have had a lean time against veteran Jock Shaw.

Ever the sportsman, after the 1952 Scottish Cup semi-final at Easter Road, when Dundee beat Third Lanark 2-0, Jock sent a telegram to Dundee congratulating them with the message, 'All the best. I think it is your turn.' Dundee had in their ranks another Annathill lad in the shape of Bobby Flavell, of course.

Flavell was born in Annathill 1921, and was nine years younger than Tiger. He joined the senior game by signing for Airdrie in 1937 as a teenager. During the war Flavell made guest appearances for both Arsenal and Tottenham. When the Scottish Football League resumed in 1946, Flavell scored over a goal per game for Airdrie and won two caps for Scotland, which convinced Heart of Midlothian to pay £10,000 to acquire his services.

He again scored frequently at Hearts, but he became a football outcast on 12 June 1949 by signing for Millonarios, of the breakaway Colombian league, a move that Hearts manager Dave McLean said meant he would 'never play for Hearts again'. Flavell played alongside the legendary Alfredo Di Stefano in Bogota, but at the end of the Colombian season, in December 1950, returned to Scotland and was punished heavily for his actions in going to Colombia, attracting far stronger sanctions than English players who had made a similar move. He was fined £150, then a record fine for a Scottish player, and suspended from playing until May 1951. He was transfer-listed by Hearts in February 1951, before signing for Dundee in April, making his debut for the club in a Dewar Shield game against St Johnstone on 5 May 1951. Flavell scored goals in both the 1951 and 1952 Scottish League Cup finals, which helped Dundee win the cup in successive years. He played in the 1952 Scottish Cup Final, which ended in a 4-0 defeat by Motherwell, and also played for Kilmarnock and St Mirren before retiring as a player.

It was apparent Jock's time as a first-team player was coming to an end and Johnny Little was signed as his replacement in the summer of 1951 from Queen's Park, after three seasons with the Spiders. Little had also started teacher training during this time. Applying Mr Struth's mantra 'the club is greater than the man' Jock helped to groom his young replacement in the proud tradition of doing the right thing for the club, which could not have been easy but to Tiger was the natural thing to do as he could not go on for ever.

As Little recalled, 'It was quite a task taking over from someone like Tiger Shaw, but he was a great character and gave me as much help as he could.'

As part of this change, it made sense that a new captain would be required on the pitch too. So, on a pre-season trip to Inverness in August 1951, the transition was agreed. George Young recalls the historic moment: 'We were in the Highlands on a pre-season trip and Bill Struth called myself and Jock Shaw together in our Inverness hotel. Mr Struth then explained that, as I had been captain of Scotland for some time, he felt that the national team captain should also be the club captain, and announced that he was appointing me skipper. I must emphasise the whole business was settled very amicably and the first man to wish me all the best as captain was Jock Shaw. But although I was the captain, there were no privileges on the field. We were a team and every player had to work as hard as the next man, so I saw my duty as captain as being more of an off-field role. And in the same way as I saw Bill Struth as a father-figure, I made a point of taking up a similar position, particularly with the younger players at the club.'

While the move had a certain inevitability, it must still have been quite difficult for Tiger, with him still being an active player at the club. Whatever his personal feelings were, he kept them to himself and was, as ever, the consummate professional.

Corky did go on to explain that his appointment as captain caused one or two Ibrox men's brows to furrow. 'Some of the lads weren't too happy at the prospect of me being captain. The thought of lifting me on their shoulders after a cup win certainly didn't appeal!' he joked.

In these three final seasons, while appearances were sporadic, Jock always gave his all when called upon and perhaps this is best illustrated by the 1952 Ne'er Day game against Celtic, which has gone down in Ibrox folklore. Little had picked up an injury in the 3-2 win at Ibrox against Queen of the South so coming into the fray for his first league appearance of the season was the Tiger, and it would be quite a day, even by Old Firm standards.

The crowd of 50,000 were treated to quite a spectacle including a hail of bottles being thrown and spectators invading the track and outskirts of the pitch, seeking safety. Police were snowballed and bottles were thrown at them. The ambulance service dealt with 20 stretcher cases, among them four women. Seven men were arrested in the ground and four outside, and a strong police presence restored order after about a quarter of an hour. Play was not interrupted.

The catalyst for the mayhem in the crowd came midway through the second half, after Tiger was injured in a tackle with Charlie Tully. He was carried off on a stretcher, and from the east terracing, behind the Celtic goal, rose a chant of 'We want Tully'. Then when Rangers scored a fourth, to make the score 4-1, a fight broke out in the centre of the west terracing. The crowd in the vicinity surged back as police climbed the barriers and made for the centre of the trouble. They emerged, frogmarching a man to the pavilion. Immediately afterwards, another fight started in the packed covered enclosure. Here, spectators, including women and children, had to jump on to the track to get to safety. While the players continued the game, spectators scuttled across behind the Rangers goal and were headed off by scores of policemen. Ambulance crews were continually in action carrying stretcher cases to the pavilion. Police reinforcements appeared from under the stand, and police horses also arrived. The four women carried to the pavilion by stretcher were all suffering from head wounds, and among the men injured was a soldier. One man was able to walk to the pavilion, blood-stained bandage around his head. Three of the casualties were taken to hospital, and it was certain that the scenes would prompt yet another inquiry into crowd behaviour when the Old Firm meet. Celtic, for their next match at Parkhead, displayed posters warning against unruly behaviour.

As for our hero Jock, he sat in the dressing room sweat-stained and his face twisted in pain imploring Mr Struth, 'Please Boss, let me go on, I'll be all right. I simply must get out there and help the boys, honestly Boss I'll be all right.' His pain was secondary to the team in his mind. Mr Struth was much more pragmatic.

Rangers The New Era described the scene: 'The second half of the New Year match with Celtic at Parkhead was just underway. The man who pleaded to get back into this grim, shut teeth fight was the crippled Jock Shaw, Jock the Ibrox lion heart. Taken off with a badly injured leg, this iron man, who had fought a hundred fights for us at left-back after coming from Airdrie during the 1938 close, was ready, in fact insistent, to get back even if it meant crawling on to the field. Surely Jock was the first Tiger to rank with those who began to find their way into certain tanks? [A reference to the 1959 slogan, "Put a Tiger in Your Tank", introduced by ESSO to boost sales.]

'But the Boss, manager William Struth, told him, "Jock you stay right where you are. Never fear lad, we'll win with ten men. The lads out there are adding a bit more for you and the colours."'

To the actual football, Rangers marched to a convincing and comfortable victory, but actually the remarkable feature of the game was that their dominance only became complete after they had been reduced to ten men by the loss of Tiger. The veteran left-back was in the first team for the first time this season. This was generally viewed as an astute move as the veteran frequently baulked Celtic's best and most dangerous forward, Collins. Up to the 12th minute of the second half, he had played as well as ever. Then came the clash with Tully. Tiger went down, and Tully was booked. A few minutes later he was carried off unable to continue. Rangers were then leading 2-1. Cox moved from inside-left to left-back and took the free kick. The ball went straight down the left wing, was crossed by Liddell, Paton promptly fired it home and the ten men were in complete control. Eight minutes later a free kick was awarded just outside the penalty box against Evans in the face of strong Celtic protests. Waddell's fierce rising drive beat Bell all ends up. That was the signal for the uproar previously described. The remaining minutes were played out in a tense atmosphere, with players of both sides intent on avoiding anything that might cause further trouble. The pity of it was that the first half had been a credit to Scottish football. Despite the snow/mud combination on the playing surface the football was of excellent quality, fast and packed with goalmouth thrills. In the 14th minute Liddell took a Thornton pass in his stride, carried on for 20 yards then neatly side-footed past Bell. Five minutes later a clever Tully lob-come-shot beat Brown from all of 25 yards to level the scores. However, it took Rangers only 60 seconds to go in front again, and once more most credit went to Liddell. He slid a perfect pass in front of Paton to make the inside right's scoring shot easy. Rangers were the more powerful outfit physically. They played their passes more accurately and crisply. They had match-winning wingers in Waddell and Liddell, allied to the usual defensive solidity of Tiger, Woodburn, Young and Brown.

Jock's only other league appearance of the season came on the final day at Pittodrie when he played in a 1-1 draw.

On 1 May 1952 he signed his penultimate contract for the club. Witnessed by Mr Struth and Jimmy Simpson, Tiger signed up for one year for £12 a week in the close season and £14 a week during the season. The bonus structure was not included in the contract.

In 1952/53 he made only one league appearance, at Methil against East Fife in a 3-2 defeat on 18 October 1952, and this was his final competitive match for the club.

It was interesting to hear, though, that even folk outside of Ibrox did not foresee an end to Tiger's days as a Rangers player and the supporters' view of the team in December 1952 was, 'This boy Grierson is terrific. What a team.' The Grierson in question being Derek, who had signed that summer from Queen's Park, and had lit up the early months of the season. The Rangers support, though, it was fair to say, while feeling somewhat happier, was still far from satisfied. A typical comment reported in *The Sunday Post* said, 'I know that Rangers have some promising forward reserves such as the youngsters Woods and MacMillan, but I'm worried about one or two defensive positions. Who is going to replace Woodburn when he gives up football? What happens if Little is off for any length of time with an injury? Rangers surely can't expect to keep calling on Jock Shaw!'

One reporter said, 'I asked an East Fife player, who a few weeks ago played against Rangers, the day when Young and Cox were on international duty at Cardiff, what he thought of Shaw these days. "If Jock's finished, I'm dead and buried long ago!" came the reply.' Again, further testimony to Jock's fitness.

Jock remained very much in demand around North Lanarkshire and in April 1953 was in attendance at the Chryston OAP Association, as reported in the *Coatbridge Express*: 'In the Public Hall on Saturday evening, the OAP Association enjoyed a full attendance of dancers for the selection of a Coronation Queen for the Muirhead area. The judges, who had a very difficult task amongst so many pretty entrants, were three Rangers football players, Jock Shaw, Duncan Stanners and John Dunlop. The ultimate winner of the competition was Miss Jessie Scott, Campsie View, Chryston, and the runner-up was Miss Pearl Rae, Pentland Road, Chryston. Music was expertly provided by the Concords Dance Band, with Mr T. V. Clark and Mr S. Leckie fulfilling the duties of MC. Councillor Thos. Hailstone, in a few brief remarks, thanked the large company for their support and assistance making this function so successful, both socially and financially.' Yes, it really was tough at the top.

While signing a further one-year contract in the summer of 1953, he subsequently only played a couple of further friendly matches and his very last appearance as a Rangers player took place in far-flung Quebec on 16 May 1954, when he came on as a substitute for Sammy Cox in a 1-0 friendly win over Chelsea.

Following the club's return from the summer tour in June, Jock announced his retirement from the game and so brought down the curtain on a glittering playing career.

It was reported in the *Sunday Post*: 'Glasgow Rangers who landed at Greenock yesterday after their tour of Canada and the United States, will be crossing the Atlantic again in two years' time if the sporting community of Vancouver, British Columbia, get their way. Vancouver, which stages this year's Empire Games, has a 40,000-capacity stadium and is planning star attractions for the future. Organisers there are working on a plan to bring star soccer teams over from the "Old Country". Already Rangers have been approached to see if they will be willing to return in 1956 to play a series of games against Arsenal. Naturally the club are in no hurry to give a definite answer yet.

'A more urgent problem is the appointment of a new manager. Another priority job is the treatment of Derek Grierson's leg injury which put him out of action in the first few days of the tour. Grierson was the Rangers' only serious casualty thanks largely to the Canadians' fondness for substitutes. Rangers took full advantage of this rule and many of the older hands were called off about 20 minutes from the end of games to be replaced by younger stars. Two veterans in great demand were Willie Thornton and Jock Shaw, who have now played their last games for Rangers. Both free transfer men, their special temporary engagements for the tour ended when the ship docked. Thornton is now free to take over as Dundee's manager.'

As for Tiger, he hung up his boots, but even at his age, two Scottish First Division sides tried to sign him with a guaranteed first-team place but he politely declined the offers saying, 'Thanks but although I feel I could continue playing for some seasons, I want to end my days as a Rangers player. The 16 years I spent with them were the happiest days of my life. In fact, they were my life. I could never play for any other team, gentlemen. No matter how hard it is to give up the game feeling as fit as I do.'

In the club book *The New Era* he was described thus: 'How typical of the Lanarkshire man, steadfast to an ideal, unflappable in the cauldron of the most searching fight, and so proud of the colours he wore that, as I have told you in the opening chapter he would go back to the field although crippled with injury. What a player! What a man to have on your side. They have never come more dogged than the Tiger. Yes, if there was a synonym for pluck it would be the name Jock Shaw.'

This was a long era of unrivalled dominance coming to an end as several of the most pivotal figures in the history of Rangers ended their time at the club along with perhaps the greatest and most influential figure in the club's history – Bill Struth, who Jock held in the highest esteem. Even after he left the club, the Struth influence was still clear as Jock fondly explained: 'There will never be another Bill Struth: he lived by the motto that he wouldn't ask someone to do something he wouldn't do himself. He was a very, very true man who had a lot of respect for his players and we in turn respected him. Bill Struth liked to see his players as well dressed which meant part of our uniform was a bowler hat. However, both Torry Gillick and I didn't like them so when we went across to Ireland by boat for a five-a-side tournament once, we threw them into the sea and told the manager they had blown off. He was very strict about coming in to Ibrox in cars. He had this thing about players seeming cooped up in them, and felt they were too cramped and we could run the risk of pulling muscles. He had a list of all our car registrations and he used to send our trainer Willie Cameron around the district to see if anyone had brought their car. I used to park down at the Clydeside and walk up to the ground, but I was still caught once or twice and told off.'

Fairgrieve wrote in the 1964 book *The Rangers*, 'Let's take for instance the case of Dougie Gray who came to Rangers [in] season 1925/26 and who was to form with Tiger Shaw, a full-back partnership comparable with the Smith-Drummond duet of the nineties.'

High praise indeed. The partnership lasted for seven years till Gray's departure in 1945/46.

Speaking in November 1971, Jock said, 'My wages were £8 a week, which was good money [around £300 a week equivalent in today's money], a journeyman was maybe making about £3 a week. No, a lot of folk have asked me "do you wish you were born 20 years later?" I always say no. I was well paid in those days, quite satisfied.'

This is a very interesting point, as while the riches on offer to today's players are mind-boggling, players from Tiger's era considered that they were very well-off. For example, Ralph Brand always said he drove a top-of-the-range car and bought his first house in his early twenties. That was a lot more than folk of a similar age in other professions were able to do.

The 1955 Rangers Supporters' Association annual had a tribute from Ian McColl to Jock, as follows: 'Jock was the first face to greet you when players arrived for training, and he was always the first one on to the track and training with spikes and he had a sharp turn of pace.' McColl also spoke of the banter that would be missed with the departure that summer of both Jock and Willie Thornton. By all accounts, despite being firm friends, they argued constantly, continually challenging each other in running, jumping, billiards, golf, and so on. In reality, however, the challenges never took place as they could never even agree on the rules.

Football had come naturally to Tiger but he was also respectful of opponents. The best he said were Jimmy Delaney, Stanley Matthews and Alex McSpadyen of Partick Thistle. He gave high praise to Delaney: 'I doubt there was ever a sportsman like Jimmy. He was the cleanest player I ever opposed. When you took the ball away from him, you did it with the knowledge that you wouldn't be tripped or pushed. I could have played Jimmy Delaney in bare feet and finished the game without a scratch, so fair was Jimmy in a tackle.'

Of Sir Stanley, Jock said, 'Undoubtedly the greatest of them all, different from anyone else. He could beat you on a threepenny piece, and he did if you let him get the ball.' Of McSpadyen, he said, 'There's always the argument about who is the fastest footballer. Most say the honour went to Jimmy Crawford of Queen's Park, who did evens for the 100 yards on the track, but I maintain McSpadyen was the fastest of the lot. He was deceptive, with an unusually long stride that gave him an ambling appearance as he ran relaxed on his heels, but once he was past you it was impossible to catch him.'

Jock was one of the fittest players of his era and he loved to train. Following the press launch of Bob McPhail's autobiography in 1988, Tiger was pictured along with Bob McPhail, Davie Kinnear, Willie Woodburn and Jimmy Smith looking as fit as ever. This prompted a gentleman called Norman Gilzean to write to *The Herald*, 'The photograph of Mr Bob McPhail and his colleagues revived some interesting memories having seen all five in football action for Rangers and Scotland. I was present in the record crowd at Hampden in 1937, and Bob McPhail of course scored two of the goals that day in the 3-1 victory over England. Crushing among the spectators that day was so intense that when people were fainting right, left and centre not one of them could fall down (I know, I was one of them). Mr Jock Shaw has apparently retained his magnificent physique. I used to work in the orthopaedic department to the Victoria Infirmary where the Rangers players came every Monday morning for a physical check-up by Mr Miller the surgeon therapist to the club, and Mr Shaw was then acknowledged as the finest example of physical fitness. Mr Woodburn was a most polite and pleasant patient whose *sine die* punishment on the field amazed us all at the Vic. I notice that they continue the genial, pleasant disposition in features and sartorial elegance in advancing years as they displayed in Mr Struth's time as manager of Rangers. He set the public image of a Rangers professional performer without all today's extravagant publicity.'

Another tribute was relayed by Willie Allison, Rangers' historian of the time, who said of Jock, 'He was strong-limbed, steel hard, steadfast to an ideal, unflappable in the cauldron of the most searching fight and proud of the colours. What a man to have in your side. They have never come more dogged than the Tiger.'

The *Wee Blue Book* for the 1954/55 season also recorded its own tribute: 'Jock, a lion-hearted defender, has said it was the proudest day of his life when he became a Ranger. For our part we can answer by recording that we have never had a more wholehearted or true Ranger. His enthusiasm and inflexible purpose could not have been surpassed and his name and spirit will always be an inspiration to those who will follow in his wake.'

Speaking in 1958, Willie Waddell was asked what type of captain Jock was. 'Jock was one of the most consistent and whole-hearted players in football. As a player and a captain his bearing and keenness were a splendid lead to all his colleagues. No player enjoyed his football more. He was a hardy lad, was Jock, and he took knocks with a smile. I don't believe there is a player at Ibrox who less visited the treatment room.'

Jock Shaw played his last competitive match for Rangers on 18 October 1952 against East Fife, aged 40 years, eight months, 26 days. Officially his final appearance for the club was in Canada as a substitute on 16 May 1954, aged 41 years, five months and 17 days. He was the oldest player to turn out for Rangers until David Weir in 2011. Speaking in 2011 Jock's granddaughter Elaine said, 'David Weir is definitely a man my Papa would have classed in the Rangers mould because he's so humble and dignified and I can't think of anyone more fitting to take this record from him.

'He has done a fantastic job for the club particularly as he was only supposed to be here for an initial six months.'

Brothers in Arms

TO HAVE one family member play for and captain his country was significant enough but to have the distinction of two brothers playing together and then captaining Scotland within months of each other was quite unprecedented. In recent years Gary and Steven Caldwell have matched this feat but in purely the strictest sense. Their ability bore no comparison to the Shaw brothers: they were in a league of their own. Jock and David were not just brothers but best friends too.

David was a few years younger than Jock so was naturally later to the professional game, but once he was signed up, they became the fiercest of rivals. From the point Jock joined Rangers in 1938, till he retired in 1954, 12 of the 16 League Championships had one of the Shaw brothers as a title winner. The only blots on the landscape were Celtic's win in 1954 and two Hibernian wins after David left for Aberdeen.

David was also a left-back, as his father and older brother were. He signed for Hibernian in 1938 from Grange Rovers and would stay there till the end of the 1949/50 season when he was transferred to Aberdeen.

He had to be patient to make his debut and the *Airdrie and Coatbridge Advertiser* tracked his progress and reported in January 1939, 'David Shaw, popular right-back of Grange Rovers, was out with Hibs A against Queen of the South A at Easter Road. Shaw, who hails from Annathill, a younger brother of Jock Shaw, the Rangers left-back.'

He would not have too long to wait for his debut, making it in April 1939 against Motherwell. He was not at all like Tiger as he was physically slender, so relied much more on his intelligent reading of the game. He was identical in height to Tiger though, at 5ft 7in.

David was part of the emerging Hibernian side during the war years and beyond, who were Rangers' main rivals until the mid 1950s. His greatest honour apart from captaining his country was being captain when Hibs lifted the league title in 1947/48.

He signed for Aberdeen in 1950 and the signing was reported in the *Aberdeen Evening Express* as follows: 'David Shaw, international left-back of Hibernian, who was signed by Aberdeen on Saturday, will not turn out at Pittodrie to-day when the Dons begin training for the new season. He has finished his holiday in Aberdeen and is meantime back in Edinburgh. The signing of Shaw has solved a problem for the Pittodrie officials. With the new season looming large they had only two full-backs on their books, Don Emery and Pat McKenna. The latter is meantime recovering from an appendix operation and it does not seem likely that he will be fit before the beginning of the season. Shaw, a brother of "Tiger" Shaw, the Rangers captain, is an astute, strong-tackling player, and his presence in the Aberdeen team should stiffen the defence considerably. He is a native of Annathill, Lanarkshire, and began his football career with Banknock Juveniles. He was signed by Hibs as a half-back in 1939 from Grange Rovers.'

David would go on to make 81 appearances for the Dons over three seasons, scoring one goal before being appointed coach by manager David Halliday. He would be first-team coach when Aberdeen won their first-ever league title in 1955, and he was to be described by inside-forward Bobby Wishart as the secret ingredient in the title success. He was introduced as Aberdeen coach in *The Sunday Post*, as follows:

There could be a friendly tip to my Aberdeen player friends,
be most polite this afternoon to left-back Davie Shaw: if

you're not – well, don't blame me if, in the near future, you have to run round Pittodrie 20 extra times. Davie Shaw, you see, is to be your new trainer and coach! I take great pleasure in exclusively announcing this imminent appointment. I know no man who has been a better servant to football as a player than Shaw, nor one who is better fitted to pass on knowledge to others. Before his studied tacticianship was rewarded with the captaincy of Hibs.

Having an elder brother can be useful, especially if he happens to be like Tiger Shaw. The Ranger, when playing for Scotland, had tried first-time methods against Stanley Matthews. They failed. In 1948 Davie, who had played against Wales the season before, was chosen to succeed his brother as Scotland's sacrifice at the altar of Matthews. He was told the Shaws of Annathill are proud, too proud to be a sacrificial repeat for anyone, and Tiger instructed Davie to play a waiting game. 'Force Matthews to make the first move.' It worked, as everyone who saw that international will remember. Davie Shaw was easily the most successful left-back tried by Scotland against the master dribbler. Unfortunately, a cartilage injury deprived Scotland of Davie's services the following season against England and as so often happens in football Davie couldn't even regain a first team place with Hibs, when fit again.

The Aberdeen trainer-coach job is a Scottish Soccer plum. To show his appreciation of having been chosen for it, Davie will sell his business in Portobello and move house to Aberdeen. And unless I'm much mistaken, he will move Aberdeen's standing in the game up and up in the next few years.

The importance of the man in charge of the dressing room isn't generally fully appreciated. A first-class man can make a first-class team. Hasn't president of the SFA Harry

Swan often told me: 'My appointment of Hugh Shaw as chief trainer was the start of the new Hibs.'

Davie took over as manager from the 1955/56 season after Dave Halliday left to go to Leicester City. His appointment was reported in *The Sunday Post*, 'Is there a bigger hero than your dad? Aberdeen skipper Davie Shaw's son disproved the old adage, like father like son, last week. Davie has been training at Pittodrie and Mrs Shaw called at the ground one day with the two youngsters. When she stopped to speak to a friend the two youngsters nipped in the main door and met Davie Halliday. The manager asked what they were wanting for. The older Shaw replied, "I want to see my daddy, Mr Shaw." "Oh," said Halliday. "And are you to be a footballer like him?" "Yes," was the answer, "but I'll no play for Aberdeen! I'm to play for my uncle's team!" What has Tiger Shaw got that his brother hasn't?' The boy had clearly had a very good upbringing!

Davie held the role for four seasons before reverting to his role as coach (which he much preferred) till he retired in 1967. He had to step in though, to lead the team one more time in the 1967 cup against Celtic after manager Eddie Turnbull became unwell. He won the initial League Cup for the Dons in 1955/56.

On 12 June 1999 the *Aberdeen Evening Express* printed this summary of his time at the club:

Keeping up Aberdeen's tradition of promoting trainers to the vacant managerial position following Dave Halliday's departure, it was filled by Dave Shaw. The new man had a tough act to follow but the nucleus of the title-winning side was still together. Shaw was no stranger to Pittodrie having been signed in July 1950. Three years later, following the departure of Jock Pattillo to St Johnstone, Shaw was installed as club trainer after captaining the Dons for three years. During an eventful playing career Shaw also captained the

Hibs side which lost to Aberdeen in the 1947 final. Brother of Tiger Shaw of Rangers, Dave developed into a reliable left-back although his career was cut short by World War Two. He also gained eight Scotland caps.

A native of Annathill in Lanark, Shaw finished his playing career at Pittodrie in 1953, his last appearance coming in the Scottish Cup Final replay against Rangers on April 29, 1953. His appointment as Aberdeen manager came at a time when there was much acrimony at the club. Having apparently resolved the row over players' bonuses for winning the title, the Dons were rocked by the SFA decision to put Hibs forward as Scottish representatives in the European Cup. Shaw was also surprised to learn his appointment had led to differences of opinion within the Aberdeen board. Undaunted, the players responded in the best possible way by taking the Scottish League Cup, defeating St Mirren 2-1 in the final.

Unfortunately for Shaw the side was beginning to break up. He earned the reputation of being a players' manager, which didn't endear him to the board. And it was that loyalty to the players that led to his ultimate departure in November 1959. The Dons had been in steady decline and couldn't arrest their slump into mid-table mediocrity. Shaw reverted to his role as club trainer, a role he remained in until 1967.

After leaving football he worked for some years as a PE teacher in the north east where he remained, till he sadly passed away in 1977 from a heart attack, aged only 59.

Scotland and the Annathill Defence

JOCK WAS like many other players of his generation whose careers were seriously impacted by the war. Had it not been for the conflict he would surely have received many more caps. For some, just one cap would have been reward enough: to have played, captained your country and done so while your own younger brother was in the same team, well, that is just the stuff of schoolboy fairy tales. John Shaw from Miners' Row in Annathill lived that dream

Now, depending on which pen pictures or summaries of Tiger's career you read, there are several different figures attributed to his Scotland appearances. So, I will try and clarify that once and for all. In total Tiger turned out for the Scotland international team on 12 occasions.

In full internationals he was capped 12 times. Eight were 'unofficial', played during the war. He partnered David twice, once in the Victory International of 1946, a memorable 1-0 win with a last-minute goal from Jimmy Delaney before 139,468 people, which I will come back to in more detail shortly, and in a 3-1 defeat to Switzerland on 15 May 1946.

His first international appearance was on 3 May 1941 against England, where Scotland succumbed 3-1 despite Alex Venters giving them an early lead. Tiger's direct opponent was Sir Stanley Matthews, who he would go on to face three times in total. Interestingly, during the war Sir Stanley guested for Scotland on 19 April 1941 against Scottish Command.

The last pre-war official international was against England on 15 April 1939. The English players wore numbers on their jerseys for the first time but so torrential was the downpour of rain in the first half they had to borrow Queen's Park jerseys for the second half.

The official series of matches did not resume until 12 April 1947. Any internationals played between April 1939 and April 1947 are not recorded in the official records and no caps were awarded. In addition, due to the special wartime conditions, many rules were relaxed a little, for example substitutions were permitted.

Having said all that, there could have been nothing unofficial about the games against the Auld Enemy when Bill or Willie Shankly (as he was known as a player) was involved. He was a player who always applied to himself his own maxim delivered as a manager to his players concerning the offside rule: 'If one of ma players is no interferin wi' play a' the time, he shouldnae be on the park.'

During the war there were what were considered 36 unofficial internationals played, in the main against England who Scotland faced 17 times, or a variety of army selections. The record against England during the war was pretty atrocious, only featuring two wins and two draws in the 17 encounters.

Tiger next appeared almost exactly two years after his debut; he again faced Sir Stan but England were even more convincing winners, running up four goals without reply at Hampden on 17 April 1943. The injured Bill Shankly was heard to comment after this match with typical candour, 'Scotland had no chance. That is probably the best England team of all time.'

It would not be until the final season of the war emergency conditions in 1945/46 that Tiger established himself and he appeared in a further ten internationals, skippering the side during all of these matches. Of his 12 internationals, only the final four are officially recorded appearances. His final outing for Scotland came in Belfast in October 1947, when he was aged 34 years and ten months, partnering club-mate George Young in the full-back berths.

May 41	Scotland 1-3 England
April 43	Scotland 0-4 England
Nov 45	Scotland 2-0 Wales
Jan 46	Scotland 2-2 Belgium
Feb 46	N.Ireland 2-3 Scotland
April 46	Scotland 1-0 England
May 46	Scotland 3-1 Switzerland
Aug 46	England 2-2 Scotland
April 47	England 1-1 Scotland
May 47	Belgium 2-1 Scotland
May 47	Luxembourg 0-6 Scotland
Oct 47	N.Ireland 2-0 Scotland

Brother David would go on to take over his place at left-back in the national team and also had the honour of captaining his country against Northern Ireland. A truly unique family honour to have two sons captaining their country.

Jock also appeared twice for the Scottish League, once while still at Airdrie in 1937 and then against the Irish League in 1947.

The highlight of Jock's international career was undoubtedly the Victory International Championship win over England at Hampden on 18 April 1946. The occasion would not just be a colossal moment for the country but a truly momentous one for the village of Annathill.

Scotland's record against England during the war years had been appalling and included a number of really heavy defeats, 8-0 being the worst. So, the Scots were determined this time it would be different. They had made a perfect start in the Victory International Series, beating Ireland and Wales, and a win over England would see them claim the coveted trophy.

In the week leading up to the match Scotland had its perennial round of call-offs with George Young, pencilled in as centre-half, and right-back Jimmy Stephen (Bradford Park Avenue), both dropping out. Two new caps were to be drafted in and it was Annathill to the rescue.

Frank Brennan of Airdrie would take the place of Young, who had been struck down by a severe attack of laryngitis. Brennan had been attracting a lot of interest from clubs south of the border. Newcastle United were particularly keen, and director Stan Seymour had had another look at him in the previous Saturday's cup tie with Clyde. Airdrie were reluctant though to do business at that stage of the season whilse still in the Southern League Cup.

Brennan was young and muscular, only 22, he stood 6ft 2in tall, weighing in at 13st. His size and stride gave him a terrific turn of pace and the previous year he had won the Bedlay Sprint. As well as playing for Airdrie he was also a mining engineer at Bedlay Pit. He would eventually sign for the Toon at the end of the season for £7,500.

The next replacement was another Bedlay Boy in the shape of one David Shaw, of Hibs. The situation was quite unique in Scottish football: David would be playing alongside his older brother, Jock. David was also a left-back but was considered talented enough to fill in on the opposite flank as he had originally played on the right before being switched, not long after arriving at Easter Road. Quite an imposing task considering the opposition. However, there was a friendly, experienced face in the ranks to guide the Annathill boys through proceedings.

The local paper the *Airdrie and Coatbridge Advertiser* wasted no time in arranging a photo opportunity and their issue on the morning of the match had a picture of the three Annathill boys with old pit colleagues at Bedlay Colliery. The previews of the match were intense, focusing unsurprisingly on the Annathill factor. One preview in the *Airdrie and Coatbridge Advertiser* was typical:

Annathill provides Scotland's defence as the Shaw Brothers
and Brennan bring honour to the Village of Footballers.

Nowhere in Scotland is excitement about the football International so concentrated as in the little mining village of Annathill. On Wednesday they gave a rousing send-off to three of their own lads who are representing Scotland against the Auld Enemy at Hampden Park this afternoon. The small, hard pitch in the village where little boys are wont to play is probably the most outstanding nursery of footballers in the country. Locals were agog at the large number of reporters who called at the village at the beginning of the week and it tickled the villagers considerably. Our photographer saw the three of them in the home of the parents of Jock and Davie. Mr David Shaw, father of the two backs, looked in for curiosity but hearing of the photograph to be taken he shyly departed, saying he was away up to attend to his 'doos'. Talk among the men was of anything but football. The older David, too, won football distinction. He was a Junior with Carrick XI and in one season gained a Junior Cup, and has the reputation of having been able to play with outstanding skill in any position. Thus, Annathill or Bedlay, as it is sometimes called, has provided Scotland with its defence. The amount of football talent which has been produced by this village is truly amazing. It has now provided Scotland with four footballers of international standard. The other one is Bobby Flavell, Airdrieonians, who returned from service with the Royal Navy this week in time to add his congratulations. At the present time Annathill could provide a senior football team, including four internationalists. Prospective Team: McBride (Third Lanark), D. Shaw (Hibs), Jock Shaw (Rangers), Frew (Morton), Brennan (Airdrie), Mooney (Third Lanark), Burke (Albion Rovers), McMurray (Third Lanark), Flavell (Airdrie), Connelly (Luton Town), and Gardner (Third Lanark).

You must know Annathill and realise the size of it to appreciate fully just what this small village has achieved in the football world. The village confidently asserts they will not let Scotland down. Provost Bonner has sent Frank Brennan a telegram expressing the best wishes of all Airdrieonians and hoping he has a good game, free from injury. Scouts would comfortably encircle the area in which all these players were born. The village can surely claim to have produced more prominent footballers to the square inch than any other place in the world.

To the match itself: despite it taking until the final minute for Delaney to score the winning goal, Scotland were totally dominant. The stats did not lie; they clearly showed the measure of Scots superiority. There were 12 corners – ten for Scotland! Bobby Brown made four saves, only one in the second half. Swift was called on 22 times, 16 of them before the interval. There were 16 free kicks, seven of them against Scotland, 58 'shies', and 33 bye kicks. Six Scots needed the trainer's attention: Husband. Brennan, Liddell, Waddell, Jock Shaw and Delaney. Three Englishmen had first aid: Mercer, Swift, and Hardwick. In the car parks were 22,000 cars, 900 buses, and 50 policemen continuously patrolled round the pitch.

With just a minute to go, there was a cathedral hush as the renowned Hampden Roar had died away from 138,000 throats, and Scotland were awarded a free kick just outside England's penalty area. Husband lifted the ball into the goalmouth and pandemonium broke out as baldish, thirtyish Delaney ended Scotland's dismal record of defeats by England since pre-war days. It was reminiscent of the day Alex Cheyne scored Scotland's winning goal from the wing when most of the reporters were busily writing up a drawn match. Then the wind played havoc to England. This time a costly error of judgement by young Shackleton brought catastrophe. Shackleton had dropped back to help out a hard-pressed defence, and in his excitement held Liddell's jersey, as they tussled for possession. Some English referees might have overlooked the tug. Not so Mr Craigmyle who immediately blew his whistle and coincidentally sounded England's death knell.

Another gamble which failed for England was the inclusion of Elliott on the right wing, as he had not the required craft to master Tiger. The Scots had men who could manoeuvre the ball into the penalty area. England on the other hand had no penetration and relied upon square passes from Bennett and Whitchurch which never threatened to trouble Scotland. Fair-haired Wright was the only England player to rise to the occasion. Franklin at the back found Delaney an awkward handful and seldom distributed the ball effectively. The England defence came through a gruelling test with a reasonable amount of credit with Scott twice clearing off the line when all seemed lost. Keeper Swift after a shaky opening brought off some spectacular saves.

Match reports of the time recorded that 'the brothers Shaw and Brennan, who come from the same Lanarkshire village, took the defensive honours'. Waddell, who nodded down the ball for Delaney's goal, was the best of the forwards on show. His curling corner kicks taken with that lethal foot into the middle were an object lesson in how it should be done.

All the good things in the game were crammed into the first half. If Lawton had scored instead of hitting the crossbar three minutes after the start, the game may have played out very differently, and also Hagan missed a gild-edged opportunity 12 minutes from the end. All in all, Scotland had two-thirds of the play and won deservedly.

The overpouring of joy at the result in beating England and the circumstances of the last-minute winner had the country waking up with a smile on its faces. *The Sunday Post* was keen to get the low-down on its heroes and needless to say headed for Annathill. 'This Village Went Daft Last Night' screamed the headline.

Two women stood at the head of the cheering crowd in the little Lanarkshire village of Annathill yesterday afternoon.

They were the mothers of Jock and Davie Shaw and of young Frank Brennan, the centre-half who subdued Tommy Lawton. They'd just heard the radio commentator announce Scotland's great victory. The whole village went daft over the success of their three boys. At 3pm Annathill was a deserted village, and the only sound was an excited voice on the radio. For a long time, the village remained hushed. Then suddenly the commentator's voice rose to shout 'Goal!' A minute later the shout was taken up all over the village. Doors opened, folk rushed into the street, which quickly became a mass of cheering people. Little boys in the street chanted, 'We've won, we've won!' Some girls climbed up trees and straddled the road with a large homemade banner inscribed: 'Well done, Bedlay boys'. When the crowd dispersed into little groups to discuss how 'their boys' had played, Mrs Shaw and Mrs Brennan went back to their houses arm in arm. 'I had a worried five minutes there, but I knew our Frank wouldn't let us down,' Mrs Brennan told *The Sunday Post*. Along the street, at the Shaws' house, Mr David Shaw, father of the Shaw brothers, just smiled happily. 'I didn't think they could do it,' he said, 'but, man, I'm glad they did!'

Last night, while the village was illuminated by the light from a fairground, everybody from the youngest lad to the oldest inhabitant waited impatiently on their heroes' arrival home.

The paper also had a more detailed interview with the proud Mrs Shaw. The headline on the day after the match emblazoned 'Mrs Shaw Is Real Proud of Her Laddies'. The article went on:

In the little village of Annathill, Lanarkshire, lives Scotland's proudest mother. She has just cause for pride. Yesterday her sons, Jock and Davie, made football history when they played side by side in the international against England at Hampden Park. Only once before have brothers been so honoured. That was in 1913, when Andrew and David Wilson played against England. A *Sunday Post* representative visited Mrs Shaw in the little Miners' Row where her sons were born. Seated at the fire beside her daughters, Alice and Margaret, she talked about the boys. 'Jock was born twenty-nine years ago in a wee house further down the row. Davie came three years later. Like most babies, they started kicking the minute they came into the world. My laddies have been at it ever since. Jock was kicking a ball round the kitchen as soon as he could walk. Three years later Davie was following the same path across the linoleum with a ball at his wee feet. Nobody was surprised. The Shaws of Annathill have aye been footballers. Fine I remember when my man, along with his brothers and his cousins, fielded an Annathill team with nobody but Shaws in it! My man played for Croy Celtic. One of his dearest possessions is an old cap with 'Lanarkshire League v Dumbarton Junior League, 1903-4', written on it in gold letters. So the neighbours just smiled when they saw my lads practising wee heidies against the wall of the house, or running home, dirty and red-cheeked after a game in the school playground (Annathill Public). They weren't so pleased when Jock put one of his shots through a window, or Davie's penalty kick landed in a bed of chrysanthemums. I was never done clouting the pair of them for wasting their boots. Gey lean times we lived in then'.

Mrs Shaw went on 'Their dad was a miner, and there were other four weans to feed and clothe: Jeannie, Alice, Margaret, and Charlie. Jock and Davie went through more boots and shoes than all the others put together. They came home with the toes kicked out, the soles hanging off, or the heels gone. If there wasn't a ball to kick, well there were aye stones and bricks in the streets. I couldn't imagine Jock or Davie ever passing a tin can! Jock never came straight home when I sent him for message. I aye had to send one of the lassies to interrupt him in "a wee game wi' the boys." His empty message basket would be one of the goalposts.'

It was in the Annathill Boys' Brigade team the boys got their first real football boots. They both left the school at fourteen, and went to work with their father in Bedlay Colliery. It was hard work, but it kept them fit. So did the platefuls of broth, tatties and mince and stew cooked for them every day. Then Jock signed for Benburb Juniors. Davie began to look at his brother with a wee bit of hero-worship in his eyes, but his chance wasn't long in coming. A few years later he joined the Grange Rovers. When Jock left Benburb for Airdrie, he stopped working the pit. Davie went on playing for the Rovers. Every night he rushed home from the pit for a wash and a change, and then away again to do some training.

In 1939 Jock signed for Rangers. A week later he got married. Davie wasn't far behind. He went to Hibs in 1940, and got married not long after. Jock played his first game for Scotland in 1941. Yesterday's was his sixth international. It was Davie's first. The boys were fair delighted at the thought of playing together for Scotland. They've always been the best of pals. They train together at Ibrox. Twice a week they come to Annathill to see their old mother and father. Davie sits at the fire, reads the paper, blethers with his dad about last week's game. In the summer he likes a game of bowls.

'The minute Jock comes in he's out again, to the billiard-hall. He's an awfy' lad for his billiards, and a handy man with a gun, too. Many's the time he's brought me home a tea-set he won at the shooting. Jock and his wife live at Muirhead. They've two children – David's seven, and daft on football, of course. Margaret's two. Davie's home's in Coatbridge. His three-year-old lad's a Davie, too. My man and I have never seen the boys playing. We aye liked just to be at home waiting for them when they came back after the game. Their brother Charlie's their biggest fan. He used to be in a Mount Ellen team, but he hasn't played since he got a bad knock on the leg. Charlie, Jeannie, and Alice were at Hampden yesterday shouting for their brothers. All the folk in Annathill who couldn't get tickets for the international were running about last week getting their wireless batteries charged so they could hear it on the wireless. Father and I had to listen-in next door. Our wireless broke down!'

This was quite an insight into the life and times in Annathill and what struck me was the parents had never seen their sons play professionally. It's perhaps also worth stating that locally and according to family members, brother Charlie was meant to be the most talented of the three brothers.

The Motherwell Times also had its own postscript to the victory. 'The County Lanarkshire can be proud of its part in Saturday's international victory at Hampden Park. There were five county men in the team, and one of them Delaney, from Cleland, scored the winning goal. The other four did very well too: Waddell (who comes from Forth, and started his football career with Forth Wanderers) and the three Annathill stalwarts, Jock and David Shaw, and Frank Brennan.

'The Annathill lads made football history. I believe it was the first time that the Scottish defensive line had been recruited from one village. The size of Annathill a pocket village, makes this all the more remarkable. They came off the field a very happy trio, with Brennan between the two Shaws, his arms round their shoulders. And they had something to be happy about. It isn't every day that three local boys so spectacularly make good. By the way, Annathill is sometimes called Bedlay. It lies down Glenboig way. But I still shudder for the man who said to me, with a chuckle "They didn't do so Bedlay, at that." Football Village There must be something in the atmosphere of Annathill that inspires football skill.'

Later in the week as a memento and to mark the occasion, Frank Brennan, Jock Shaw and David Shaw were very pleased to be informed that the members of the Scottish team had been allowed to keep their International jerseys.

There may have actually been more than three boys from Annathill on the Hampden turf that great day as according to local folklore there was a fourth Annathill man, as Button Cairns played in the pipe band.

I make no apology for devoting so much detail to this match as while researching the book I confess I was unaware of the back story. It's quite remarkable that a village, which back then was inhabited by around 1,500 people, produced such a high level of footballing talent. Often when I am running, I take a route through Annathill. The village has changed beyond recognition as you might expect. The Miners' Row of houses is long gone, replaced by a typical modern housing estate. It numbers less than 400 residents now. That this village produced two captains of Scotland and the Scottish defence is a quite remarkable story.

Football talent emerging from the small villages of Glenboig and Annathill into the professional games was disproportionate in all probability to the size of the villages and here are but a few of the names I came across during the course of my research: David Arbuckle (Queen's Park), John Bennett (Third Lanark), Francis Burns (Manchester United), Willie Fowler (Motherwell), James Gray (Celtic), Drew Jarvie (Aberdeen), Bertie Kelly (Third Lanark), Johnnie McCann (Hibs), John McNeil (Albion Rovers), William Morrison (Queen of the South), Joe Reilly (Celtic), Johnnie Veitch (Celtic).

With apologies to anyone I have omitted, as it's not meant to be an exhaustive list, but that is quite an impressive array of talent when you add the Shaw brothers, Frank Brennan and Bobby Flavell.

A few months later and Scotland were on the road to Manchester on Saturday, 24 August 1946 to play the Auld Enemy at Maine Road in a match to raise funds for the Burnden Park disaster. At Burnden Park, Bolton on 9 March, 33 supporters were killed and over 400 injured after crushing in the crowd during a sixth-round FA Cup tie against Stoke City. The disaster brought about the Moelwyn Hughes report, which recommended more rigorous control of crowd sizes. The disaster was the worst in the UK until, sadly, 2 January 1971.

Although labelled an unofficial international as the last of its type prior to the launch of the official status once more, it was still serious stuff, with 22 players staking claim to further honours, so it was unofficial in name only. When blue shirts clash with white, how can there be any other outcome?

Despite four goals, it was reported as being a very drab affair, that drabness being relieved only by the displays of the opposing right-wingers, Matthews and Waddell. These two brought the only thrills into the play and although neither were scorers themselves, they were each prominently associated with the work leading up to the goals. Unfortunately for Jock, in the first half it was Matthews who provided the entertainment and in the second it was Waddell. Right from the start, Matthews completely mesmerised Jock with his trickery. Despite getting a bit of a roasting, Jock never once resorted to foul play. England's first goal came during the period when they looked as if they could have scored when they liked. Matthews made the opening for Welsh to give Miller no chance from close in.

Matthews, though, thankfully did fade in the second half and Jock was able to shackle him much more effectively. Jackie Husband, who had been deployed to assist Jock dealing with Matthews, was then released to have a more positive influence on proceedings. To the vociferous delight of the hundreds of tartan-bedecked Scots who had made the journey south, Waddell was brought more into the play and he demonstrated that his power of penetration, if perhaps less artistic than Matthews's, was every bit as effective. His strong running and feinting and his ready shot revealed him as the danger man of the Scottish front line. His close co-operation with Thornton was Scotland's salvation, for in the last five minutes the winger made the opening before laying on the most perfect of passes for the equalising goal by the centre-forward. Play never rose to any great heights of brilliance and as a matter of fact at times it was decidedly poor. Both teams were said to have had a number of weaknesses, England more so than Scotland, but on the day on the balance of play Scotland should have won, and by a considerable margin. The Annathill defence was once more on show and while the first period had been decidedly difficult for all concerned, Jock takes full credit for the way he played Matthews, keeping his head where many others would have lost theirs. David Shaw also improved as things went on. Frank Brennan was not quite his Hampden self.

The third meeting within a year against England was the Wembley trip in April 1947, and after the two most recent meetings Scotland were supremely confident.

As they set off by train from Central Station in Glasgow for London, other than a bit of excitement over the late arrival of SFA president, Provost David Gray (Airdrie), who caught the train with only a few minutes to spare, the advance guard of the SFA party left in high spirits. There were only a few well-wishers, the majority of them young autograph hunters, who were present to see off the home Scots players – Shaw, Young and Woodburn (Rangers), Steel (Morton), Miller (Celtic) and Smith (Hibs); the travelling reserves were Thornton (Rangers) and Husband (Partick Thistle). The party would be joined in London by the Anglo Scots. Also present were SFA secretary George Graham, Councillor Bob McKinnon (St Johnstone) and trainer Hugh Shaw (Hibs). All the party were quietly confident of success. Captain Jock summed up the thoughts of the boys, saying they all knew the size of the job on hand but that would make them all the keener to go out and win. 'And we have the spirit to bring back a victory,' he added. While the main party gathered at the entrance to the platform, Gordon Smith slipped up alone and on to the train.

This was to be Jock's finest match in a Scotland jersey and he was roundly proclaimed man of the match.

It was a proud Tiger who led his team out at Wembley. Pre-match the players were introduced to Prime Minister Clement Attlee – not bad for a wee boy from Annathill.

Jock clapped his hands, spurred on his lads to inspire them to overcome the disappointment of the bizarre failure to award a spot-kick after clear handball by debutant Billy Wright. The defence was watertight to the extent that Tommy Lawton must have been thinking he would have been as well slipping away to play for Chelsea. The wing-halves were probing and pushing forward and with a little more composure from the forwards Scotland could have had several goals. Willie Miller in goal had a comfortable Wembley baptism; cool and confident he was very much more impressive than his counterpart Frank Swift. George Young didn't put a foot wrong despite being up against Jimmy Mullen, England's slickest forward on the day.

Jock, well he had the game of his life. 'I'll show them,' he seemed to say. He had Matthews in his pocket. One wag recalled that for every time Jock was chasing Stan, there were nine times Stan was chasing Jock. The Ranger was just simply outstanding.

'Scotland's best team since the Wembley Wizards,' declared Provost John Lamb, of Arbroath, the SFA vice-president. He went on, 'It has lifted Scotland from the depth of depression to great triumph. Every player was above criticism.'

A tartan-bedecked fan from Perth was wandering in the Underground at midnight and advised: 'We've had a good day, we've seen a good game, Scotland has a good team, and so, pal, we're all happy,' was how he was feeling. The game may not have gone down in the history book as the 'Tam and Tartan' international but never before had London seen as many tartan and kilted people. One wag commented that it could be called 'The Red Heads' international', to honour the display of Forbes and Macaulay. Dynamic Jimmy Delaney (scorer of the Hampden winner a year previous) jumped right into the picture from the start of the game. He was all-action. In the first minutes he cut through the defence, but Swift nipped the ball from his toe. Then he screwed a shot outside the post. England's response saw a cross from Pearson hit the side net. A smart touchline move by Gordon Smith brought a corner. A lovely cross into the box and Delaney sent the ball screaming just past the post. All this in the opening five minutes. England's defence was reeling, and Scotland might well have been three goals up.

The tartan bonnets of the spectators were certainly up in the air. Scotland kept moving up field with precision passing and in 15 minutes the reward came. A ground pass from Shaw to Delaney. A neat interchange of positions between the centre and McLaren, and the inside-right cracked the ball well and true past Swift.

Scotland's tower of strength was now apparent. The foundations lay in the half-back line of Macaulay, Woodburn and Forbes, who were magnificent. They were all stronger in the tackle than the Englishmen, and were sending their forwards away with perfect passing. The way Macaulay was bringing down high balls with his feet, and even first time placing such balls, was masterly.

Stanley Matthews stood 20 minutes on the line without touching the ball. The first time he got it, Jock was on him, and after a thrilling tackle, robbed him, which gave Jock the confidence required, and he never allowed the Stoke wizard to work his spell. He had learnt his lessons from the August clash and ensured there would be no repeat – the sign of the consummate professional.

So closely in turn did the Scottish wing-halves mark Carter and Mannion that they seldom got a pass through to Lawton, and when he did get the ball, Woodburn dealt with him comfortably.

It was not until ten minutes into the second half that England were able to show anything like their expected form, and for the first time Scotland's defence was put into some discomfort, and Raich Carter scored to equalise.

Gordon Smith was getting over some fine crosses, but it was not until the latter part of the game that he saw much of the ball. One feature of the clash was the manner in which all four wingers were being kept out of the game.

M. De la Salle, the French referee, had a good game, though England appeared to benefit from any breaks that were going. For example, he awarded a foul against McLaren when the ball struck the player's hand. A minute later, the ball played Scott in the same way inside the penalty box, and there were loud cries for a penalty, but the referee ignored the appeals.

The Frenchman's ultimate misjudgement nearly cost Scotland the match. Carter got the ball in an offside position and stopped, knowing he was offside. The Scottish defence stopped, too, the linesman waved his flag, but the referee waved Carter on. He went on, and with a little care should have scored, but Miller came out to smother the shot, and all with only eight minutes to go.

Scotland had played well and the team played studied, expansive football. They had more than two-thirds of the play, and even Englishmen confessed they were lucky.

So that was three games where Jock had captained his country against the Auld Enemy and emerged undefeated: not many could claim that distinction. His performance in 1947 was particularly impressive and one English scribe was heard to comment, 'And most breathtaking of all was Tiger Shaw cutting the telephone line between Matthews and his men. Never in all my experience of Matthews have I seen him so helpless.' Other testimonials included, 'Gimme the tools he seemed to be stating, but it was the Tiger who finished the job', and finally, 'Shaw was an inspiration. Whenever the ball showed out, he pounced on it. Never has he played a better game in his life. If ever there was a way to stop Matthews, this was it.'

Willie Woodburn also played in the game and speaking in 1982 said, 'Jock Shaw was our skipper that day and it was a tremendous feeling just to walk down behind him in the tunnel, and hear the roar of the fans.'

Speaking of the two England games in 1946 and 1947, Jock recalled, 'The first game in 1946 was a Victory International to mark the end of the war, and the match really fired the public's imagination.

'There were about 140,000 at the game at Hampden and England had all their big guns out – Britton, Cutlass, Matthews and Finney. As they were in the team, the English elite of the day, the press just didn't give Scotland a chance. We were written off by the fans too but that didn't stop them turning up, and they saw a fair bit of a game too.'

Jimmy Delaney was the man who got the only goal, netting from close range, but Jock recalls it was his team-mate Willie Waddell who was the architect. 'He got the ball out on the right wing and held it a bit, inviting the English players to come and tackle him. They duly came and he dribbled past them and managed to get to the touchline. His cross was perfect for Delaney to knock home.'

Jock also recalled that this was the first time Scotland had been taken to the seaside to prepare for a match. 'We were taken to Loch Awe for a couple of days. It was a good break for us because we had never done it before and it set us up nicely for the big game.'

The following year the selectors took the players down to Reading to prepare for the bi-annual clash against the Auld Enemy at Wembley and once again Scotland were not given a hope.

'Well England had their big stars out again and I suppose it was only natural,' Jock said. 'Stan Mortensen played, so did Tommy Lawton and Wilf Mannion, and I distinctly remember they had a boy making his England debut, Billy Wright of Wolves.'

Jock also played against England when he received one of his two Scottish League caps, in 1938.

'I was still with Airdrie at the time, in fact it was just before I signed for Rangers. The game was at Goodison Park and was a Scottish League v English League fixture but we lost 0-2.'

Speaking more about his international experiences, he went on to recall, 'Delaney, Matthews, Finney – all great players with different styles. Jimmy Delaney, you know, always tried to beat you on the outside, Gordon Smith inside. It was up to you to figure out how to play them. Many was the time I remember chasing Gordon Smith right across the park from touchline to touchline simply to stop him getting inside me. Of the English wingers I reckon that Finney was the better of the two. Sure, Matthews was a wonderful ball-player but Finney was more direct and he had two great feet.'

The winger who caused him most trouble, though, was none of those mentioned so far. He gives that credit to Johnny Crum of Celtic. Interestingly, during the war Crum worked alongside Willie Woodburn and Jimmy Smith so the build-up to Old Firm games was very, very interesting. Crum used to do nothing but wind Woodburn up and it would really impact him. Smith would try and calm him down, and it would normally work with only one exception when Woodburn gave away two penalties in one match due to fouls on Crum.

'He didn't always play on the wing,' said Jock, 'but when he did, he was a good player. I think he more than any other gave me the most bother.'

Jock, though, loved the Old Firm games. 'I don't know whether it was the atmosphere or what but I enjoyed these Old Firm games more than any other.'

His record against Celtic illustrates why he loved those games so much. In all competitions, he played 51 times in Old Firm clashes, winning 36, drawing six, and only losing nine.

In May 1947 Scotland embarked on an end-of-season European trip to play Belgium and Luxembourg. The official party were suitably kitted out in smart official dress. This included a new international tie which raised the standards and professionalism off the park. There was, though, time for relaxation in the evening after a long season. The players always prefered golf to track work for training, and the Friday was the big tournament day on the putting green before the Luxembourg course. Tommy Pearson, who was a scratch golfer, was an easy winner. There was talk of Pearson being lost to football the following season. The Newcastle United outside-left advised reporters that he was considering a very attractive offer to become a full-time golf professional, but it must be full-time. Interestingly, Pearson played for England against Scotland as a guest player during the war.

Alex Forbes (then of Sheffield United) had just taken up the game of golf, and had been getting lessons from Arthur Lees, a member of the British Ryder Cup team. The lessons were clearly paying off, as on the first hole he secured a hole in one. There was some ribbing going on, of course, 'Where were Rangers and Hibs when the prizes were being dished out?' Well, they were represented but were probably best to stick to football. Jock and brother David shared the booby prize. 'There's something queer about a game,' said Jock, 'where you've got to score as few as you can to win.'

The train journey from Belgium to Luxembourg, through the famous forest of Ardennes, was rather tedious, if picturesque. The train had to slow down constantly to cross the many bridges on the route. At every stop poor Billy Steel, who had travelled on the journey with the 21st Army Group, got the blame for blowing up all the bridges. According to this Scottish team, every piece of destruction in Europe was accomplished by Billy in his soldiering days.

Jock couldn't resist the sight of a pair of real old-fashioned 100 per cent elastic braces in a shop window. In a twinkling he had made the purchase and donned the braces, considering himself to be quite gallus. Then to demonstrate their efficiency George Young stuck in his thumb, pulled them well out and let them smack back – ouch! Jock looked as if he had been on the receiving end of a Jackie Paterson body blow.

In Luxembourg the players found it a rather strange experience as they got the impression of being transported into the world of an old-fashioned fairy-tale picture book. The stadium was a different matter altogether and some commentators noted it as beautiful and awe-inspiring. It was owned by the corporation of the town, and had a beautiful, compact small-scale enclosure, set amidst gorgeous scenery. It was like a miniature copy of the Yankee baseball stadium. The terracing was all seating and the spectators sat in sports shirts, flannels and straw hats to watch the play. Sadly, the weather in Scotland was more suited to heavy coats and flat caps. Outside the stadium was a statue of one of their most famous players, and it was lamented that someday at home we would put one of our sporting heroes on the same pedestal as we did our poets and generals.

The trip also saw the formation of the Scottish band in Luxembourg, the home of the mouth organ: Jackie Husband, Jock and secretary George Graham were now harmonising on harmonicas!

Trainer Hugh Shaw suggested the players were being overfed, so one course was cut from every meal. The players were not particularly perturbed at this development. The trip ended with a comfortable 6-0 victory over Luxembourg, and all in all the short trip had been a great success.

Jock took his duties as captain at both club and international level very seriously and was accustomed to high standards of professionalism on and off the field. At this time, those standards were not universally embraced within the international set-up: there was no team manager, and he had to make representations on behalf of the players during a trip to Belfast to play Northern Ireland in February 1946. Jock persuaded the SFA to alter the trip itinerary to allow the players to do additional training before embarking on a long sightseeing bus trip. Jock's point was many players had already travelled long distances to meet up with the squad, such as Paterson and Chisholm who had been on the road for three days. Some training and loosening up was essential before any further long bus trips. Thankfully common sense prevailed and the trip was put back to enable the players to do some training at Windsor Park after breakfast. Scotland would go on to win 3-2.

Even after his international career was over, Jock was still having some influence and setting standards. For the 1949 clash at Wembley the challenge was set for Sammy Cox who would fill the left-back berth. John Lamb (Arbroath) SFA vice-president, said, 'We have a good fighting team, and that means we have a good fighting chance. At the last Wembley game, the success in achieving the draw was largely down to the outstanding play of Jock Shaw and Alex Forbes on the left flank, when they kept a firm grip of Matthews, and Scotland surprised everyone by drawing with the all-conquering English side. Today the job is handed to Sammy Cox (ex-Dundee and Rangers) and George Aitken (East Fife), and they have only to play to their team form to make a Scottish victory possible.' Succeed they did, with the Scots running out emphatic winners by 3-1.

Life on the international stage was a bit of an adventure post-war and, of course, there was no team manager, with the team being selected by committee. Jock's namesake, Hugh Shaw, was trainer to Scotland's international teams and was a quiet, mild-mannered individual. Yet, when he gave a simple team-shape-altering message to Gordon Smith during an international against Belgium at Hampden, he almost started a football war. All sorts of stories have developed out of the incident. Stories of authority flouted, of players ignoring orders, of Jimmy Delaney refusing to switch positions. So, what prompted this chain of events?

With about seven minutes to go, George Graham saw, as everyone saw, that a forward switch might have helped get the team back into the game. The SFA secretary told trainer Shaw to pass on the message that Smith and Delaney should change places. The trainer went out on to the track, Gordon Smith, the nearest player, was summoned to him and told, 'Pass it on that you have to change places with Delaney.' Note well the words 'Pass it on'. Gordon, of course, went straight to Delaney with the information. The reply he got from the Celt was, 'I want to hear that from my captain.' Had the message reached Jock Shaw, all would have been well. Celtic's Delaney was quite insistent though in waiting for instructions from captain Tiger. Just think how Shaw would have felt had he seen two of his forwards making a change, and he, as the captain, knew nothing about it.

Hats off to Delaney for giving due respect to Tiger and his role. Who would have known best: an SFA committee man, or the captain of Rangers and Scotland? As was also the case back then, the players ran the game, facilitated by the captain, and it was a sign of the amateurish set-up where councillors were suddenly making tactical adjustment. So, there you are, everything hinged on Gordon Smith's interpretation of trainer Shaw's 'Pass it on' message. The player concerned did only what he thought right during the heat of the game but really should have gone to Tiger in the first instance, and not Delaney. In the circumstances his actions implied endorsement of the ill-thought-out tactical change. A case of a simple misunderstanding but resulting in mayhem.

After the match there was an article in *The Sunday Post* about the role of the captain.

> What exactly are the duties of a football captain? Each club has its own ideas, but I think all will agree with Dave McLean, Hearts' manager. When he signed Bobby Baxter and made him team captain, Mr McLean told me 'a good captain is worth a two-goal start'. In my opinion a team captain should make any move on the field which he thinks is for the benefit of a team. At the same time, I also think that if an instruction comes on to the captain from his manager, he should accede immediately to the request. After all, the manager is the one who answers to the directors for the team's results Still, I know of clubs who consider their captain's only job is to toss up before the start. And I'm still looking for the day when

I'll see captain win the toss then suddenly turn around for a consultation to see which way he'll kick.

Lessons were learned on Wednesday. One of the most important points was that a few words pre-match about in-play etiquette would not be amiss to some of our players. Little things happened which must have looked particularly bad to our visitors. I'm thinking now of Delaney invariably showing disgust at the referee's decisions. But Jim wasn't the worst offender. We had young Walker, when, finding a throw-in was against us, deliberately throwing the ball away from an opponent so he could take his position. If Walker had manfully handed the Belgian the ball, he'd probably have found this gentleman waiting till he took up his stance before making the throw-in. Just don't look for actions like these in British jerseys. Players must have it knocked into them that they are not only representing just Scottish football. They are representing land. There's no point in sinking to those levels.

Reading this passage makes you yearn for the days when gamesmanship wasn't so embedded as it is in the modern game.

Tiger was to make a further appearance for the Scottish League in a clash with the Irish League in April 1947. To say it was an eventful 90 minutes was something of an understatement. Star of the show was to be another Annathill pal, Bobby Flavell.

Once again, an Irish team had been declared one of the weakest to have represented the Old Country, and considered wisdom pre-match was that they would have been much improved from recent showings. Ralph the Rover of the *Belfast Telegraph* described the action:

The Irish League team although beaten 7-4 at Windsor Park on Wednesday by an admittedly clever Scottish League XI, carried off the honours up to a stage. When captain Jock Shaw won the toss for Scotland and set the Irish boys to face a gale, blowing from the mountain end, most pressmen prepared themselves for a cricket score, and a conservative guess was about a 6-0 half-time lead.

The score was six right enough, but equally divided. The gale actually proved a disadvantage, and the Irish boys had decidedly better control of the ball against it. Inside a minute Flavell, the Scots centre-forward, gave an indication of what was to follow later, when from a throw-in he took the ball on the fly and drove a fiercely hit shot over the bar. For 20 minutes it was mainly a Scots attack but when Campbell was sent through to open the Irish score the crowd were on their toes immediately, and from then till that last 15 minutes, when the three Scottish inside-forwards ran riot, the game was a series of thrills.

Almost unbelievably the Irish boys went further ahead when Feeney beat Miller, after clever work by Denvir. Flavell got two for the Scots to level matters. There then followed a further exchange of goals – another by Campbell for the Irish League, and then Flavell made it three each at the interval.

Upon resumption it was the Scots who took the lead with Billy Steel the scorer. Then there followed a grand piece of work by Feeney to make it four-all within ten minutes and it was hammer and tongs and the crowd were on their feet. That was until Gillick surprised Smyth with a 25-yard drive, and that was followed by three further strikes by Flavell, one from a penalty in the closing 15 minutes, and gave the Scots a rather flattering three-goal winning margin.

There were only two failures on the Irish side. Molloy had no reply to the thrusts of the Scots inside-forwards, particularly Gillick, who helped Flavell to several of the centre-forward's five goals. Brennan opened auspiciously but faded out completely in the second half. Denvir was the equal to Gillick in the Scottish line, and shared with him the honours of the most dangerous players on the field. McHorren gave Woodburn a tough evening's work, Feeney held his own with Hewitt, and had Brennan supported him in the second half, would have been more dangerous. The defence, with the exception of Molloy, stood up staunchly to a clever forceful attack, but training and patience told in the closing minutes, however the honours go to a team that were not rated to have even a sporting chance. Miller, the Scots goalie, had a nervous and unhappy evening, and might have saved two of the goals.

Not a bad evening's work for Flavell, in fact a record-breaking night with his five goals and I am not aware of any other Scottish representative who scored as many in a single match.

Life after Playing

AFTER HANGING up his boots, Jock initially joined the staff on a part-time basis as a scout for the Lanarkshire area.

By this time, he had taken ownership of a newsagent business in Glenboig on the main street and also a confectionery shop in the Oval. The newsagents was attached to the family home.

The transition could not have been easy, having spent 22 years as a professional sportsman and 14 of those at his beloved Ibrox. However, after spending 12 months working in his paper shop Rangers had another offer for him, this time to join the ground staff and help to maintain his beloved Ibrox turf.

The first August after leaving Rangers it was reported in *The Sunday Post* that, 'One can be lonely in a crowd even in a group of pals. Jock Shaw, the Tiger of Ibrox, poignantly realised that yesterday. Jock was at the Rangers' ground when the players carried through their training under the eyes and cameras of assorted pressmen. But, for the first time in 22 years, he was on the sidelines watching.

'He stood there looking fit-though-40 in his outdoor clothing while Rangers players did their lapping, exercises and ball practice. "You should do well in that jersey," he cracked to Johnny Little as the young full-back passed him wearing the numbered training sweater that used to be Jock's. Jock has no complaints about the years outstripping him. "I've had a good innings – 22 years," he says. But it must have been a wrench for him to be standing idle. At these sessions down the years, one has always been able to pick out The

Tiger as the keenest of all in a pre-season workout, but he would now arrange to have Saturday afternoons off. "I may find myself doing a bit of scouting," said Jock. Of course, there is no need to ask for which club he'll seek talent.

'He is such a keen Ranger that I wouldn't doubt he has blue blood in his veins.'

In December 1954 it was reported that there would be two Tigers at Ibrox for the Rangers v Rapid Vienna game. One would be playing, the other growling from the sidelines. Walter Zeman, the Austrian goalkeeper, is an almost legendary hero with his countrymen, who affectionately called him the Tiger, but they took the copyright from Ibrox, where two generations of Rangers' fans knew only one Tiger, the one who used to stalk wingers then pounce.

In April of 1955 Jock Shaw lost his motor car when it went up in flames. He had been carrying out some repairs at the rear of his house on Main Street, Glenboig, and left the car for a few minutes to go in and listen to his former colleague, George Young, speaking on the wireless. Minutes later a neighbour shouted that his car was on fire. When Coatbridge Fire Brigade arrived at the scene the car, an Austin saloon, was almost a total wreck.

Jock could not kick the football habit and at the end of May 1955 he was taking part in an Old Crocks match to show the younger generation how it should be done. Fans flocked to Broomfield, Airdrie's ground, to see Celtic veterans from pre-war putting the clock back 17 years. The old hands took down their boots to see if they could teach the younger generation how the game used to be played. Many of the Celtic team that won the famous 1938 Exhibition Cup were in a side called Lanarkshire Old Crocks. The Crocks included stars like Torry Gillick (Rangers) and Tommy Brady (Hibs and Aberdeen), as well as Jock. At outside-left was the Scottish Players' Union secretary Johnny Hughes, formerly of Third Lanark and Morton. In the Exhibition team were famous former Celts like Malky MacDonald (now manager of Kilmarnock), George Paterson, John

Divers and Bobby Hogg. Two famous veterans acting as linesmen were Partick Thistle's Jimmy McGowan and Tommy Kiernan, formerly with Celtic and Albion Rovers. The game caused such interest with Celtic fans that a football special train ran from Glasgow.

On the subject of our friends from the East End Jock was held in very high esteem. It was interesting to note a passage I came across in Celtic's match programme for the game against Motherwell on 17 March 1992. It was reviewing an old match against Airdrie and recalled Jock as the 'most renowned left back in Scotland who barely game Delaney a kick'. It then went on to describe a Celtic Supporters Rally in the 1950's where Tiger was rather surprisingly the guest of honour. 'To the Celtic support's credit he was given a standing ovation when introduced and Willie Maley presented him with Celtic scarf subsequently formed part of the exhibition in the Peoples Palace celebrating Celtic's Centenary in 1988. Oh how times have changed.'

Baillieston

IN SEPTEMBER 1955 it was announced that Tiger Shaw had been appointed coach at Baillieston Juniors, which was only a short six-mile car journey from his home. It was a move which was welcomed from all quarters, and the Baillieston support hoped that Jock would be able to instil a little bit of the Ibrox 'Iron Curtain' policy into their defence, for it had been leaking goals at an alarming average of about two per game.

Davie Wilson, speaking of his emergence in the Rangers team, talked fondly of Jock, and the role he played in his development at Baillieston. 'When I arrived at Ibrox in 1956 I could hardly believe that all I had dreamed about had come true, that I was a member of this wonderful club. I was 14 when given a trial by the club on the strength of my promising displays for my school team. I was then loaned to Baillieston Juniors, and it was with them that I linked up with that staunch fellow Jock Shaw, among the most loyal and steadfast players Rangers ever signed. There is no truer blue fan than Jock.'

In Alistair Aird's excellent book on Davie Wilson, Wilson recalled the insight and wisdom Tiger was able to impart while he was the coach at Baillieston and Davie was setting out on his fledgling career path. 'Jock was part of the coaching team at Baillieston and for a young lad like me working with someone like him was fantastic and Jock can take credit for turning me into a winger. He suggested watching the full-back I was against and looking out for what foot they favoured. He advised that I should take them on the opposite side, and I beat many a full-back in my time as a result of that guidance.'

The Thirds' Coach

TOWARDS THE end of the 1950s Rangers decided to set up a third team to play in the Combination Reserve League and the chosen man to lead the team was Tiger. The date this happened is a little unclear and the club has retained nothing in its records to verify the position, and the first reference to Tiger that could be traced was in the *Daily Express* of October 1958.

However, from what information is available about the Combined Reserve League in which the Thirds participated, it seems to have been set up following the abolition of C Division, and the subsequent formation of the Scottish (Reserve) League. The lower league clubs had no competition for their reserve sides to play in. A Scottish Alliance was played during 1956/57 but it wasn't popular and disbanded. However, a meeting in Glasgow on 3 July 1958 saw the formation of the Combined Reserve League for Second Division reserve sides, as well as the youth sides of Celtic, and later Rangers and Heart of Midlothian.

The meeting was organised by Morton chairman J.S. Thomson who became the chairman of the new league, John Hosie (Dumbarton) was elected treasurer. Robert Kelly of Celtic agreed to represent the league in view of any matters that the SFL and SFA might be concerned about. Called colloquially the 'wee' league, it kicked off on 20 September 1958. Because of the small number of clubs involved, the league was normally played over an autumn and spring series with a flag being awarded to the winners.

A fixture list was arranged for the first part of the season and the games on the opening day were Morton v Celtic, Albion Rovers v Ayr United and Queen's Park v Dumbarton. The matches ran up until 22 November, with two 'wind up' games on 6 and 29 December.

Another aspect of the league's membership was the frequent inclusion of some non-league clubs. One of these was Clydebank. Formed in 1966 from the ashes of the ES Clydebank merger, they would go on and obtain full Scottish League status, reaching the Premier Division, before being bought out in 2002 and moved to Airdrie as Airdrie United.

From the records that are available, Rangers appear to have joined in 1963, and remained till 1969/70. Success was not the principal purpose for Rangers, player development being the priority. In terms of performance, the most successful years were finishing runners-up in 1968/69 and finally winning the flag in 1969/70.

Although the league disbanded in 1972, the Scottish League used the name for its competitions for minor reserve sides. Rangers' third team ceased around the same time.

During Tiger's involvement he had some future Rangers legends in his charge and helped develop the careers of many future stars including Sandy Jardine, John Greig, Colin Jackson, Jim Forest, Willie Mathieson, Alex Miller, Davie Wilson, Alex Willoughby and Willie Henderson.

The extent of the role has over time become a little ambiguous and it's arguable that there was day-to-day involvement from Tiger. Speaking to journalist/author David Leggat it's clear this was very likely a part-time role, taken in tandem with his job on the ground staff. The obvious parallel was with Bob McPhail, who for many years looked after the reserve side and combined this with running his very successful electrical business on the Broomielaw. There is every likelihood this was how Jock's role was carried out. To add a little more credence to this view, the pre-season full playing staff picture included neither Tiger nor Bob McPhail.

It's also interesting that when Scot Symon was appointed manager, those in charge of all the teams were Struth men. This was no accident as the continuity helped continue the standards and expectations from the Struth era and those in charge of the club recognised the merits in using this approach.

Bob McPhail was brought in around 1948 by Mr Struth to look after the reserve team in order to pass on to these emerging talents the requirements and standards expected of a Ranger. It is apparent that McPhail along with Scot Symon played an instrumental role in bringing Jock back to fulfil the role of overseeing the third team. It was really a very early version of something akin to Liverpool's famous Boot Room ethos. There was a thread flowing from Struth to McPhail to Jock. Jock's job was to educate the fledgling players on the standards and discipline expected of a Rangers player, and in turn pass out any tips he could. Standards such as shirt tucked in, socks held up with the appropriate amount of red visible on the socks and boots shined immaculately. There would then follow a debriefing with manager Scot Symon and later Davie White on the Monday/Tuesday following the weekend's match.

The team was invariably picked by the manager, though Jock would have offered his views naturally enough, as he was seeing the players perform in the flesh. These were in the days long before clubs employed video analysts.

David Leggat recalls as a very fresh-faced young pup of a journalist being sent on his first assignment to report on a Rangers third-team match against Jordanhill College in season 1966/67. He was being shown the ropes by highly respected reporter Gair Henderson and was instructed to get the team line-up from 'Mr Shaw'. A nervous David entered the away-team dressing room while the players were getting changed, and things were organised so informally then that Jock had to write the Rangers team down in the young reporter's notepad.

Players in action that day who got some first-team experience, albeit very limited, were Kenny McFarlane and Derek Traill.

Over the years Tiger's tips, so to speak, helped many a young player who was tentatively making their way in the game. These players included a very young Craig Brown, who joined Rangers in 1958, and he was quoted as saying, 'Jock was in charge of the third team when I signed for Rangers and spent a short time at the club. He was someone to look up to, someone you gave instant respect to. I know how much he helped me as a young player and I always appreciated that.'

John Greig also said, 'He would give me runs to the station and I'd look at him and it made me ponder. He used to be the captain of Rangers. I wondered if I could ever be like him?' He could not have picked a better role model.

Willie Mathieson (one of the legendary Barca Bears), who joined the club in the summer of 1962, recalled one of his first experiences. 'Scot Symon always had the idea on the first day back to play a mixture of the first team and second team against a mixture of the second team and the new boys. It was his way of seeing just how the new lads would shape up and react. I was up against Craig Watson who was on the fringe of being a first-teamer, and who had actually played in the first team. Craig was a real flier of a winger and the first time he came down the wing he went speeding past me. It was a hot sunny day and there was an old grey-haired man at the side of the pitch with shorts on, and he asked what my position was. I told him I was a left-back and he said the next time Craig came at me I was to go and clatter him.

'I did just that and Mr Symon was very angry about things. The old man told me to do it again and that's exactly what I did. This time Mr Symon gave me a real shouting at but the old man was still there, and said I should do the same again. I wasn't too sure but decided to go in hard again. The third time Craig came at me my tackle was perfectly timed and I came out with the ball.'

It was only later Willie discovered the old man was Jock. 'He shouted then that I'd do for him, and it was only after the game that I found out who he was. From then on he was my mentor and in fact was like a father to me as I developed.'

There was no fast-tracking into the first team packed with stars like Jim Baxter, Willie Henderson, Ralph Brand and so on. Willie recalled, 'I was lucky that old Jock Shaw took such good care of me and that when I went into the reserves Bob McPhail looked after things and taught me an awful lot too.'

A personal favourite of Tiger's, though, was Alex Willoughby. This would be a bond which would last a lifetime and they became and remained close all their days. While researching this book I saw countless pictures of social occasions, functions and parties in Tiger's home where Alex and his wife shared many happy times with the Shaw family. Even when Alex was in Hong Kong they kept in touch and he would post pictures of his children as they were growing up to let Tiger see how they were doing. It was completely fitting that Alex should read the eulogy at Tiger's funeral in 2000.

Alex recalled his introduction to Rangers, joining as he did along with his cousin Jim Forrest and Willie Henderson as the club's first-ever ground-staff signings. 'There were 32 clubs from all over Britain chasing me but it was never a contest. It was Ibrox for me even though it did mean having to polish the boots of the first-team stars. I arrived at the stadium in the summer of 1960, reporting for training for the first time on the same day as Jim Baxter. I was the Scottish Schoolboy signing and he was the big-money signing.

'The first mistake I made was hanging my clothes on Eric Caldow's peg. I was the new boy and there he was the captain of Rangers and Scotland. He was very polite about it and asked me to move my gear along. They were a tremendous bunch who knew how to get down to work and who were just as dedicated when it came to going out and having fun. I don't think it is just nostalgia but there was a closeness about that team. They looked after us kids. Folk like Jimmy Millar made sure you weren't messed about, as did Harold Davis.'

A usual day for the ground maintenance staff back in the day started at 8.30am and the boys would help Dave Marshall and Jock tend to the pitch before training. Alex fondly recalled, 'After lunch we went back to our duties until 4.30pm, and between us we had to clean about 100 pairs of boots. But there were advantages too. We also had to help sweep the terraces, and pile the rubbish into a corner and burn it. In those days, crowds of 80,000–90,000 were not uncommon, and neither were the beer bottles. After every match we had to stack them up and crate them, then the cleansing department came and took them away. But there was always a deposit given on returned bottles so that gave us a wee bung which went into a kitty for all the staff behind the scenes to have a night out at Christmas.

'These were great times but the work was hard. I used to get the number 55 bus from the top of Copland Road home to Springburn, and I was always fast asleep by the time it reached Paisley Road Toll.'

While reminiscing about his playing career Alex recalled returning to the stadium after returning to Glasgow from a period overseas – the last stop of which was a spell managing in Iceland for KA Akureyri, where he took them from the Third to the First Division in three seasons – to work as bar manager in the Rangers Supporters' Association Social Club. 'It is really wonderful to be back in Glasgow and even better to be working so close to Ibrox. On matchdays people like Jock Shaw and Eric Caldow drop in before they go to the games.'

Another player coming under the Tiger influence was a young Bobby Watson who signed for Rangers in 1964 from Airdrie schools football. 'I first went to Ibrox as a 15-year-old from Airdrie Academy. At that time Lanarkshire was quite an area for producing footballers as I'm sure it still is today.

'It was a marvellous education particularly in the travelling sense. I used to go into training on Tuesday and Thursday nights with Ian McMillan, who also lived in Airdrie. I was a part-timer in those days actually along with Jim Baxter who was in the army at the time. The coach then was Jock Shaw and he was a marvellous character. It was like missionary work in the third team travelling to places like Cumnock and Dunoon.'

Sandy Jardine, another Rangers grade-A legend, recalled being called up to the Rangers third team in 1965, when he was 16. 'After a year on the ground staff, I'll never forget my first appearance in a light blue jersey. It only came after I had staged my own low budget version of "The Great Escape". The match was a pre-season friendly in Millport. The lads had travelled over by boat with Jock Shaw in charge of the side. Luckily for me the manager decided to pick me. I was to make my first appearance in a twin centre-half role. It wasn't exactly the most auspicious or glamorous surroundings in which to make your Rangers debut. The changing facilities were in a school pavilion and made the term 'spartan' seem like a compliment. Even so, I was a bit nervous about my first game for the club and I had to pay a visit to the toilet before the match started. To my horror, I discovered that the rest of the team had trotted out for the kick-off and the groundsman had locked up, leaving me imprisoned in the bathroom. For five minutes I was left to make frantic calls for help that seemed to fall on deaf ears. I also tried in vain to bang the door down. Eventually I made enough of a racket to attract the attention of the groundsman to come and let me back out. If I had been an actor, it would have been the equivalent of forgetting my lines on my stage debut. Although I can look back and laugh about the incident now, at the time the whole episode had a nightmarish quality about it. I remember all too vividly breaking out in a cold sweat and rushing out on to the park to be greeted by the cry from Jock of "Where the hell have you been?" I think I had missed the first couple of minutes of the game and I had to blurt out my abashed story of how the groundsman had locked me up in the toilet. Fortunately, my delayed arrival didn't damage the team's chances and we went on to win 3-2.'

During his time with the third team, Jock took them on visit to Peterhead Prison where, as luck would have it, he bumped into an old pal from Glenboig in the shape of Johnny Ramensky. Ramensky was originally born Jonas Ramanauckas to Lithuanian immigrant parents in Glenboig in 1905. He worked down the pit in Bedlay where he became familiar with the use of dynamite, which he would put to some significant use in his other chosen career.

Throughout his life, Ramensky demonstrated great strength and gymnastic skill which he used to begin a career as a burglar, followed by graduating to safe-cracking. During his criminal career, Ramensky maintained that he never targeted individuals' houses but only businesses and he became famous for never resorting to violence despite being arrested numerous times, resulting in the nickname 'Gentleman Johnny' or 'Gentle Johnny'. Detective Superintendent Robert Colquhoun, one of his old adversaries, when taken ill, was sent a message by Ramensky wishing him a speedy recovery, suggesting he had been working too hard in pursuing him.

Having been denied a licence to attend his wife's funeral, Ramensky began another series of feats which led to part of his fame. Ramensky was the last man to be shackled in a Scottish prison cell, as well as the first to escape from Peterhead Prison, going on to escape and being ultimately recaptured a further four times. He spent more than 40 of his 67 years in prison.

Ramensky was released after serving a sentence in Peterhead Prison in 1943. During his time there he had written to various officials seeking references to join the army. Due to the intervention of a senior police officer from Aberdeen he had attracted the interest of Robert Laycock who was seeking people with skills which could be used in commando raiding forces. As a result, he was enlisted with the Royal Fusiliers in January 1943 and transferred immediately to the commandos, where he was trained as a soldier while also instructing on the use of explosives. Although being officially enlisted with the Royal Fusiliers he never actually served with them, spending his entire wartime service with the 30 Commando.

Ramensky, using his safe-blowing skills, performed a number of sabotage missions, being parachuted behind enemy lines to retrieve documents from Axis headquarters, including Rommel's headquarters in North Africa and Hermann Goering's Carinhall in the Schorfheide. This culminated during the Italian campaign, where 14 embassy strong boxes or safes were opened in only one day.

He remained in the army after the cessation of hostilities as a translator for the Allied forces who were repatriating approximately 70,000 Lithuanians from camps in the Lübeck area. Following this, he had a short spell as an officer's batman before being demobbed in 1946.

Ramensky did not give up his safe-cracking lifestyle and spent the time after the war in and out of jail, eventually dying in Perth Royal Infirmary after suffering a stroke in Perth Prison, where he was serving a one-year sentence after being caught on a shop roof in Ayr.

Ramensky's friend Sonny Leitch, also a career criminal who served in the armed forces, said that Ramensky told him that he had stolen a hoard of Nazi loot from the Rome area during the Allied march on Rome in 1944, and that this hoard was later kept at the Shepton Mallet military prison in Somerset, and the Royal Navy supply depot at Carfin, Lanarkshire, after the war. He claimed that the hoard contained portraits of Hitler, Eva Braun, Goering, Goebbels and Himmler, and a treasure trove of jewellery and gold. Although this was never proven, there were certain looted items of little monetary value which survived him and remain, along with personal items, in a vault in a Glasgow bank. These include banners from Goering's Carinhall, and Ramensky's commando beret, compass and commando knife.

During his wartime service Ramensky was also known to have sent various items looted from German and Italian targets to friends and associates in Scotland, including the governor of Peterhead Prison.

Ramensky was quite a character and, upon spotting Tiger on his prison visit, tapped Jock for some cigarettes. He duly handed over a full 20 pack. Several years later Ramensky turned up in Tiger's shop and asked for 20 cigarettes; after handing over the money, he promptly handed the fags back to Tiger, advising that he had now repaid his debt from all those years ago.

Ground Staff

PRIOR TO taking on his role with the third team, Tiger's day-to-day job was with the ground maintenance team. Needless to say, he applied himself with the same diligence and dedication as he did when a player. While some may have considered this to be a relatively menial role for an ex-Rangers and Scotland superstar (as he would have been described today in modern parlance), as it was for Rangers, Tiger was only too happy to be involved and making a contribution to his club.

Head groundsman at the time was Davie Marshall and he described a typical week and their routine:

Sunday: tidy up pitch after Saturday's game, replace divots, roll the turf. (Remember this was in the days when the first team and reserves would be at Ibrox on alternate Saturdays.)

Monday: clean up terracing and stand.

Tuesday – Saturday: carry out general maintenance duties.

Unsurprisingly a Celtic match created the most work, and there could be up to 12 tons of rubbish to clear. There was also an agreement that the club would cut the pitch at nearby Tinto Park on a weekly basis to support Benburb, which continued into the 1970s.

During winter the routine changed a little, as the pitch had to be attended to immediately after the match in order to protect it from frost and to avoid rutting.

That sometimes meant it could be midnight before Jock got home; a mighty long shift.

In the early 70s the turf used at Ibrox came from a farm in Kilmarnock and was the same as laid at Rugby Park at the time, and Tiger took great pride in ensuring the playing surface of his beloved Ibrox was kept in tip-top condition.

It was not just footballers Rangers helped though, and continuing Mr Struth's tradition of supporting top athletes by making Ibrox available for training purposes, in the mid-60s this extended to boxing.

Olympic Champion in 1956, Richard 'Dick' McTaggart made his Commonwealth Games debut at the 1958 Games in Cardiff, winning gold in the lightweight category. He then went on to win bronze at the 1960 Rome Olympics before making his second Commonwealth Games appearance and taking his second medal, with silver in the 1962 Games at Perth, this time competing in the light welterweight category. He went on to compete at the 1964 Olympic Games in Tokyo, becoming the first British boxer ever to compete at three Olympic Games.

His overall record was phenomenal, winning 610 of 634 amateur bouts. Alongside Commonwealth and Olympic glory, he was crowned European champion in 1961 and won three ABA lightweight titles and two light welterweight belts.

Dick remains Scotland's only Olympic boxing champion to date. He was voted into the International Boxing Hall of Fame in 2000 and was one of the inaugural inductees into the Scottish Sports Hall of Fame in 2002.

So it was from Tokyo in 1964 that Dick sent a postcard to Jock which read, 'Well over here at last and still doing my usual morning running only it's at 7 o'clock in the morning, but I am sure feeling fit. My regards to everyone at the park. Dick.'

During this period Jock also had a role in the club's Centenary match on 17 January 1973 against the great Ajax side of that time with Johan Cruyff pulling the strings. Jock's role was to escort veteran striker Andy Cunningham pre-match to the centre circle for the ceremonial kick-off. Jock was resplendent, smart as always in his sheepskin jacket and club tie, immensely proud of this great occasion for his club.

A young fresh-faced 16-year-old, Willie Scott, left school to embark on life's adventure in December 1973 and his father was friendly with head groundsman Davie Marshall. Over a pint in their local, talk turned to young Willie and his future prospects. Davie said he would sort him out and he was to report to the ground the following Monday morning and he would arrange a role for him up till the summer.

Living in Copland Quadrant he did not have far to walk to start his new job.

On his first day he was introduced to Tiger, and was paired up with him so he could be shown the ropes, so to speak. He had not at this point realised exactly who his new workmate was. An added bonus of this job was that he was literally given the keys to heaven – his own set of keys to Ibrox.

Anyway, a couple of days had passed and Willie was immediately impressed by the hard graft of the rugged man who was his new work partner and indeed his kindness. One evening his father asked how the new job was going and he explained it was going really well and he had been paired up with someone called Tiger. 'What, Tiger Shaw?' his father exclaimed, and it was only then he realised he had been in the company of Rangers Royalty.

Tiger clearly left a lasting impression on young Willie, and even after all these years he thinks back fondly to the kindness extended to him by this humblest of heroes. These were salad days in the company of a legend who took him right under his wing. The ground staff in those days were given two complimentary tickets for the enclosure which were duly passed on to Willie's father, as the youngster was on duty on matchday tending to the pitch. On one occasion Willie was telling Tiger how much of a hero he was to his father. At this point Tiger asked him where was his dad in the crowd that day and when he pointed him out Tiger asked to be introduced. So proud as punch Willie took Tiger over to the enclosure where his father was stood, where there then followed a lengthy chat with his dad about past games and incidents as his father stood in awe. Tiger didn't have to do that, but it was a perfect illustration of the man's kindness.

Willie also vividly recalls how the players of the time extended Tiger the utmost respect as an ex-Rangers captain and called him 'Mr Shaw'.

On another occasion, while Willie was sweeping the terracing, John Greig was doing some recuperation from a hamstring injury, working on the track. Upon seeing this, and knowing John was his hero, Tiger said, 'Come on down and I'll introduce you to John', which he duly did and they spent another few minutes chatting.

Willie walked out with £10 a week but it could have been a million, for what he was experiencing was what money really could not buy.

He also recalled Derek Johnstone being really good to the ground staff and bringing them in clothes he had been given by sponsors or as gifts. He was also regularly sent to a chemist in Cardonald to collect a prescription for Jock Wallace and was always told to keep the change. Another source of a wee bit of extra cash was the weekly task of taking the players' cars inside and washing them. The tips for this were always generous.

As they got to know each other there were many stories from Jock's playing days that would be relayed, but the one Willie most remembers is that just prior to a Celtic game Tiger had tweaked his hamstring which was causing him 'murder', the adjective he used. Mr Struth, though assured him it would be okay, and that he would be sent to the trainer to sort him out. The trainer duly arrived with a brown case from which he removed some lotion and proceeded to rub it on to brown paper, and then bandaged the brown paper to his leg. Tiger was not at all convinced, and said the hamstring was still too tight to play. Mr Struth assured him everything would be fine. Anyway, the minutes passed and by the time he got on the park he did notice an easing of the pain: the only problem was it was now being gradually replaced by a burning sensation! Tiger did finish the game but as a memento of the occasion was left with a lasting burn mark on his leg. All in a day's work, I guess.

In summary and thinking back, Willie can still see in his mind's eye Tiger with his yard brush grafting for the club he loved, the lasting impression being that no one would work harder for Rangers than Jock in whatever role he had to serve.

Speaking of his time on the ground staff in 1971, Jock said, 'I'd just hate to leave Ibrox. Thirty-three years I've been here and that's a long time. If I were to have my time again, I wouldn't like anything to be altered.'

A proud moment arrived in August 1972 when his grandson John aged 12 joined as a ball boy, where he stayed till the end of the 1975/76 season, at which point he handed over to his brother Alan.

In May 1975 an out-of-the-blue but very welcome phone call from his home in Glenboig was made by Meg to Jock, who was busy at work on the Ibrox pitch, carrying out one of the critical close seasons tasks which follow the end of a long season. The phone call was from a delighted Meg to advise him that lady luck had shone on the Shaw household in the shape of Rangers Pools. To his pleasant surprise Tiger had bagged £1,402.84 in the weekly draw as one of the ten winners that week; it's the equivalent of around £12,000 today. 'It's about time I won something,' Jock joked. 'I have had three tickets in the pools since it started, so I reckon they owed me a pay-out. This is quite fantastic. I haven't really had time to think about what I'll do with the money, but I'm sure I will find something.' His agent Isobel Howson was equally pleased as she picked up £140 as her agent's prize share.

A further memorable moment arrived on 4 May 1976. After Rangers clinched the treble against Hearts in the Scottish Cup Final on 1 May, they still had one home game to play against Dundee United at which they would be presented with the league trophy. To make the evening a bit of a gala affair, Willie Waddell decided that as some pre-match entertainment the Rangers treble-winning teams of 1949 and 1964 would have an old crocks match, which was to be refereed by George Young. Tiger proudly led his team out and, on the evening, the following old team-mates followed him on to the park – Bobby Brown, Willie Rae, Ian McColl, Willie Woodburn, Sammy Cox, Willie Waddell, Willie Thornton, Jimmy Duncanson and Eddie Rutherford.

The main match against Dundee United was played out as a fairly innocuous affair and ended as a 0-0 draw, which secured United's Premier League survival. One of the few highlights of the evening was the sight of keeper Hamish McAlpine missing a penalty, then having to sprint frantically back to his goal.

In 1975, Rangers were due to play Dublin Bohemians in a first-round European Cup tie at Ibrox on 17 September – this was during the height of the troubles in Northern Ireland and therefore was considered something of a high-risk encounter.

Reporters asked Rangers general manager Willie Waddell if the club would be following the usual tradition of flying the flag of the visiting nation during a European Cup match. There was the potential for a little local difficulty, however, as the visitors were from the Republic of Ireland, and that particular country's flag had never before been flown at Ibrox Stadium. In addition, the only place a green, white and orange tricolour was readily available was across the city at Celtic Park, where its existence had been the subject of considerable controversy over the years.

Give Rangers their due, they were going to fly the flag and photographer Tommy Fitzpatrick and a reporter from the *Scottish Daily Express* were sent across town in a taxi to capture the scene. As they arrived and after explaining the purpose of their visit, they were summarily escorted from the premises. Asking if they could have a picture of Jock 'Tiger' Shaw running the tricolour up the flagpole probably was going a step too far. At the end of the day, after taking police advice, the Rangers' directors decided that the flag should not be flown because it was felt that it would lead to trouble on the terracing. Even so, the story still made front-page news in the next day's *Express*, and naturally it caused considerable comment later.

Jock was always keen to support local sport in the Lanarkshire area. In June 1981 Carluke Bowling Club members travelled to Bathgate for the annual game for the George Martin-Tiger Shaw Trophy and the Carluke Club brought the cup home, winning by 30 shots. The Carluke members were delighted that Tiger himself was able to be present at the game as he had been ill for some time, but the close relationship with Carluke and his close associate George Martin made the date too important to miss. Carluke president, Alan Orr, thanked the Bathgate Club for their usual hospitality throughout the day.

Jock also put forward an athletics trophy to be competed for by the Boys' Brigade (BB) in Glenboig. It was at some point passed over to Gartcosh BB, then went missing for over 30 years. The trophy has only relatively recently been rescued by Rev. David Slater of Glenboig Parish Church and returned to the family.

Retirement

TIGER FINALLY retired in November 1980 and was presented with a portable colour TV as a parting gift. He would also receive a pension from the club of £7 a week. This does not seem a lot for his 42 years of loyal service, and is equivalent to £30 today. That would just about buy you a concession ticket at Ibrox. Tiger, though, did not complain.

Interviewed for the *Rangers News* in July 1981, just a few days after his 68th birthday, Jock said, 'There's no doubt about it, we were definitely the top dogs. We were always there or thereabouts when the cups were being dished out, and to be honest there was not a team in the country who could live with us when we were on our game. A defeat for Rangers was a real big event in those days. The defence picked itself: Brown, Young, Shaw, McColl, Woodburn, Cox, the Iron Curtain. We certainly didn't lose many goals with that line-up.

'Up front we usually had Waddell, Gillick, Thornton, Duncanson and Rutherford.

'With Waddell and Thornton's almost telepathic understanding, Torry Gillick's magic and Jimmy Duncanson and Eddie Rutherford's clever stuff on the left, there were few if any better combinations.

'In reserve we had the likes of Billy Williamson, Willie Findlay and Jimmy Caskie who would have automatically walked into the first team if they'd played for anyone else but Rangers. Aye, we were a really good team and I'll never tire of reliving those days.'

Recalling his debut, he said, 'We were playing Arsenal at Ibrox and I was in direct opposition to a player called Bryn Jones who had joined Arsenal for a big fee during the close season and was keen to make a good impression, but it was our night and I didn't do too badly against Jones. It was a good start to my Rangers career with a victory, and things continued in that way throughout my time with the club. We won just about everything that was going on during the war and since the leagues restarted after it, we just kept on winning.'

In terms of the famous Moscow Dynamo game in 1945, he said, 'I think the entire population of Scotland wanted to see that game. The game was played on a Wednesday afternoon, but everyone took time off their work to be there and the atmosphere was something special.

'The Russians had beaten all the top teams in England and I think many people expected them to do the same to us. Mind you, it looked like that early on because they went 2-0 ahead and we missed a penalty so things weren't looking too good.

'Jimmy Smith though pulled one back just before the interval and that set us up for the second half when we really piled on the pressure. Their keeper Tiger Khomich played a stormer but we knew that a goal had to come and it did when George Young scored from a penalty. Then we set our sights on a winner but Khomich was unbeatable and we had to settle for a draw. Afterwards the Russians admitted they'd been more than a little lucky and they said we were the best team they'd ever come up against.

'We played all the top teams in European friendlies. Believe me these games were played like cup ties. We beat the best so I reckon we would have won any European Cups that were going in those days.'

When asked about his greatest achievement he answered without hesitation: 'Winning the treble in 1949 was really something. No team had ever won all three major honours before and as I remember no one really expected us to do it because although we had already won the League Cup and Scottish Cup no one fancied us for the flag. We were a point behind Dundee on the last day of the season and while we played at Albion Rovers, Dundee played Falkirk at Brockville. No one really expected Dundee to slip up but we went to town on Albion Rovers just in case.

'We were sat in the dressing room when news filtered through Dundee had lost 4-1 and we were champions. For a while it didn't sink in that we had done what no other side had managed to do, but Bill Struth brought it home to us when we saw tears in his eyes. It was a happy day for us all, make no mistake about that.

'There was such a great team spirit at the club that my job was mainly as a figurehead among the players. It was of course a great honour to captain Rangers and they will always be the only club for me.'

How did he manage to play on so long? Speaking in 1993 he said, 'What amazes me is that they say players are old men once they reach 34 or 35. I won the last of my ten Scotland caps when I was 37, and I reckoned I played the best stuff of my career between the ages of 34 and 39. I never felt fitter, I always told Bill Struth that if I ever felt, it, he would be the first to know but I never did.'

He went on to say he had rarely missed a match at Ibrox since 1938. 'Saturday can't come quickly enough these days so I can see the team, although I still hate to see them beaten. The club has never forgotten me and I've always been very well treated. For instance, they always invite me to cup finals. I'll never hear a bad word said about them. The game and Rangers have been good to me. I enjoyed playing and it took me all over the world to America, Portugal, Sweden and Denmark. I was a miner. What would I have seen if it wasn't for football? If I had stayed in the pits, I would never have left my home village of Annathill.

'The happiest days of my life were as a Rangers player and that was the way I wanted to be remembered so I bowed out when we came back from the Canadian tour (in 1954). This club has been great to me. My playing days were glorious and if I could go through it all again then I would.'

It was not just Rangers that Jock provided his support to and he was especially keen to support the local Boys' Club, and their ground was a mere stone's throw from his front door. He made the Aberdeen local press in December when he was spotted watching juvenile side Sunnybank Swifts in their under-12s Scottish Cup tie away to Glenboig United Boys' Club. It was to be the Aberdeen youngsters who prevailed though, as they twice came from a goal behind to win 3-2, with one of their scorers being Jim Bett (junior), the son of the Aberdeen star of that era.

It is a mark of the esteem in which he was held by the support that in August 1990 the Rangers Supporters' Association named the new lounge in their club on Edmiston Drive after him. In attendance on the opening night were ex-players George McLean, Alex Willoughby, Jim Forrest and Eric Caldow.

By this time Alex had taken over as bar manager and ensured Tiger had his own table which was located as you came down the stairs on the left-hand side, where he would hold court before every home game.

One of the regular guests at Tiger's table was Tom Purdie, who became close friends with Tiger. They would watch games from a spot generally next to where the Rangers blind party were based to the right of the control room above the tunnel. Long-serving Rangers Supporters' Association president Jimmy Clements was invariably there too. Tom recalled one occasion he took his daughter who was 13 at the time to a match and she went to the wall at the front of the enclosure to get a better view. Tiger on this occasion was about halfway down the enclosure. Tom then spotted a huge argument breaking out between Tiger and some of the support and it was clear Tiger was far from happy about something. At half-time Tom's daughter came up to speak to him and he asked her what Tiger was unhappy about. He was told there had been a lot of swearing and Tiger had pulled some supporters up for it, as that was behaviour not expected at Ibrox and in particular when there was a young girl around. To Tiger this was behaviour that was not good enough for a Ranger, whether a player or supporter. It was all about standards.

Tom also relayed a story Tiger had told him about an incident with Mr Struth shortly after signing. It was the day of his home debut, 20 August 1938, against Motherwell. Every first-team player at the time was given two complimentary tickets in an envelope. Tiger opened up the envelope to find two enclosure tickets. The mischief-maker Bob McPhail pointed out to him that there must be some mistake as all the players normally got main stand tickets. He was advised to go and take it up with Mr Struth, and point out the obvious mistake. So, off went a nervous Tiger, up the marble staircase to Mr Struth's office. Duly invited in, he pointed out the error in Mr Struth's ticket allocation, at which point he was asked to hand over the tickets. Mr Struth studied them for a moment, then proceeded to rip them into tiny pieces and drop them in the bin, saying, 'No mistake here laddie' and he sent a sheepish Tiger on his way. As he made his way back into the dressing room his face transparently gave away how that discussion had gone and he was then met with roars of laughter. Yup, he had been stitched up like the proverbial kipper – welcome to Ibrox!

During the 1990/91 season he went back on to the pitch to take the acclaim of his adoring public, when being introduced to the crowd before kick-off prior to Rangers' 1-0 victory over Motherwell. It was perhaps fitting that on the day the only goal was scored by someone cut very much from the same cloth as Tiger in the shape of John Brown.

Frank Bennett runs the very successful local boys' club Glenboig United from the village. Every season they have an awards night and a guest of honour is selected to be recognised for their career. In the mid-90s they were racking their brains for the identity of that year's recipient. After much contemplation Frank suggested Jock Shaw and as the discussion developed everyone was astonished the village had not actually done anything like that for him before. So, the die was cast – the Tiger was going to be honoured. The matter was very much kept secret from Jock so as not to alert him. There was also only one choice for the person to make the presentation: Alex Willoughby. On the night I think it's safe to report Jock was blown away by the honour and it had been a plan well made and executed as he genuinely had no clue about it. It was an event which touched Jock deeply and it meant so much as it was his 'ain folk' who were honouring him. There was a touching moment when Jock came up to Frank later in the evening with tears in his eyes and sincerely thanked him, saying no one had ever done anything like that for him before and that they had 'taken the feet away from him'.

Tiger always had time for the supporters: he was one himself after all and was more comfortable mixing with them in the Wee Rangers club or enclosure at Ibrox than anywhere else. No distance was too far for the Tiger to travel, from Campbeltown in deepest Argyll to hand out the prizes at an end-of-season function, or to Luton in Bedfordshire to open a new extension to the local supporters' club.

In 1999 Rangers set up a poll for the greatest-ever Ranger, which, of course, was won by John Greig. The one minor flaw in this type of poll, though, is they will be heavily weighted towards the memory of those voting and therefore players from the more recent past are always likely to attract more votes. It's just the nature of these polls, and I am sure if you ran it again today the outcome would be different.

In addition, though, on the evening there were three initial inductees into the Rangers Hall of Fame. Fittingly Tiger was one of the first to be admitted along with Bob McPhail and Willie Woodburn.

Donald Findlay introduced the inductees and had this to say about Jock: 'His nickname perhaps tells you all you would need to know about him. He truly epitomised everything of the Rangers fighting spirit. Respected by the Rangers support and the supporters and players of every club he played against. Indeed, it is tremendous when you go about supporters' functions and this man you still meet and he is still popular with people who are only in their teens because they rightly know the name of Jock Tiger Shaw.'

Jock, accompanied on the night by his son David, took to his feet to proudly acknowledge the acclaim from the assembled audience at the Hilton. His was the first picture to appear in the opening montage for the official video of the event too.

Following the event, through a discussion between Sandy Jardine, David Mason (club historian), Donald Findlay and TV presenter Dougie Donnelly, the concept of an annual Hall of Fame event to honour many more of the greats in the long and illustrious history of Rangers was born. It is quite some accolade for Jock to be the first name on what would become a very, very long list over the years.

Death and Legacy

AROUND 1998 Tiger's health started to fail. By then he was 86, and he had the onset of dementia and latterly his eyesight was also badly affected. It's only looking back now the family can see that significant change in him, as it's not always obvious when you see someone day in, day out. He passed away peacefully with his family around him on 13 June 2000.

His funeral took place in Glenboig Parish Church on 17 June. Fittingly, the hymns played were the Boys' Brigade hymn 'Will Your Anchor Hold' and 'How Great Thou Art'. His final journey was then to Daldowie Crematorium.

Alex Willoughby had the honour of delivering the eulogy and it was an emotional but truly heartfelt tribute to his great friend.

'Jock Shaw hung his boots up in 1954 at the age of 42, although some accounts reckoned he was 38. You see Jock was a crafty old character. He never told anyone his age. Whenever Rangers played abroad and the players had to fill out entry cards, Jock would go into a corner. He never wanted anyone to see his date of birth. On the field he could easily have been half his age. Even at 42 he could have gone on for many more years because he looked after himself. Today's players are encouraged to eat properly and train well. Jock was doing that 50 years ago.

'When he announced his retirement from the game, two Scottish sides wanted to sign him, but he told them "Thanks, but although I feel I could continue playing for some seasons, I wanted to end my days as a Rangers player. The 16 years I spent with them were the happiest of my life. They were in fact my life. I could never play for another team, gentlemen."

'Rangers were Jock's life and he achieved the ultimate accolade from the club recently when he was entered into the Rangers Hall of Fame. It tells you something of Jock when you consider that he was among the first three names selected. And there was never any doubt he would be revered in Rangers' history. Here was a man who played over 600 games for Rangers. Determination was his game, and he earned the name Tiger. Jock Tiger Shaw or simply Tiger to many.

'His career began at Benburb, then he joined Airdrie in 1933. Five years later Rangers signed him for a fee of £2,000, a substantial sum in those days, but he was well worth it, because he led the side to many trophies. As a member of Bill Struth's great sides of three decades he won four League Championships, three Scottish Cups and two League Cups.

'He also won the Southern League Cup five times, the Southern League Championship six times, the Summer Cup once, the Glasgow Cup five times, the Charity Cup six times and the Victory Cup. A born winner and few Rangers teams lost with Tiger in their side. With the famous Iron Curtain defence alongside him, who could get past him?

'In that glorious spell he won nine successive championships through the war years and led the side to an 8-1 victory over old rivals Celtic in the New Year fixture of 1943. He was the first captain of any Scottish side to lift the domestic treble, a truly remarkable achievement, and one which, although equalled on many occasions by succeeding Rangers captains, can never be surpassed.

'He was also capped four times by Scotland, passing on the left-back berth to his brother Davie who played for Hibs. He captained the national side to a win over England in the Victory International of 1946.

'With that kind of record, is it any wonder they call him a legend?

'When he finally gave up the game Rangers found a role for him as trainer and then groundsman, nursing the Ibrox turf he had graced for many years. When he eventually retired, Ibrox was never far from his thoughts. On match days you could find him in the "Wee Rangers Supporters' Club", sitting in the seat they always reserved for him. At the game he would never hear a bad word about us.

'And through all of that devotion and determination in a blue jersey, this spirit of Ibrox, will to win, if you like. Ask anyone who knew him what he was like and they will sum him up in one word – gentleman. Because that's what Jock Shaw was. Forget the glamour of the game and the roar of the crowds. Here was a true gentleman who was liked and respected by everyone.

'He once told me that "You're never a legend until yer deid." Sadly, he has fulfilled that final criteria. But never has a man worn that label more fittingly.'

Among the mourners was Ally McCoist who had been abroad commentating on the European Championship, but flew back for the day specially so he could pay his final respects.

Following his cremation, Tiger's ashes were interred behind the Copland Road goal and a few years later his great pal Alex Willoughby, who sadly lost a long battle with cancer, joined him in 2004. Both resting for ever more in their own Blue Heaven.

While supporters, colleagues and others mourned the loss of a football hero it was, of course, his family who had the biggest chasm left in their lives; after all they had lost a beloved husband, father and Papa. Meg survived him by six years.

Shortly after his death a letter arrived from the House of Commons, it was from Tam Dalyell. In the handwritten note he said, 'Dear Mrs Shaw, As a child I was a great admirer of your husband from the terraces. As an MP I met him at Ibrox, where it was a pleasure to chat with him. With deepest sympathy, yours sincerely Tam Dalyell.'

From speaking to the family, it's clear he is still greatly missed, and was someone of whom they were immensely proud. He was a great character and a loving family man. He could bring you back down to earth right enough though, as granddaughter Elaine Campbell fondly recalled. Elaine is a very accomplished pool player, clearly taking her skills from her Papa and his billiard prowess. She recalls what happened when she was first selected to play for Scotland.

'When I'd heard I was picked to play for Scotland, I was eager to tell him because I was so chuffed and so were my mum and dad and I was high as a kite. So I went to tell him and he said, "Aye, good hen, that's you the fourth in the family to play for Scotland." Not as cutting as it might sound, but it was just his way of making me keep my feet on the ground and not get carried away with myself before I'd even hit a ball for Scotland. He was so proud.

'After he died, I played in the World Championships for Scotland. A few of the girls were speaking to me to see how I was doing as I was getting very nervous. One of them, Kathy Paton, said to me, "Don't worry, he'll be looking down on you in this event." Next thing, team Scotland were announced to make their entrance. Our walk-on music was "Eye of the Tiger". Kathy and I just looked at each other, gobsmacked. The organisers picked the music, not the teams, so that was just sheer chance that was ours.'

Was it though? I am sure one proud Papa might have had something to do with it. Needless to say, there really was only one title that could be used for this book.

Elaine and her sister were reminiscing about going to Ibrox with Tiger. 'He never wore Rangers colours, apart from his tie and blazer, when he went to the games on Saturdays. Was always suited and booted when he went. When we were growing up, we were never allowed to wear Rangers colours either. I was of the age that I had to use my own money to buy a Rangers replica shirt before I could get one. Even when I went to the game with him, I always had to be dressed "in case we end up in the directors' box", which wasn't often to be fair, as he preferred sitting in the stand or the enclosure. But aye, no Rangers colours for me and Lorna growing up.'

Elaine then went on to say, 'It's funny because I sometimes don't associate this period of his life [playing for Rangers] and pics of him during this period as "him". If that makes any sense. The "him" in these pictures I never knew. I knew the older man, the grandfather figure. The one that played about with us in the garden, that made us dinner when my mum was at work and we came home from school. The one that taught us to ride a bike, that kept the pigeons, that went to all the pigeon meetings and worked with Johnny Burns' dookit [pigeon house].

'The one that went to his pal Charlie's garage and drove cars for him to customers, the one that dressed up as Santa on Christmas morning and went round all the weans in the wee bit where we live with an "extra" Christmas present from Santa himself no less, and then the one that took me to Ibrox until he was unable to, when the tables turned and I returned the favour by taking him.

'Sometimes when I was younger at Ibrox I didn't "get it" – I didn't understand why all these people wanted to talk to MY Papa, he couldn't possibly know them all, and what did they want his signature for? It was stopping me getting in to Ibrox to catch the players in the indoor training area under the stand [before the seats went in the enclosure and new tunnel was constructed] to get MY signatures from the current crop of players. Oh, the irony, eh?'

I can empathise with what Elaine is talking about here; there was a certain generation who looked the same age no matter the passing of the years. My own Papa, for example, looked exactly the same the age when I was born in 1962 until he passed away 24 years later.

The story about the car deliveries did make me chuckle. Charlie Gallagher had a garage in Glenboig not far from where I now live and when a new car arrived or a repaired vehicle was being returned it must have been quite a sight when Tiger turned up with your keys. There must have been a few double takes. 'It's not, is it?'

A post on the Glenboig Friends page on Facebook caught my eye, when, on the 20th anniversary of his passing, Elaine posted some pictures. One of the comments related to the garage. It was written by Ellen McPake: 'Jock was a really nice man; when I worked in the community centre he used to come round every morning from Charlie Gallagher's garage and sit and have a cup of tea then say, "can I borrow some tea bags as we've run out at the garage". I used to look forward to him coming in every day.'

The other comments which followed Elaine's post perfectly summed him up and I have copied a few of these below as examples:

'Gentleman'.

'Great Man'.

'Lovely man and great player – Legend'.

'Handsome man'.

'One Word – Legend'.

'A lovely gentleman'.

'The best sliding tackler ever'.

'My granda played for Celtic at same time Jock played for Rangers. Whenever he came up to Glenboig he always made an effort to go and see Jock.'

'Had the pleasure of sitting next to him in Church for Sunday service. A lovely man.'

There were many, many more but they all display a clear theme: Jock Tiger Shaw was a lovely, gentle man.

Tiger left behind a fine legacy, and his surviving family are as humble as he was about his achievements and I am only too happy to play a small part in getting his story out there. My only regret is that this has taken me quite as long as it has to complete.

The family had a Rangers scarf made out of his final Rangers jersey as a memento, and there is also a lasting tribute to him in the place he loved more than anywhere in the world – Glenboig.

As part of the regeneration of the village a lot of new housing is being built and just a short walk from my front door is the suitably named Jock Shaw Drive; I am sure the great man would have been very humbled by that.

He was not just a great player, though, as I hopefully have been able to suitably convey; he was also a great family man and I am sure he would be both pleased and proud at the family he and Meg created.

Jock and Meg were married for 63 years and were as proud as punch to get the Royal seal of approval on their 60th wedding anniversary. They had two children, a son David and daughter Margaret.

David was in the merchant navy, then became a police officer and finally, prior to retirement, he worked for Caterpillar in Birkenshaw, Uddingston, where he still lives.

David and his wife Jean, who was a nurse, have four boys: David (jnr) who works in construction, Paul in insurance, Alex in racing and William also in construction. David (jnr) has two daughters, Sharon and Alexis.

Margaret is a fully trained shorthand typist, and worked in Colville's and the steelworks in Gartcosh before settling to work for most of her career in the Department of Employment. Margaret and husband Hugh, who was an engineer, have two daughters Elaine and Lorna, both of whom work for the Department for Work and Pensions.

Margaret, Hugh, Elaine and Lorna lived in the same house as Jock and Meg in Glenboig for most of their lives, and Margaret and Hugh still live there. Lorna and her husband Colin have two children, Ryan and Abbie.

Sadly, Jock did not live long enough to meet any of his four great grandchildren as the oldest of them, Ryan, was born only six weeks after his death. However, I'm sure that he would be extremely proud of the fine young people they have become in their own right.

I am certain there would be no doubt about that.

Playing Record

Rangers

	P	W	D	L	F	A
League	173	118	31	24	405	178
Regional League	28	21	3	4	64	30
Southern League	174	129	23	22	507	176
Scottish Cup	27	19	5	3	57	18
League Cup	42	28	6	8	96	38
Southern League Cup	50	42	5	3	132	39
Emergency Cup	6	4	2	0	17	7
Victory Cup	8	6	2	0	20	4
Summer Cup	18	13	2	3	51	24
Charity Cup	23	17	3	3	51	16
Glasgow Cup	35	25	5	5	83	42
Friendlies, etc.	20	11	3	6	43	34
Total	604	433	90	81	1526	606

For Airdrie: 174 appearances and five goals.

Honours (38)

League	1938/39, 1946/47, 1948/49, 1949/50
R/League	1939/40
S/League	1940/41, 1941/42, 1942/43, 1943/44, 1944/45, 1945/66
Emergency War Cup	1939/40
Scottish Cup	1947/48, 1948/49, 1949/50
League Cup	1946/47, 1948/49
Summer Cup	1941/42

Victory Cup	1945/46
Charity Cup	1938/39, 1939/40, 1940/41, 1941/42, 1943/44, 1944/45, 1945/46, 1946/47, 1947/48, 1950/51
Glasgow Cup	1939/40, 1941/42, 1942/43, 1943/44, 1944/45, 1947/48, 1949/50
Lanarkshire Cup	1934/35
Glasgow Junior Cup	1931/32
Goals for Rangers	11 October 1941 v Dumbarton in 7-0 win
	14 February 1942 v Hamilton in 6-0 win
	6 April 1942 v Clyde in 8-2 win
	1 November 1947 v Airdrie in 3-0 win

Bibliography

The British Newspaper Archive Website
Scottish Referee
Mr Struth the Boss, David Mason and Ian Stewart
Struth, David Leggat
We Will Follow Rangers, Hugh Taylor
Rangers Historian, Robert McElroy
*Rangers The New Er*a, Willie Allison
The Rangers: Scotland's Greatest Club, John Fairgrieve
Possilpark to Ibrox, Donald Caskie
Wilson On the Wing, Alistair Aird

Also available at all good book stores

9781785316333

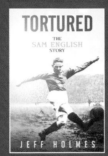

9781785317255

9781785315510

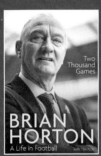

9781785316685

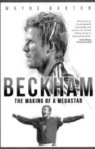

9781785316760

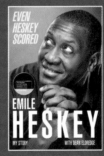

9781785315008

9781785316548

9781785316807

9781785314995